Understanding the Mind

Also by Geshe Kelsang Gyatso

Meaningful to Behold
Clear Light of Bliss
Buddhism in the Tibetan Tradition
Heart of Wisdom
Universal Compassion
The Meditation Handbook
Joyful Path of Good Fortune
Guide to Dakini Land
The Bodhisattva Vow
Heart Jewel
Great Treasury of Merit
Introduction to Buddhism
Tantric Grounds and Paths
Ocean of Nectar
Essence of Vajrayana
Living Meaningfully, Dying Joyfully
Eight Steps to Happiness
Transform Your Life

Profits received from the sale of
this book will be donated to the
NKT-International Temples Project
A Buddhist Charity Building for World Peace
UK email: kadampa@dircon.co.uk
US email: info@kadampacenter.org

GESHE KELSANG GYATSO

———

Understanding the Mind

LORIG
AN EXPLANATION OF THE
NATURE AND FUNCTIONS
OF THE MIND

THARPA PUBLICATIONS
Ulverston, England
Glen Spey, New York

First published in 1993
Second edition reset 1997
Reprinted 2002

The right of Geshe Kelsang Gyatso
to be identified as author of this work
has been asserted by him in accordance with
the Copyright, Designs, and Patents Act 1988.

Tharpa Publications
Conishead Priory
Ulverston
Cumbria LA12 9QQ, England

Tharpa Publications
47 Sweeney Road
P.O. Box 430
Glen Spey, NY 12737, USA

Cover painting of Manjushri by
the Tibetan artist Chating Jamyang Lama.
Cover design by Tharpa Publications.
Cover photo of Geshe Kelsang Gyatso by Kathia Rabelo.
Line illustrations by Gen Kelsang Wangchen.

Library of Congress Control Number: 2002104949

British Library Cataloguing in Publication Data
A catalogue record for this book is
available from the British Library.

ISBN 0 948006 53 6 – papercase
ISBN 0 948006 54 4 – paperback

Set in Palatino by Tharpa Publications
Printed on acid-free 250-year longlife paper and bound
by Interprint Ltd., Marsa, Malta.

Contents

Illustrations

Acknowledgements

This book, *Understanding the Mind*, is a comprehensive explanation of the mind based on the experiences of accomplished meditators. Traditionally, Buddhist books on the mind are written from the point of view of the Sautrantika Buddhist school – an intermediate view taught by Buddha for the sake of disciples who could not immediately grasp his final view – and therefore such books are difficult to relate to meditative experiences. This book, however, is written from the point of view of the Madhyamika-Prasangika Buddhist school, which expresses Buddha's final intention. As such it is a unique and practical guide for those who seek to develop their minds through sincere study and meditation.

From the depths of our hearts we thank the author, Venerable Geshe Kelsang Gyatso, for his inconceivable kindness in composing this book, which provides for meditators throughout the world a definitive exposition of the nature, types, and functions of the mind.

We would also like to thank all the students of the author who, with great dedication and skill, edited the book and prepared it for publication.

Roy Tyson,
Administrative Director,
Manjushri Mahayana
Buddhist Centre,
November 1992.

Introduction

The subject of this book is the mind. It is very important to have a correct understanding of the nature and functions of the mind because this special knowledge will open the door to liberation for us. In the Sutras and the Mahamudra scriptures it says:

> If you realize your own mind you will become a Buddha; you should not seek Buddhahood elsewhere.

This instruction is very profound. It indicates that there are many different levels on which we can understand the mind. We can understand the gross minds, the subtle minds, and the very subtle mind; and we can understand each of these either intellectually, through a generic image, or directly, through experience. To begin with we can understand these different levels of mind intellectually by studying this book and authentic commentaries to Vajrayana Mahamudra, such as *Clear Light of Bliss* and *Tantric Grounds and Paths*. Then, on the basis of this understanding, we can gain direct experience of the gross, subtle, and very subtle minds by engaging in the special meditation practices explained in Vajrayana Mahamudra. When we realize our very subtle mind directly we shall attain the higher realization of clear light, and we shall then be very close to becoming a Buddha. Soon this realization will transform into the omniscient wisdom of a Buddha and we shall become a great enlightened being.

If we understand clearly the nature of our mind we shall definitely realize that the continuum of our mind does not cease when we die, and then there will be no basis for doubting the existence of our future lives. If we realize the existence of our future lives we shall naturally be concerned for

1

Buddha Shakyamuni

our welfare and happiness in those lives, and we shall use this present life to make the appropriate preparations. This will prevent us from wasting our precious human life on the preoccupations of this life alone. Therefore, an understanding of the mind is very helpful.

In the *Perfection of Wisdom Sutras* and in many other scriptures it says that all phenomena are like dreams. This means that just as all the things experienced in a dream are mere appearances to mind, so all beings, their environments, their enjoyments, and all other phenomena are mere appearances to mind. This is not easy to understand at first, but we can develop some understanding by contemplating as follows. When we are awake many different things exist, but when we fall asleep they cease because the mind to which they appear ceases. During our dreams we become a dreamer, and at that time the only things that appear are dream objects. Later, when we wake, these dream objects cease because the mind to which they appear ceases. Other than this there is no specific reason why they should cease. If we think deeply about this we shall understand how all phenomena are mere appearances to our mind, just like objects in a dream. Then we shall realize that we can cause all the unpleasant things that we dislike to cease simply by abandoning impure states of mind, and we can cause all the good things that we desire to arise simply by developing a pure mind. In this way we shall be able to fulfil all our wishes. Therefore, understanding the mind is a real wishfulfilling jewel.

Although everyone has a mind, most of us have only a vague understanding of its nature and functions. For example, if we have not trained in Dharma we shall probably know very little about the different types of mind, how they are generated, and what effect they have on our lives. We shall not be able to distinguish virtuous minds from non-virtuous minds, and we shall not know how to cultivate the former and abandon the latter. Why is it necessary to understand all this? The reason is that all happiness and suffering depend upon the mind, and so if we want to avoid suffering and find true happiness we need to understand how the mind works

3

and use that understanding to bring our mind under control. Only in this way can we improve the quality of our life, both now and in the future.

In recent years our understanding and control of the external world have increased considerably and as a result we have witnessed remarkable material progress; but there has not been a corresponding increase in human happiness. There is no less suffering in the world today, and there are no fewer problems. Indeed, it might be said that there are now more problems and greater unhappiness than ever before. This shows that the cause of happiness and the solution to our problems do not lie in knowledge or control of the external world. Happiness and suffering are states of mind and so their main causes are not to be found outside the mind. If we want to be truly happy and free from suffering we must improve our understanding of the mind.

When things go wrong in our life and we encounter difficult situations we tend to regard the situation itself as the problem, but in reality whatever problems we experience come from the side of the mind. If we were to respond to difficult situations with a positive or peaceful mind they would not be problems for us; indeed we may even come to regard them as challenges or opportunities for growth and development. Problems arise only if we respond to difficulties with a negative state of mind. Therefore, if we want to be free from problems we must learn to control our mind.

Buddha taught that the mind has the power to create all pleasant and unpleasant objects. This is a view held in common by all four Buddhist schools: the two Hinayana schools – the Vaibashikas and the Sautrantikas – and the two Mahayana schools – the Chittamatrins and the Madhyamikas. According to this view the world is the result of the karma, or actions, of the beings who inhabit it. A pure world is the result of pure actions and an impure world is the result of impure actions. Since all actions are created by mind, ultimately everything, including the world itself, is created by mind. There is no creator other than mind. Buddhists believe this because they rely upon the explanations given by Buddha.

4

Normally we say 'I created such and such', or 'He or she created such and such', but the actual creator of everything is the mind. We are like servants helping our mind, which is the actual creator. Whenever our mind wants to do something we have to do it without any choice. Since beginningless time until now we have been under the control of our mind, without any freedom; but if we now practise Dharma sincerely we can reverse this situation and gain control over our mind. Only then shall we have real freedom.

Within the four Buddhist schools, the Chittamatrins in particular believe that all phenomena, including the world itself, are the same nature as the mind that apprehends them and have no existence outside the mind. They say that if we dream of a mountain, for example, that mountain is the same nature as the dream mind and has no existence outside the mind. If it existed outside the mind we would have to say that a huge mountain existed in our small bedroom, which is clearly absurd. They say that just as it is with dream objects, so it is with all phenomena – they are all the same nature as the mind, like a dream mountain.

The highest of the four Buddhist schools, the Madhyamika-Prasangika school, says that all phenomena are merely imputed by mind and have no existence from their own side.

The essential point in all these views is that liberation from suffering cannot be found outside the mind. Permanent liberation can be found only by purifying the mind. Therefore, if we want to become free from problems and attain lasting peace and happiness we need to increase our knowledge and understanding of the mind.

The explanation of the mind in this book is in two parts. The first part explains the nature and function of the different types of mind, and how we develop and increase knowledge and understanding. First, each type of mind is clearly defined so that it can be correctly identified, and then the different varieties of each type of mind are enumerated and illustrated by examples. Then there follows an explanation of how each type of mind is generated, and finally there is advice on how to apply our understanding of each type of mind to our Dharma practice. These explanations help us to understand how we develop and increase valid knowledge and Dharma realizations.

The second part of the book explains primary minds and mental factors. Here the emphasis is on distinguishing virtuous states of mind from non-virtuous states of mind so that we can cultivate the former and abandon the latter. First there is an explanation of the six primary minds and their relationship to their accompanying mental factors. Then there follows an explanation of the definitions, divisions, and functions of each of the fifty-one mental factors. These explanations help us to control our deluded minds and attain permanent freedom from suffering.

PART ONE

Types of Mind

Nagarjuna

Object-possessors

In general, all phenomena, including minds, are objects because they are objects of knowledge, but some objects, namely expressive sounds, persons, and minds, are also object-possessors. Besides these three, all other phenomena are only objects and not object-possessors.

DEFINITION OF OBJECT-POSSESSOR

The definition of object-possessor is a functioning thing that expresses or cognizes an object.

DIVISIONS OF OBJECT-POSSESSOR

There are three types of object-possessor:

1 Expressive sounds
2 Persons
3 Minds

Expressive sounds are object-possessors because they express particular objects; persons are object-possessors because they cognize objects with their minds; and minds are object-possessors because their principal function is to cognize objects.

As mentioned above, besides being object-possessors, expressive sounds, persons, and minds are also objects because they are objects of knowledge. In general, objects and object-possessors are mutually dependent because whatever exists is an object of mind and there is no such thing as a mind without an object. More specifically, it is not possible for any of the three types of object-possessor to exist without its particular object.

EXPRESSIVE SOUNDS

DEFINITION OF EXPRESSIVE SOUND

The definition of expressive sound is an object of hearing that makes its expressed object understood.

Not all sounds are expressive sounds. The sound of the wind or the sound of the rain, for example, do not express any meaning. An expressive sound is necessarily the speech of a person that is produced through the power of the motivation of that person. Sometimes it is possible for the sound of Dharma to arise from the movement of trees in the wind, but in such cases either that sound is a manifestation of Buddha's speech, or it is simply the subjective experience of the hearer.

It is possible to convey a meaning without using sound, for example by using sign language or by writing, but these are not object-possessors and they are not real language. They are representations of language that are methods for understanding something, like traffic lights. However, this remains a subject of debate.

DIVISIONS OF EXPRESSIVE SOUND

There are three types of expressive sound:

1 Letters
2 Names
3 Phrases

LETTERS

DEFINITION OF LETTER

The definition of letter is a vocalization that is a basis for the composition of names and phrases.

When we say 'A', this sound is the letter A, and it is letters such as this that are the basis for the composition of names and phrases. Letters that appear on paper are not actual

10

letters but representations of letters. Actual letters are necessarily expressive sounds. In *Commentary to Valid Cognition*
Dharmakirti says:

Letters are generated from motivation;
They are sounds produced by mind.

NAMES

DEFINITION OF NAME

The definition of name is an object of hearing that principally
expresses the name of any phenomenon.

When we say 'Peter', this sound is a name. The name 'Peter'
depends upon putting together the five letters: P, E, T, E, and
R. The basis for the composition of the name Peter, therefore,
is these five letters, and if any of them is missing the full
name is not produced. Thus, the name Peter is a collection
of several letters.

There are two types of name: original names and subsequent names. An original name is the name that is originally applied to an object and is the principal name for that
object. An example is the name given to a child by his or her
parents. A subsequent name is a name that is subsequently
applied to an object and is a secondary name of that object.
There are two types of subsequent name: subsequent names
based on similarity and subsequent names based on relationship. Examples of the first are nicknames such as calling
someone who resembles a monkey 'Monkey' or calling someone who looks angelic 'Angel'; and examples of the second are
calling the rays of the sun 'the sun', such as when we say 'The
sun comes into the front room', and calling a grey-coloured
horse 'a grey'.

The name of an object is not a natural characteristic of that
object but is merely imputed onto the object according to the
conventions of a particular language. All objects of knowledge are merely imputed by their names, therefore they do
not exist from their own side. However, they do exist because

their names are valid names. For example, when we see a close friend called Peter, in reality we see only his body, but still we say 'There is Peter.' In this case, the name Peter is a valid name because his body is a valid basis for imputing Peter. For this reason, whenever we see his body we develop the thought 'There is Peter.' The same can be applied to other persons, and indeed to all other phenomena. If we study this subject deeply we can develop valid knowledge of the two truths – conventional truths and ultimate truths. This valid knowledge is the actual path to liberation from suffering.

PHRASES

DEFINITION OF PHRASE

The definition of phrase is an object of hearing that indicates a meaning by connecting a name with a predicate.

The basis of a phrase is a name, for example, 'dog'. When we add a predicate to a name, such as 'The dog is black', or 'The dog runs', we create a phrase. Phrases are the basis of all more complex verbal constructions such as sentences and discourses.

GENERATION OF EXPRESSIVE SOUNDS

All expressive sounds are produced through the motivation of a speaker and therefore have their origin in the mind. Names are produced in dependence upon letters, and phrases are produced in dependence upon names. Discourses and commentaries arise in dependence upon collections of many phrases. Thus, all Buddha's instructions of Sutra and Tantra, as well as all the commentaries to them, are expressive sounds.

APPLICATION OF EXPRESSIVE SOUNDS TO
DHARMA PRACTICE

Expressive sounds are very useful because they are the principal means of communication. Our understanding of Dharma is based on listening to teachings and discussing their meaning with others. Moreover, since the written word is based on spoken language, everything we read also depends on express-ive sounds. Expressive sounds, therefore, are essential for our spiritual development.

By relying upon the supreme expressive sounds of Dharma instructions, eventually we shall attain a realization of the ultimate nature of all phenomena, emptiness. To begin with we shall attain a generic image of emptiness, but through continually meditating on this generic image eventually we shall experience a direct realization of emptiness, and through this realization we shall be released from the ocean of sam-saric suffering. In summary, all realizations of Sutra and Tantra come from the study and practice of the supreme expressive sounds of Dharma instructions. Knowing this, we should strive to study and practise Dharma sincerely.

PERSONS

DEFINITION OF PERSON

The definition of person is an I imputed in dependence upon any of the five aggregates.

Person, being, self, and I are synonyms. The function of a person is to perform actions and experience their results.

The five aggregates of a person are the aggregate of form, which is a person's body; the aggregate of consciousness, which is a person's primary minds; and the aggregates of feeling, discrimination, and compositional factors, which are a per-son's secondary minds, or mental factors. Here, from within the fifty-one mental factors, feeling and discrimination are selected and listed as the third and fourth aggregates, and the remaining forty-nine mental factors are included within the fifth aggregate, the aggregate of compositional factors. From this we can see that all five aggregates are included within a person's body and mind.

The function of a person, to perform actions and experience their results, is completely dependent upon the aggregates of feeling and discrimination. If a person lacked discriminations he or she would not be able to perform any actions, and without feelings he or she would not be able to experience the results of any actions. It is to highlight this that these two mental factors are listed separately within the five aggregates.

The definition of person given here is used by all four Buddhist schools. Through investigating 'Where is the I?' and 'What is the I?' the lowest Buddhist school, the Vaibashikas, believe that they find the I to be just the collection of the five aggregates. Some Sautrantikas believe the same as the Vaibashikas, whereas others believe the same as the Madhyamika-Svatantrikas, that the root mental consciousness is the I. The Chittamatrins believe that the consciousness-basis-of-all is the I. The Madhyamika-Prasangikas reject all these assertions. They realize that the I is merely imputed in dependence upon any of its aggregates. If we are satisfied with this merely imputed I, we can say 'I am going', 'I am hungry', and so forth; but if we investigate further, trying to find a substantially existent I that is not a mere imputation, we shall find nothing. This is because in reality all phenomena, including our I, are merely imputed by mind, and do not exist from their own side in the least.

DIVISIONS OF PERSON

There is a twofold division of persons into Buddhas and non-Buddhas; another twofold division into ordinary beings and Superior beings; and a fivefold division into Buddhas, Bodhisattvas, Solitary Conquerors, Hearers, and migrating beings.

GENERATION OF PERSONS

As already mentioned, a person is imputed in dependence upon any of the five aggregates. For example, our present self, or I, is imputed in dependence upon our aggregates of this life. Our aggregates are the basis for imputing our I, and our I is the phenomenon imputed upon them. When our consciousness entered our mother's womb at conception, our gross body of this life gradually began to develop, and the assembly of that mind and body became the basis for imputing the self or I of this life. When we emerged from the womb our parents gave us a name, and we subsequently came to identify with that name. As we pass through life we assume a number of different identities, such as child, adolescent, employee, husband or wife, or senior citizen. In each case the basis in dependence upon which this identity is imputed is our aggregates of body and mind and the particular function we are performing. For example, if we qualify as a solicitor, others will refer to us as a solicitor and we shall identify ourself as a solicitor; if we reach retirement age others will refer to us as a senior citizen and we shall identify ourself as a senior citizen; and so on.

When we die, our consciousness will leave this present body and enter a new body, and that new mind and body will then become the basis for imputing our self or I of the next life. For example, if after death we take the aggregates of an animal we shall become an animal and if we take the aggregates of a god we shall become a god. Since beginningless time we have taken countless rebirths, each time developing a new identity upon the basis of the aggregates we have taken. However, if we search for a truly existent person in any of these rebirths we shall not find one because, whatever kind of rebirth we take, our self or I is merely imputed by thought in dependence upon the aggregates of that life. If we understand this clearly and meditate on this knowledge it will lead us to a realization of the emptiness of the I, or person.

APPLICATION OF OUR UNDERSTANDING OF PERSONS TO DHARMA PRACTICE

We need to develop an understanding of both the conventional nature of the person and the ultimate nature of the person. From an understanding of the conventional nature of the person we shall see that the function of a person is to perform actions, or karma, and to experience their results.

Thus, if we accumulate positive karma we shall definitely experience beneficial results, and if we accumulate negative karma we shall definitely experience unpleasant results. In most cases the results of karma are experienced in future lives. Although the person of our future life who will experience the results of actions we have committed in this life will not be the person of this life, nevertheless it will be 'us' who experiences those effects. If we deny this, we deny a fundamental principle of Dharma, that the results of an action cannot ripen on another person. Therefore, death and rebirth alone do not protect us from the consequences of our actions. By thinking deeply about this we shall make a firm decision to avoid negative actions and perform only positive actions, and we shall put this decision into practice in our lives.

By understanding that the person is merely imputed in dependence upon the aggregates of body and mind, and is not to be found anywhere within them, we shall come to understand the ultimate nature of the person – emptiness. By familiarizing ourself in meditation with the emptiness of persons, and in particular with the emptiness of our own self, gradually we shall abandon self-grasping, which is the root of all suffering, and eventually we shall attain complete freedom from the sufferings of samsara.

MINDS

DEFINITION OF MIND

The definition of mind is that which is clarity and cognizes.

In this definition, 'clarity' refers to the nature of mind, and 'cognizes' to the function of mind. Mind is clarity because it always lacks form and because it possesses the actual power to perceive objects. Mind cognizes because its function is to know or perceive objects. In *Ornament of the Seven Sets* Khädrubje says that thought, awareness, mind, and cognizer are synonyms.

It might be felt that since persons are not form but do cognize objects, they too fit this definition. However, this is not the case, because although persons themselves are not form but non-associated compounded phenomena they nevertheless possess form because they possess physical bodies. Even persons in the formless realm lack form only temporarily. In previous lives they possessed physical bodies, and in future lives they will acquire them again. Mind, on the other hand, always lacks form. Moreover, although persons cognize objects, they do so only through the power of mind. Cognizing objects is the principal function of mind, not of persons.

There are other phenomena, such as uncompounded space and emptiness, that always lack form, but these are not clarity because they do not have the power to perceive objects. If something is clarity it necessarily possesses the power to perceive objects.

Although mind lacks form it can nevertheless be related to form. Thus, our mind is related to our body and is located at different places throughout the body. We can understand this by considering the following. From the point of view of how it is generated, there are two types of mind: sense awareness and mental awareness. There are five types of sense awareness: eye awareness, ear awareness, nose awareness, tongue awareness, and body awareness. These are generated directly in dependence upon their particular sense powers, which are located within the respective physical sense organs. The eye sense power is located within the eye organ, the ear sense power within the ear organ, and so on. The body sense power is located throughout the body, apart from certain parts such as the hair and the nails. When a sense power meets an appropriate object, a sense awareness is generated. Thus, when an eye sense power, for example, meets a visual form, an eye awareness apprehending that form is generated. Therefore, we can say that the various sense awarenesses are related to the body and are located at various places throughout the body.

When we die, the mind usually leaves the body gradually rather than immediately. For some people it begins to withdraw from the feet and finally leaves through the crown of the head, or through any of the upper doors such as the mouth or the eyes, whereas for others it withdraws first from the top of the body and finally leaves through the lower doors. If we watch a dying person we can observe this process. For example, if the mind absorbs upwards, the dying person first loses all awareness in the feet because the body sense power has ceased to exist there, and then this process continues with the dying person gradually losing awareness from the lower parts of the body upwards. By observing this process we can see how sense awareness is related to, but different from, the physical body.

There are three levels of mental awareness: gross, subtle, and very subtle. All our normal waking minds are gross minds. Subtle and very subtle minds manifest only during sleep, during death and, for completion stage practitioners, during meditative equipoise. According to Tantra all minds, including mental awarenesses, are mounted upon inner winds, which are subtle forms. Since these winds have specific locations within the physical body, the minds that are mounted upon them can also be said to have the same locations. In this way we can identify specific locations for the different types of mental awareness. Thus, discursive thoughts, dull minds, and confused minds are said to exist mainly in the region of the crown chakra; love, compassion, hatred, and self-grasping in the region of the heart chakra; and desirous attachment in the region of the navel chakra. With practice we can learn to identify the movement of these various winds in the different parts of our body as their associated minds manifest.

Subtle minds manifest when the inner winds gather and dissolve within the central channel. A detailed explanation of how this occurs is given in *Clear Light of Bliss* and *Tantric Grounds and Paths*. The very subtle mind and its mounted wind are located within the tiny vacuole inside the central channel at the centre of the heart chakra. This mind is known as the 'root mind' because all other minds arise from it and dissolve back into it. It is also known as the 'continually abiding mind' because it is the only mind that survives from one life to the next. It is this very subtle mind that finally leaves the body at death and goes to the next life. By focusing on an object such as a seed-letter within the vacuole inside the central channel at the heart chakra, completion stage practitioners are able to bring all the winds into the central channel at this point and thereby cause the very subtle mind to manifest there. This is why the very subtle mind is said to exist at the heart chakra.

To summarize, there are many different types of mind – sense awarenesses, mental awarenesses, gross minds, subtle minds, and very subtle minds – but they are all the nature of clarity and they all function to cognize; and even though none of these minds is form they can all be related to form and can be identified as having specific locations within the body.

DIVISIONS OF MIND

There is a twofold division of mind into conceptual minds and non-conceptual minds; a twofold division into sense awarenesses and mental awarenesses; a sevenfold division into direct perceivers, inferential cognizers, re-cognizers, correct beliefs, non-ascertaining perceivers, doubts, and wrong awarenesses; a twofold division into valid cognizers and non-valid cognizers; and finally another twofold division into primary minds and mental factors. These will be discussed in detail below – the first four divisions here in Part One and the fifth division in Part Two.

GENERATION OF MIND

To understand how mind is generated we first need to understand that mind and body are separate entities that have separate continuums. Practitioners who have mastered the practice of transference of consciousness know this from their own experience because they are able to eject their mind from their body and go wherever they wish, even entering into different bodies. Moreover, when we fall asleep and dream, our mind leaves our physical body and wanders through dream worlds experiencing dream enjoyments and dream sufferings while our physical body remains in the same place.

At present we cannot witness this separation, but accomplished meditators who can retain mindfulness throughout the sleep and dream state are aware of their mind leaving their gross physical body, travelling through different dream worlds, and later, when the dream is finished, re-entering the physical body. Until we are able to experience this separation of mind and body directly we need to rely upon the following reasoning to develop conviction that mind and body are separate entities.

One way to realize that mind is non-physical is to consider the differences between what obstructs physical objects and what obstructs mind. Physical objects are obstructed by other physical objects. Thus, a chair cannot exist where there is a table. Even subtle matter such as light or radio waves can be obstructed by physical obstacles. Mind however cannot be obstructed by physical objects. The presence of a wall, for example, does not prevent the mind from thinking about what is on the other side of the wall. Similarly, even though there is a whole planet between Australia and England, nevertheless we can think about Australia from England.

Physical objects take time to travel distances, and the greater the distance the more time is needed, but the mind can think of distant objects immediately. For example, the mind can think of the sun as quickly as it can think of this book. Thus, even though our body remains still, our mind can move immediately to an object, no matter how distant and no matter what physical obstacles might be in the way. Mind is not even obstructed by time. Simply by thinking of an event that occurred in our childhood our mind goes to the past, and if we had clairvoyance we would even be able to see that event directly. Physical phenomena cannot establish a connection with the past in this way.

Although mind is not obstructed by physical phenomena, it does have its own obstructions – delusions and their imprints. However, these are completely different from the things that obstruct matter.

Another characteristic of matter is that it can be reproduced and shown to others. Visual forms can be photographed and sound can be recorded, but mind cannot be reproduced or recorded. We cannot photograph attachment or bodhichitta. Even if we extracted chemicals from one person's brain and injected them into another person's brain we would not be able to transfer that person's thoughts, memories, or knowledge to the other.

If mind and body were one entity, then whatever developed or increased the body would also develop and increase the mind, and vice versa; and whatever damaged or destroyed the one would also damage or destroy the other. However, this is clearly not the case. Eating large amounts of food, for example, increases the size of the body but it does not necessarily enhance the mind. On the other hand, physical illness harms the body but does not necessarily harm the mind. Indeed illness may even lead to an increase in mental good qualities such as patience, renunciation, and compassion. Moreover, a person who has greatly improved his or her mind through Dharma study and practice does not necessarily show any physical improvement, and a person whose moral conduct and views have degenerated does not necessarily deteriorate physically. Of course there is often a relationship between the quality of our mental state and our physical condition, but this merely indicates that there is a relationship between the body and mind, not that the body and mind are the same entity.

Through contemplating how mind completely lacks form and how it is a separate continuum from the body we shall understand clearly that forms such as the brain or the central nervous system cannot be mind. We shall also understand that mind cannot be produced from physical causes. Mind has two types of cause: substantial and contributory causes. The substantial cause of any mind is its own previous continuum. Thus the substantial cause of the first moment of the mind of this life is the last moment of the mind of the previous life, and the substantial cause of the first moment of the mind of the waking state is the last moment of the mind of the sleep state. The contributory causes of a mind assist the substantial cause in generating that mind. All minds are included within sense awareness and mental awareness. A contributory cause of a sense awareness is its particular sense power, and a contributory cause of mental awareness is the mental power. Eye awareness, for example, is generated from its previous continuum with the assistance of the eye sense power. The generation of the remaining four sense awarenesses can be understood in the same way. Mental awareness is generated from its previous continuum with the assistance of the mental power.

APPLICATION OF OUR UNDERSTANDING OF MIND TO DHARMA PRACTICE

Through understanding the nature, function, and causes of mind mentioned above we shall also understand that when we die our mind will leave our present body and go to the next life, and in this way we shall develop a clear understanding of the existence of future lives. When this knowledge arises clearly within our mind we should make a strong decision, thinking 'I must protect myself from lower rebirth and create the causes of happiness in my next life by sincerely practising Dharma now.' We should meditate on this determination and put it into practice sincerely day and night.

Conceptual and Non-conceptual Minds

From the point of view of how they engage their objects minds can be divided into two types: conceptual minds and non-conceptual minds. Whereas non-conceptual minds engage their objects directly, conceptual minds engage their objects through the medium of a generic image. Until we become a Buddha we need both conceptual and non-conceptual minds. Even the highest Bodhisattvas, for example, realize the two truths simultaneously only with their conceptual minds.

Some people believe that all conceptual thoughts are bad and should be abandoned. This mistaken view was taught by the twelfth-century Chinese monk Hashang, who misunderstood what Buddha taught in the *Perfection of Wisdom Sutras* and believed that the way to meditate on emptiness was simply to empty the mind of all conceptual thoughts. This view still has many adherents today, but if we hold this view we shall have no opportunity to progress on the spiritual paths. For one thing, if we prevent conceptual minds from arising we shall not be able to remember anything, and as a result all our spiritual development will cease. Moreover, conceptual realizations are the main causes of the realizations of yogic direct perceivers, and without these the attainment of liberation is impossible.

CONCEPTUAL MIND

DEFINITION OF CONCEPTUAL MIND

The definition of conceptual mind is a thought that apprehends its object through a generic image.

Although other scholars have different explanations, this definition is explained by Khädrubje in *Ornament of the Seven Sets*. When we think of or remember an object, say an elephant, there appears to our conceptual mind an object that is the opposite of non-elephant. This appearance is the generic image of elephant. Even though there is no actual elephant in front of us, nevertheless there is a generic image of elephant appearing to our mind. Thus our conceptual mind apprehends elephant through the generic image of elephant. We can apply this to all other phenomena.

There are five types of object: appearing object, observed object, engaged object, apprehended object, and conceived object. When we see a table with our eye awareness, for example, that table is the appearing object of our eye awareness because it appears directly to our eye awareness. The table is also the observed object, engaged object, and apprehended object of our eye awareness because at that time our eye awareness is focused on the table, understands the table, and apprehends the table. However, the table is not a conceived object of our eye awareness because only conceptual minds have conceived objects. For us, non-conceptual minds cannot conceive an object.

When our eye awareness sees a table we may develop the thought 'This is a table.' This thought is a conceptual mind that apprehends the table through a generic image of the table. For this conceptual mind, the table is the observed object, the engaged object, the apprehended object, and the conceived object. However, it is not the appearing object of this mind because the appearing object of this conceptual mind is a generic image of the table, not the table itself.

The definition of generic image is the appearing object of a conceptual mind. Although other texts give a different explanation, this definition is Khädrubje's intention. A generic image of an object is like a reflection of that object. When we look in a mirror we see directly the reflection of our face, and through this we know what our actual face looks like. In a similar way, conceptual minds know their object through the appearance of a generic image of that object, not by seeing the object directly. If we speak precisely, we must say that table appears to a conceptual mind apprehending table because the general aspect of table appears to that mind. The general aspect of table and the generic image of table are synonyms. However, table is not the appearing object of a conceptual mind apprehending table. This can be applied to all other objects.

As with other types of mind, the nature of conceptual mind is clarity that completely lacks form and possesses the power to perceive objects. However, its function is different from that of other types of mind. The principal function of conceptual mind is to impute names by thinking 'This is a table', 'This is a chair', 'I am Peter', 'He is John', and so on. All phenomena are merely imputed by conceptual mind in this way.

Another function of conceptual mind is to find the object of meditation. Whenever we meditate we first need to find the object on which we are going to meditate. This means trying to perceive clearly the generic image of the object of meditation, and this is achieved by conceptual mind. Moreover, the root of meditation is to maintain mindfulness, which means to hold the object without forgetting it, and for us this is also a function of conceptual thought because our non-conceptual mind cannot do this.

When we first realize the ultimate nature of phenomena, emptiness, we do so with our conceptual mind. If we then meditate repeatedly on this conceptual realization, eventually we shall realize emptiness directly. At that time our conceptual realization will transform into a yogic direct perceiver realizing emptiness, which is the direct antidote to the delusions. It is through this yogic direct perceiver that we shall be released from the ocean of samsaric sufferings.

DIVISIONS OF CONCEPTUAL MIND

There are three types of conceptual mind:

1 Conceptual minds that perceive the generic image of an object mainly through the force of listening or reading

2 Conceptual minds that perceive the generic image of an object mainly through the force of contemplating the meaning of that object

3 Conceptual minds that perceive the generic image of an object mainly through the force of previous imprints

An example of the first type is a thought perceiving an appearance of the opposite of non-yeti that develops mainly through the force of listening to someone else explaining about yetis. Other examples can be understood from this. An example of the second type is a thought perceiving an appearance of the opposite of non-yeti that develops mainly through the force of our own contemplation of yetis after listening to an explanation about them. Again, other examples can be understood from this. Examples of the third type are all natural conceptual thoughts, such as innate self-grasping and other innate delusions.

There is also a twofold division of conceptual mind:

1 Correct conceptual minds
2 Wrong conceptual minds

The first includes all conceptual minds whose conceived objects exist, such as conceptual minds conceiving pen, paper, and so forth; and the second includes all conceptual minds whose conceived objects do not exist, such as a conceptual mind conceiving a reflection of a face to be an actual face, a mind of self-grasping, or a conceptual mind conceiving karma, reincarnation, or enlightened beings to be non-existent.

GENERATION OF CONCEPTUAL MINDS

There are three ways in which conceptual minds are generated: through the force of hearing names, through the force of contemplating, and through the force of previous imprints. These can be understood from the previous explanation of the three types of conceptual mind.

APPLICATION OF CONCEPTUAL MINDS TO
DHARMA PRACTICE

It is very important to distinguish conceptual minds that are harmful and to be abandoned from those that are beneficial and to be cultivated. Although there are countless wrong thoughts and attitudes, there are sixteen in particular that we should know and strive to abandon because they directly prevent realizations of the stages of the path. They are:

(1) Disliking or having disrespect for our Spiritual Guide
(2) Not wishing to take the essence of our precious human life
(3) Not remembering death
(4) Being attached to the pleasures and happiness of this life alone
(5) Not fearing rebirth in the lower realms
(6) Not wishing to go for refuge to the Three Jewels
(7) Not having faith or conviction in the laws of karma
(8) Seeking to accumulate non-virtuous actions and not virtuous actions
(9) Regarding samsara as having the nature of happiness
(10) Wishing to increase delusions and contaminated actions
(11) Being uninterested in attaining liberation
(12) Not wanting to practise the three higher trainings, which are the causes of liberation
(13) Forsaking mother living beings
(14) Self-cherishing
(15) Self-grasping
(16) Disliking the practice of Secret Mantra

Corresponding to these there are sixteen correct thoughts and attitudes that we need to cultivate:

(1) Relying faithfully upon and having respect for our Spiritual Guide

(2) Wishing to take the essence of our precious human life

(3) Remembering death

(4) Not being attached to the pleasures and happiness of this life

(5) Fearing rebirth in the lower realms

(6) Wishing to go for refuge to the Three Jewels

(7) Having faith and conviction in the laws of karma

(8) Seeking to accumulate virtuous actions and not non-virtuous actions

(9) Regarding samsara as having the nature of suffering

(10) Wishing to abandon delusions and contaminated actions, which are the causes of samsaric rebirth

(11) Being determined to attain liberation

(12) Wanting to practise the three higher trainings

(13) Cherishing all mother living beings

(14) Forsaking self-cherishing

(15) Realizing selflessness

(16) Liking the practice of Secret Mantra

We should try to understand all these conceptual minds well by studying authentic explanations such as those given in *Joyful Path of Good Fortune* and then, based on this understanding, make a strong determination to abandon the sixteen wrong thoughts and cultivate the sixteen correct thoughts. Then we should put this determination into practice.

NON-CONCEPTUAL MIND

DEFINITION OF NON-CONCEPTUAL MIND

The definition of non-conceptual mind is a cognizer to which its object appears clearly without being mixed with a generic image.

DIVISIONS OF NON-CONCEPTUAL MIND

There are two types of non-conceptual mind:

1 Sense awarenesses
2 Non-conceptual mental awarenesses

All sense awarenesses are non-conceptual minds, but mental awarenesses can be either conceptual or non-conceptual. Conceptual mental awareness and conceptual mind are synonyms.

There are three types of non-conceptual mental awareness:

1 Non-conceptual mental direct perceivers
2 Yogic direct perceivers
3 Non-conceptual mental awarenesses that are neither of these two

An example of the first is a mental direct perceiver to which a form appears clearly without being mixed with a generic image, such as eye clairvoyance. An example of the second is any yogic direct perceiver, such as a yogic direct perceiver realizing subtle impermanence. An example of the third is a dream eye awareness that apprehends a dream mountain as an actual mountain. This is not an actual eye awareness because eye awareness does not exist during sleep. As Chandrakirti says in *Guide to the Middle Way*:

> Because eye awareness is impossible in sleep, it does
> not exist;
> Only mental awareness exists.

This means that since there can be no sense awareness, such as eye awareness, during sleep, dream objects that are objects of sense awareness do not exist. Only mental awareness exists during sleep. Therefore, dream eye awareness, ear awareness, nose awareness, tongue awareness, and body awareness are mental awarenesses; and because their objects appear clearly to them, without being mixed with a generic image, they are non-conceptual mental awarenesses.

It should be noted at this point that if an object appears clearly to a mind, that mind is not necessarily non-conceptual.

For example, some conceptual minds that are clear and strong concentrations perceive their object clearly but, because they are conceptual minds, their object is perceived through the medium of a generic image of that object.

There is another twofold division of non-conceptual mind:

1 Correct non-conceptual minds
2 Wrong non-conceptual minds

A correct non-conceptual mind is a non-conceptual mind whose apprehended object exists. All sense direct perceivers are correct non-conceptual minds. Also, in general, dream eye, ear, nose, tongue, and body awarenesses are correct non-conceptual minds because they are non-conceptual minds and their apprehended objects exist. For non-conceptual minds, apprehended object and appearing object are synonyms. A dream mountain that appears to a dream eye awareness, therefore, exists. It is a form that is a phenomena source, and is like a reflection of a mountain. Dream things cannot be objects of sense awareness but only of mental awareness; therefore they are phenomena sources.

Non-conceptual minds such as an eye awareness apprehending a toy snake as a real snake, or an ear awareness apprehending an echo as the actual sound of speech, are wrong non-conceptual minds because they are non-conceptual minds and their apprehended objects do not exist.

GENERATION OF NON-CONCEPTUAL MINDS

All non-conceptual minds are included within sense awarenesses and non-conceptual mental awarenesses. All five sense awarenesses are generated from their own previous continuum and the meeting of their particular sense power with a corresponding sense object. Non-conceptual mental awarenesses are generated from their own previous continuum and their dominant condition, the mental power.

APPLICATION OF NON-CONCEPTUAL MINDS TO
DHARMA PRACTICE

At present we cannot use our non-conceptual mental awareness in our daily activities. The only non-conceptual awarenesses we can use are our sense awarenesses. Although our sense awarenesses are not our I, nevertheless when they see a form, hear a sound, and so on, we say 'I saw such and such', 'I heard such and such', and so on. If we use our sense awarenesses for virtuous activities we shall experience beneficial results and develop good qualities, but if we use them for non-virtuous activities we shall experience suffering and problems. Knowing this, we should make a determination not to use our sense awarenesses for non-virtuous purposes but to use them only for virtuous purposes. Then we should put this determination into practice.

One special way of using our sense awarenesses for virtuous purposes that is explained in the *Perfection of Wisdom Sutras* is, whenever we see visual forms, hear sounds, smell odours, experience tastes, or touch tactile objects, immediately to recognize that these sense objects lack true existence. By familiarizing ourself with this recognition we shall gradually reduce our attachment, anger, and other delusions, and especially our self-grasping.

Aryadeva

Sense and Mental Awarenesses

From the point of view of their uncommon dominant condition, minds can be divided into two types: sense awareness and mental awareness.

SENSE AWARENESS

DEFINITION OF SENSE AWARENESS

The definition of sense awareness is an awareness that is developed in dependence upon its uncommon dominant condition, a sense power possessing form.

As with other minds, the nature of sense awareness is clarity, but it has different functions from other types of mind. The principal functions of sense awareness are seeing visual forms, hearing sounds, and experiencing odours, tastes, and tactile objects. There are five sense awarenesses, which are called the 'awarenesses of the five doors'. The five doors are the eyes, ears, nose, tongue, and body. In dependence upon their respective doors, eye awareness sees visual forms, ear awareness hears sounds, and so on.

Insofar as they permit us to read and listen to Dharma instructions, sense awarenesses are useful for our Dharma practice, but from the point of view of their obstructing our meditation and concentration they are quite harmful. If a sense awareness manifests when we are meditating on an object single-pointedly it immediately disturbs our concentration by causing distraction to other objects. It is like a sharp thorn sticking into our flesh. This is why many meditators who are emphasizing the attainment of tranquil abiding develop renunciation for sense awarenesses.

As a result of having developed renunciation for sense awarenesses in their previous lives, form and formless realm beings have no sense awarenesses of their own. Form realm beings, for example, can see forms and hear sounds, but they do so by using desire realm eye awareness and ear awareness in much the same way as we see distant forms by using binoculars and hear distant sounds by using a telephone. They have no need of nose awareness, tongue awareness, or body awareness at all because they do not need to enjoy smells, taste food and drink, or experience tactile objects. Instead they derive continuous enjoyment from the inner food of the suppleness of concentration.

DIVISIONS OF SENSE AWARENESS

There are five types of sense awareness: eye awareness, ear awareness, nose awareness, tongue awareness, and body awareness. There are also five sense objects: visual forms, sounds, smells, tastes, and tactile objects. The definition of eye awareness is an awareness that is developed in dependence upon its uncommon dominant condition, an eye sense power. This definition can be applied to the other four sense awarenesses by changing the uncommon dominant condition to the ear sense power, the nose sense power, the tongue sense power, or the body sense power.

The eye sense power is an inner energy power abiding in the very centre of the eye organ that functions directly to generate eye awareness. The ear sense power is an inner energy power abiding in the very centre of the ear organ that functions directly to generate ear awareness. The remaining sense powers can be understood in the same way. The eye sense power itself is not form, but it possesses form. This is similar to a person. Persons are not form but they possess form, namely their form aggregate.

It is said that the eye sense power is a very hidden object. The Buddhist schools of the Vaibashikas and the Sautrantikas believe that it is form. They say that it is a very clear lucid form located in the centre of the eye organ in which visual forms are reflected. However, the Madhyamika schools reject this assertion.

Sense consciousnesses are primary minds. Their retinues of secondary minds, or mental factors, are sense awarenesses but not sense consciousnesses. Consciousness and primary mind are synonyms.

GENERATION OF SENSE AWARENESSES

Both sense and mental awarenesses are generated in dependence upon two conditions – their dominant condition and their immediate condition. According to the Sautrantikas there is a third condition – the observed object condition.

The definition of dominant condition is that which principally assists the development of a sense or mental awareness. There are two types of dominant condition: common dominant condition and uncommon dominant condition. An example of a common dominant condition is light. We cannot see anything with our eye awareness if it is dark, therefore light is a necessary condition for eye awareness. It is called a 'common dominant condition' because it is common to everyone. The uncommon dominant condition of eye awareness is the eye sense power. This is said to be uncommon because it is specific to each person. Different types of being have different types of eye sense power. For example, a human eye sense power needs a considerable amount of light to function well, whereas a cat's eye sense power functions equally well in both light and dark, and an owl's eye sense power is particularly suited to the dark.

A particular sense power can give rise only to its particular sense awareness. Thus, the eye sense power, for example, can give rise only to eye awareness. However, in *Close Placement of Mindfulness Sutra* Buddha says that although snakes have no ears and so cannot develop ear awareness they nevertheless have a special eye sense power that enables them to hear sounds with their eye awareness. Light is not a necessary condition for hearing, and so even though they use their eyes to hear, they can hear in the dark. The eye awareness of a Buddha can see, hear, taste, smell, and touch.

The immediate condition of an eye awareness apprehending a form is a mental consciousness that develops immediately before that eye awareness and that is the same continuum as that eye awareness. It exists simultaneously with the eye sense power.

According to the Sautrantikas, sense and mental awarenesses also have an observed object condition, which must be both an observed object of that awareness and a cause of that awareness. For them, blue is both the observed object of an eye awareness apprehending blue and a cause of that awareness, and so blue is the observed object condition of an eye awareness apprehending blue.

The Chittamatrins do not assert observed object conditions because they believe that a mind and its object arise simultaneously from the same seed. Thus, they say that an object cannot be a cause of the mind that apprehends it because it is the same entity as that mind. According to the schools that assert observed object conditions, an object is a cause of the mind that apprehends it and is therefore a different entity to that mind, but for the Chittamatrins this difference in entity between an object and the mind that apprehends it is the principal object to be negated.

APPLICATION OF SENSE AWARENESSES TO
DHARMA PRACTICE

This can be understood from the previous explanation of the application of non-conceptual minds to Dharma practice.

MENTAL AWARENESS

DEFINITION OF MENTAL AWARENESS

The definition of mental awareness is an awareness that is developed in dependence upon its uncommon dominant condition, a mental power.

The definition of mental power is a mentality that principally functions directly to produce the uncommon aspect of a mental awareness. For example, after the last moment of an eye consciousness apprehending blue we usually develop a mental direct perceiver directly apprehending blue. This is a mental awareness. Its dominant condition, a mental power, is the last moment of the eye consciousness apprehending blue. This eye consciousness is a mentality because it is a primary mind. It directly produces the uncommon aspect of a mental direct perceiver directly apprehending blue, which is its apprehending blue and not non-blue. After the last moment of the mental direct perceiver directly apprehending blue we usually develop a conceptual awareness thinking 'This is blue.' The dominant condition of this conceptual mental awareness is the last moment of the mental direct perceiver directly apprehending blue. All other mental awarenesses can be understood in the same way.

DIVISIONS OF MENTAL AWARENESS

There are two types of mental awareness:

1 Conceptual mental awarenesses
2 Non-conceptual mental awarenesses

Conceptual mental awareness and conceptual mind are synonymous. Examples of non-conceptual mental awareness are dream sense awarenesses apprehending dream objects and a wisdom directly realizing emptiness. According to the Sautrantikas, all mental direct perceivers, self-cognizers, and yogic direct perceivers are non-conceptual mental awarenesses.

There is also a threefold division of mental awareness:

1 Non-virtuous mental awarenesses
2 Virtuous mental awarenesses
3 Neutral mental awarenesses

The sense awarenesses of sentient beings are always neutral – they cannot be virtuous or non-virtuous. Within mental awareness, deluded mental awarenesses – such as covetousness, harmful thought, wrong view, anger, and jealousy – are non-virtuous mental awarenesses. All non-virtue arises from delusions, and delusions arise from four causes: the root, the seed, the object, and inappropriate attention. The root of all delusions is self-grasping; the seed of a delusion is a potential left on the mental continuum by similar delusions in the past that acts as the substantial cause of that delusion; the object is any contaminated object; and inappropriate attention is a mental factor that focuses on the object in a mistaken way and acts as a co-operative cause of delusions. For a delusion to arise, all four causes are necessary.

Some people believe that delusions are caused by bodily vigour because their delusions seem to be stronger when their vital energies increase, and so to reduce their delusions they try to weaken their body by engaging in harsh ascetic practices such as fasting and exposing their body to extremes of heat and cold. In reality, however, the causes of delusions exist within the mind, not the body. For this reason Nagarjuna said that physical asceticism is not very important. To overcome delusions we need the mental asceticism of practices such as meditation and patience.

The easiest way to prevent delusions from arising is to stop inappropriate attention by not allowing our mind to dwell on and exaggerate the attractive or unattractive features of contaminated objects. In this way we shall be able temporarily to prevent delusions. However, to eradicate them completely we must abandon their root, self-grasping, by attaining a yogic direct perceiver realizing emptiness. Once we have attained a direct realization of emptiness, we shall gradually eradicate the seeds of all the delusions. We eradicate the seeds of all intellectually-formed delusions on the path of seeing, and the seeds of all innate delusions on the path of meditation.

Nagarjuna said that minds can be like writing in stone, writing in sand, or writing in water. Minds that are like writing in stone are deeply ingrained and difficult to remove; those that are like writing in sand can be removed more easily; and those that are like writing in water disappear naturally almost as soon as they arise. At present, our deluded minds are like writing in stone and our virtuous minds are like writing in water. We should try to reverse this situation. It is difficult to stop delusions completely but if we conscientiously apply their opponents we can gradually weaken them so that they are no longer engraved in our mind like writing in stone. At first they will become like writing in sand, which can be removed with little effort, and then gradually as their strength continues to diminish they will become like writing in water. Eventually they will disappear altogether.

As for virtuous mental awarenesses, these include all the stages of the path to enlightenment from respect for our Spiritual Guide to superior seeing. All virtuous minds arise from four causes: imprints, the object, appropriate attention, and the empowering blessings of the Buddhas. Although all sentient beings have at least some virtuous imprints, those who have very few find it extremely difficult to generate virtuous minds, while those who have very rich imprints develop virtuous minds naturally. The objects from which virtuous minds develop are the Three Jewels and their representations – such as our Spiritual Guide and our spiritual friends. Appropriate attention is a mental factor attention possessing a special way of thinking that acts as a co-operative cause for a virtuous mind. The fourth cause, the empowering blessings of the Buddhas, is a little more difficult to understand. It is said that all the virtuous minds of sentient beings are the result of the enlightened activities of the Buddhas. The two principal ways in which Buddhas help sentient beings are by giving teachings and by blessing their minds. Without the blessings of the Buddhas it is impossible for a virtuous mind to arise. All sentient beings have at some time or another received Buddha's blessings. It is almost impossible for animals to develop virtuous thoughts on their own but there are many cases of animals naturally developing virtuous thoughts as a result of receiving Buddha's blessings. If this happens at the time of their death they will take a rebirth in one of the higher realms. As with deluded minds, all four causes are necessary for a virtuous mind to develop.

A neutral mental awareness is a thought with neither a virtuous nor a non-virtuous motivation – for example simply wishing to eat or to go for a walk.

GENERATION OF MENTAL AWARENESSES

Mental awareness is generated in dependence upon two conditions: the dominant condition and the immediate condition. The dominant condition of a mental awareness is a mental power. The immediate condition of a mental awareness is an awareness whose principal function is to produce directly the nature of a mental awareness. For example, the nature of a mental awareness apprehending blue is the clarity of that awareness. This nature is produced by its immediate condition, which is the same continuum as that awareness. In summary, mental awareness is generated from the meeting of its dominant condition and its immediate condition.

APPLICATION OF MENTAL AWARENESSES TO
DHARMA PRACTICE

The practice of meditation depends almost entirely upon mental awareness because we cannot contemplate or meditate with our sense awarenesses. Initially our meditation is conceptual mental awareness but gradually it becomes non-conceptual mental awareness. Moreover, all virtuous actions of body and speech are initiated by virtuous mental awareness. We should practise the methods for cultivating virtuous mental awarenesses that are explained in the Lamrim teachings. In this way we shall be able to reduce, and eventually completely abandon, all non-virtuous mental awarenesses.

Direct Perceivers

As mentioned before, mind can be divided into seven:

1 Direct perceivers
2 Inferential cognizers
3 Re-cognizers
4 Correct beliefs
5 Non-ascertaining perceivers
6 Doubts
7 Wrong awarenesses

All minds are included in this sevenfold division. The main purpose of studying it is to distinguish valid minds from non-valid minds, and to learn the stages by which we attain Dharma realizations.

DIRECT PERCEIVERS

DEFINITION OF DIRECT PERCEIVER

The definition of direct perceiver is a cognizer that apprehends its manifest object.

Examples are non-conceptual minds that apprehend cars, houses, trees, and so on; and conceptual minds that apprehend such objects without depending upon reasons. These are all direct perceivers because they apprehend their object in a manifest way, without relying upon reasons.

The first moment of a valid conceptual mind that realizes emptiness is not a direct perceiver but an inferential cognizer because it realizes its object through the power of reasons, not in a manifest way. However, the second and subsequent moments of a valid conceptual mind realizing emptiness are direct perceivers because they realize their object in a manifest way, without depending upon reasons. Even so, these minds do not realize emptiness directly because they are conceptual minds.

To realize emptiness in a manifest way is to realize it through experience, without depending upon reasons. Thus, for the second and subsequent moments of a valid conceptual mind realizing emptiness, emptiness is a manifest object, but for the first moment of a valid conceptual mind realizing emptiness, emptiness is a hidden object. In the term 'direct perceiver', 'direct' means 'manifest object', and so any mind that apprehends a manifest object is a direct perceiver. All re-cognizers are also direct perceivers.

The definitions of direct perceiver presented in the Lorig text by Purbuchog and in some other texts are given according to the Sautrantika tradition, which is quite different from the Madhyamika-Prasangika tradition.

DIVISIONS OF DIRECT PERCEIVER

There are three types of direct perceiver:

1 Sense direct perceivers
2 Mental direct perceivers
3 Yogic direct perceivers

SENSE DIRECT PERCEIVERS

DEFINITION OF SENSE DIRECT PERCEIVER

The definition of sense direct perceiver is a direct perceiver that is generated in dependence upon its uncommon dominant condition, a sense power possessing form.

Examples of sense direct perceivers are an eye consciousness seeing blue, an ear consciousness hearing a sound, and so on. Although all sense awarenesses are non-conceptual minds, they are not necessarily sense direct perceivers. For example, wrong sense awarenesses such as an eye awareness that, under the influence of the drug dhatura, sees the earth as yellow, or one that due to an eye disease sees snowy mountains as having a bluish colour, are not sense direct perceivers.

DIVISIONS OF SENSE DIRECT PERCEIVER

Because there are five types of sense object, there are five types of sense direct perceiver: eye sense direct perceivers, ear sense direct perceivers, and so on. These are distinguished by their uncommon dominant condition and their object. Eye sense direct perceivers, for example, are produced from an eye sense power as their uncommon dominant condition and have visual forms as their objects; ear sense direct perceivers are generated in dependence upon an ear sense power and have sounds as their objects; and so on. The remaining types of sense direct perceiver can be understood in the same way.

There is also a threefold division of sense direct perceiver:

1 Sense direct perceivers that are valid cognizers but not re-cognizers
2 Sense direct perceivers that are both valid cognizers and re-cognizers
3 Sense direct perceivers that are non-ascertaining perceivers

An example of the first type is the first moment of a sense awareness apprehending any of the five sense objects – forms, sounds, smells, tastes, and tactile objects. Such minds are not re-cognizers because they realize their object through their own power. All Buddhas' sense and mental direct perceivers are valid cognizers that are not re-cognizers because Buddhas have no re-cognizers. Examples of the second type are the second and subsequent moments of a sense awareness apprehending any of the five sense objects. These are re-cognizers because they realize their object through the power of the first moment of that awareness. The object of the first, second, and subsequent moments of such a sense direct perceiver is the same, but the way of realizing it is different. Examples of the third type, sense direct perceivers that are non-ascertaining perceivers, are the eye awareness of a new-born baby seeing its father's face, and an eye awareness seeing unfamiliar faces in a crowd.

GENERATION OF SENSE DIRECT PERCEIVERS

All phenomena are included within both the twelve sources and the eighteen elements. The twelve sources are the six object sources – visual form source, sound source, smell source, taste source, tactile object source, and phenomena source; and the six power sources – eye source, ear source, nose source, tongue source, body source, and mentality source. These twelve are called 'sources' because generally they are the sources of consciousness. The first six are objects that are sources of consciousness, and the second six are powers, or uncommon dominant conditions, that are sources of consciousness. Within the six object sources, phenomena source comprises objects that appear only to mental awareness.

The eighteen elements are the twelve sources plus their effects, the six consciousnesses – eye consciousness, ear consciousness, nose consciousness, tongue consciousness, body consciousness, and mental consciousness. When a visual form source and an eye source meet, an eye consciousness develops; when a sound source and an ear source meet, an ear consciousness develops; when a phenomena source and a mentality source meet, mental consciousness develops; and so on.

An ear consciousness, for example, develops only when a sound and an ear sense power meet. If someone shoots a pistol in the distance we do not hear the shot as soon as it is fired because it takes time for the sound to reach us. Thus, we do not develop an ear consciousness apprehending that sound until the sound and the ear sense power have met. Similarly, if we look at the moon, an eye consciousness apprehending the moon develops when light from the moon meets our eye sense power. For mental awareness to develop it is not necessary for an object and the mental power to meet.

Thus, we can think of the moon without the moon being present before us. Distance does not prevent an object from appearing clearly to a mental awareness, but to perceive distant things clearly with a sense awareness we need to use special devices such as telescopes, or to have clairvoyance.

Due to karma, sentient beings have different sense powers and can therefore perceive different objects. Thus, beings of the desire realm have contaminated sense powers with which they experience the five contaminated objects of desire – forms, sounds, and so on. We can enjoy these objects only because we have these sense powers. If we purify our sense powers we can attain certain types of clairvoyance, such as the clairvoyance of the fleshly eye, with which subtle and distant visual forms beyond the range of ordinary vision can be seen with the eyes.

To develop a sense direct perceiver a non-defective sense power and a non-deceptive sense object must meet. An example of a defective sense power is the eye sense power of a person suffering from jaundice that causes that person to see things as yellow. An example of a deceptive object is a whirling incense stick that appears to be a circle of light. If both the object and the sense power are free from such faults, a sense direct perceiver will be generated when they meet.

APPLICATION OF SENSE DIRECT PERCEIVERS TO DHARMA PRACTICE

Whenever our eye sense direct perceivers see attractive, unattractive, or neutral forms, or our ear sense direct perceivers hear pleasant, unpleasant, or neutral remarks, and so on, we must prevent attachment, anger, and confusion from arising within our mind by not allowing inappropriate attention to develop with respect to these objects. This is a great Dharma practice that we can practise during our daily activities. It is called 'restraining the sense doors'. It is very important to emphasize this practice if we want to be able to meditate without distractions.

MENTAL DIRECT PERCEIVERS

DEFINITION OF MENTAL DIRECT PERCEIVER

The definition of mental direct perceiver is a direct perceiver that is generated in dependence upon its uncommon dominant condition, a mental power.

DIVISIONS OF MENTAL DIRECT PERCEIVER

There are three types of mental direct perceiver:

1 Mental direct perceivers induced by sense direct perceivers
2 Mental direct perceivers induced by meditation
3 Mental direct perceivers that are induced neither by sense direct perceivers nor by meditation

There are five types of mental direct perceiver induced by sense direct perceivers: mental direct perceivers apprehending forms, sounds, smells, tastes, and tactile objects. For example, after an eye consciousness apprehending blue has developed we usually develop a mental direct perceiver that thinks 'This is blue.' This mental direct perceiver is a conceptual mind. Although it is induced by an eye awareness its uncommon dominant condition is a mental power, therefore it is a mental awareness; and because it apprehends its manifest object it is a direct perceiver.

Examples of mental direct perceivers induced by meditation are deep experiences of Lamrim, the stages of the path, gained through meditation. They are direct perceivers because they realize their objects through the power of experience of meditation and so realize their objects in a manifest way. Examples of mental direct perceivers that are induced neither by sense direct perceivers nor by meditation are conceptual minds that realize their objects simply by our remembering them.

GENERATION OF MENTAL DIRECT PERCEIVERS

Mental direct perceivers induced by sense direct perceivers are generated as follows. For example, an eye sense direct perceiver apprehending a form such as blue generates a conceptual mind apprehending blue that thinks 'This is blue'; an ear sense direct perceiver apprehending the sound of words generates a conceptual mind apprehending sound that understands the meaning of those words; a nose sense direct perceiver apprehending a smell generates a conceptual mind apprehending smell that thinks 'This is a pleasant smell', or 'This is a bad smell'; and so on. The same can be applied to tongue sense direct perceivers and body sense direct perceivers. All these conceptual minds are mental direct perceivers that are induced by sense direct perceivers.

We generate mental direct perceivers induced by meditation by training our mind in meditation and thereby gaining deep experience of the realizations of Sutra and Tantra. We generate the third type of mental direct perceiver by remembering, without relying upon reasons, an object that we previously understood. Such minds are re-cognizers that are mental direct perceivers induced neither by a sense direct perceiver nor by meditation.

The explanation of the nature and generation of mental direct perceivers according to the Sautrantika tradition causes many people to develop confusion and leads to many disagreements. By contrast, the supreme tradition of the Madhyamika-Prasangikas is very clear and simple.

APPLICATION OF MENTAL DIRECT PERCEIVERS TO DHARMA PRACTICE

If we are to gain authentic Dharma realizations that have the power actually to remove suffering we need to develop mental direct perceivers induced by meditation. In *King of Concentration Sutra* Buddha says:

> Just as we cannot quench our thirst by listening to the sound of water and watching it flow past, so we cannot overcome our suffering simply by listening to teachings on emptiness and understanding them intellectually, without meditating on them.

The main point of this quotation is that once we have developed some understanding of Dharma through sincere study, we then need to familiarize our mind with this understanding by meditating on it repeatedly. Only then shall we be able to gain deep realizations that will enable us to pacify our suffering and overcome our problems.

YOGIC DIRECT PERCEIVERS

DEFINITION OF YOGIC DIRECT PERCEIVER

The definition of yogic direct perceiver is a direct perceiver that realizes a subtle object directly, in dependence upon its uncommon dominant condition, a concentration that is a union of tranquil abiding and superior seeing.

An example of a yogic direct perceiver is a direct realization of any of the sixteen characteristics of the four noble truths in the continuum of a being on the path of preparation, the path of seeing, the path of meditation, or the Path of No More Learning.

Subtle objects are the two truths, the sixteen characteristics of the four noble truths, and so on. Through training in tranquil abiding observing a subtle object, eventually we shall realize that object directly, in dependence upon a concentration that is a union of tranquil abiding and superior seeing. When we attain such a direct perceiver observing a subtle object we become a special realized being, a Yogi or Yogini, and that realization is called a 'yogic direct perceiver'.

A yogic direct perceiver is a very special wisdom. By depending upon yogic direct perceivers we can eventually eradicate the two obstructions – the obstructions to liberation and the obstructions to omniscience. Without gaining this wisdom, however, it is not possible to attain permanent freedom from suffering. Once we attain a yogic direct perceiver we shall never again fall into unfortunate rebirths, and we shall never again create throwing karma that impels us into rebirth in samsara.

DIVISIONS OF YOGIC DIRECT PERCEIVER

All yogic direct perceivers are included within two types:

1 Yogic direct perceivers in the continuum of Hinayanists
2 Yogic direct perceivers in the continuum of Mahayanists

There is also a fourfold division of yogic direct perceiver:

1 Yogic direct perceivers that are paths of preparation
2 Yogic direct perceivers that are paths of seeing
3 Yogic direct perceivers that are paths of meditation
4 Yogic direct perceivers that are Paths of No More Learning

There is another twofold division:

1 Yogic direct perceivers that realize the conventional nature of phenomena
2 Yogic direct perceivers that realize the ultimate nature of phenomena

GENERATION OF YOGIC DIRECT PERCEIVERS

Although yogic direct perceivers are non-conceptual minds, the way that they are generated is quite unlike the way that other non-conceptual minds, such as sense awarenesses, are generated. For example, a yogic direct perceiver realizing the impermanence of the body is generated as follows. First we listen to teachings on the impermanence of the body and develop a correct belief that the body is by nature momentary. Then, through contemplating conclusive reasons that establish the momentariness of the body, we develop an inferential cognizer realizing the subtle impermanence of the body. This is our first valid cognizer realizing the subtle impermanence of the body, and the first mental abiding.

By placing our mind single-pointedly on this subtle impermanence we then gradually progress through the other mental abidings until we attain tranquil abiding. At this point we

have a very vivid and powerful experience of subtle impermanence, but we have still not realized it directly. Our mind
is still a conceptual mind that apprehends its object through
a generic image. Before we can realize subtle impermanence
directly, without a generic image, we first need to attain
superior seeing observing subtle impermanence. Thus, we
continue meditating on subtle impermanence with a concentration of tranquil abiding until we attain the special wisdom
of superior seeing observing subtle impermanence. At this
stage our mind is still conceptual, and subtle impermanence
still appears to our mind mixed with a generic image. If we
continue to meditate on subtle impermanence with a union
of the concentration of tranquil abiding and the wisdom of
superior seeing, the generic image will gradually fade until
it disappears altogether and subtle impermanence appears
directly to our mind.

This mind directly realizing subtle impermanence that is
generated in dependence upon the union of tranquil abiding
and superior seeing is a yogic direct perceiver realizing subtle
impermanence. All the previous concentrations from the
second mental abiding up to just before attaining the yogic
direct perceiver are re-cognizers that are mental direct perceivers induced by meditation. The way to generate yogic
direct perceivers realizing the remaining fifteen characteristics of the four noble truths can be understood from this
explanation.

APPLICATION OF YOGIC DIRECT PERCEIVERS TO
DHARMA PRACTICE

Yogic direct perceivers are essential for our spiritual development because without them we cannot realize emptiness
directly and thereby attain liberation. However, since we
cannot attain yogic direct perceivers until we become special,
realized beings, we may wonder how we can apply them to
our present Dharma practice. The way to do this is to meditate on facsimiles of yogic direct perceivers. We do this whenever we engage in correct conceptual meditation on the sixteen

characteristics of the four noble truths with the motivation of attaining yogic direct perceivers. Even though to begin with we may attain only a very rough generic image of the object, if we do the meditation repeatedly with a strong motivation to attain a yogic direct perceiver we shall sow the seeds for the object to appear more and more clearly, and create the cause to attain an actual yogic direct perceiver in the future.

According to the Sautrantika and Chittamatra schools there is a fourth type of direct perceiver – self-cognizing direct perceivers. They say that all minds have two parts – cognizing themselves and cognizing others. According to them, the first are self-cognizers, which do not depend upon an object, and the second are other-cognizers, which do depend upon an object. However, the Madhyamika-Prasangikas deny the existence of self-cognizers. They say that all subjective minds depend upon objects, and all objects depend upon subjective minds. Therefore, there are no independent minds, and so there are no self-cognizers. Detailed presentations of the Madhyamika-Prasangikas' refutation of self-cognizers can be found in *Meaningful to Behold* and *Ocean of Nectar*.

Inferential Cognizers

DEFINITION OF INFERENTIAL COGNIZER

The definition of inferential cognizer is a completely reliable cognizer whose object is realized in direct dependence upon a conclusive reason.

There are three types of object: manifest objects, slightly hidden objects, and deeply hidden objects. In general, manifest objects are phenomena such as visual forms and sounds that can be perceived directly by ordinary beings; slightly hidden objects are phenomena such as impermanence and emptiness that can be known initially only by depending upon a conclusive reason; and deeply hidden objects are phenomena such as the specific workings of the laws of karma that can be perceived directly only by Buddhas. However, these three types of object are relative. Thus hell beings, for example, are deeply hidden phenomena from the human viewpoint, but manifest objects from the viewpoint of hell beings themselves. Manifest objects can be realized initially by direct cognizers, but both types of hidden object can be realized initially only by inferential cognizers.

Inferential cognizers are very common, and we normally have many during each day. For example, if we see a person go into a room that has only one entrance, and not leave by that entrance, we know with certainty that he is still in the room even though we cannot see him. Similarly, if we see smoke billowing from the chimney of a house, we know for certain that there is a fire in the house even though we cannot see the fire directly. These are both examples of inferential cognizers that realize their object in dependence upon conclusive reasons. Most scientific and historical knowledge is based on inferential cognizers. For example, if an archaeologist finds a few bones, broken pots, and stone tools, he can infer many things about the life of the people to whom they originally belonged and, provided that he does not go beyond the evidence, his knowledge will be reliable.

There is one philosophical school, known as the Charavakas, that denies the existence of hidden objects and asserts that everything that exists can be realized directly by ordinary sense awarenesses. Thus, they do not accept inferential cognizers, and they deny that we can have reliable knowledge of anything that does not appear directly to one of our five sense awarenesses. This view is obviously incorrect because it is refuted by our everyday experiences. For example, if we stir sugar into tea we can know that the tea will be sweet without having to taste it to find out. Similarly, if we see a car we can know with certainty that there must have been a person or group of persons who manufactured it even though we may never have seen them ourself. We know these facts because we realize them with inferential cognizers.

Inferential cognizers are very important for our spiritual practice. Most of the essential topics explained in Dharma are hidden objects that can be realized initially only through inferential cognizers. Once we have realized these objects inferentially, if we continue to meditate on them we shall eventually realize them directly with a yogic direct perceiver, and then they will become manifest objects for us. There are some objects that are not presently manifest for us but that would become manifest for us if we were simply to move to a different position or just wait for something to happen. For example, we can establish that there is a fire inside a house simply by entering the house to have a look, or we can discover that a candle will eventually burn down simply by waiting for it to do so; but we cannot establish the existence of subtle objects such as emptiness or any other of the sixteen characteristics of the four noble truths in this way. The only way we can gain incontrovertible knowledge of these objects is by generating inferential cognizers in dependence upon conclusive reasons.

Whenever we realize something by means of a conclusive reason we use a special form of logical reasoning known as a 'syllogism'. An example of such syllogistic reasoning is, 'There is a fire in the house because there is smoke.' Like all syllogisms this has three parts – a subject, a predicate, and a reason. The subject is 'in the house', the predicate is 'there is a fire', and the reason is 'because there is smoke.' The combination of the subject and the predicate is known as the 'probandum'. In this case the probandum is 'There is a fire in the house', and it is this that we realize in dependence upon the reason.

A conclusive reason is a reason that is able to establish a probandum incontrovertibly. A conclusive reason must have a definite relationship with the predicate. Generally there are two types of relationship – natural relationships and causal relationships. A natural relationship obtains between objects that have the same entity, or nature. For example, there is a natural relationship between dog and animal because a dog is an animal. Similarly there is a natural relationship between re-cognizer and valid cognizer because whatever is a re-cognizer is necessarily a valid cognizer. A causal relationship obtains between objects when one is the cause of the other. Thus, causal relationships exist between acorn and oak tree, fire and smoke, and eye sense power and eye awareness. Because there are two types of relationship there are also two types of reason – those based on a natural relationship (which are known as 'nature reasons'), and those based on a causal relationship (which are known as 'effect reasons'). Examples of the first are the reason in the statement 'This white dog is an animal because it is a dog', and the reason in the statement 'The second moment of an inferential cognizer is a valid cognizer because it is a re-cognizer.' Examples of the second are the reason in the statement 'There is a fire in the house because there is smoke' and the reason in the statement 'A new-born baby's mind must have arisen from its previous continuum of awareness because it is a mind.'

The definition of conclusive reason is a reason that is qualified by the three modes. The three modes are: the property of the subject, the forward pervasion, and the reverse pervasion; and any conclusive reason will be qualified by all three. We can understand these three modes by considering the syllogism stated above, 'There is a fire in the house because there is smoke.'

The first mode is called the 'property of the subject' because for a reason to be conclusive it must apply to, or be a property of, the subject. In this case, the reason is a property of the subject because there is smoke (reason) in the house (subject). The second mode is called the 'forward pervasion' because for a reason to be a conclusive reason it must be pervaded by the predicate. In this case, the reason is qualified by the second mode because wherever there is smoke (reason), there is fire (predicate). The third mode is called the 'reverse pervasion' because if the predicate does not apply the reason must also not apply. In this case, the reason is qualified by the third mode because if there is no fire there is no smoke.

If a reason lacks any of the three modes it is not a conclusive reason. Thus, if we were to say 'There is a fire in the house because there is a chimney', the reason would not be a conclusive reason because it would not be qualified by the second and third modes. Similarly the statement 'There is a fire in the house because fire is hot' also does not have a conclusive reason.

By considering examples like the one used here we can learn to identify the different components of a syllogism and to understand the three modes of a conclusive reason. Then once we understand these we can apply them to our Dharma practice. For example, to realize the sixteen characteristics of the four noble truths we must first generate inferential cognizers of them. Thus, to realize that our body is a true suffering we can begin by contemplating the syllogism, 'My body is a true suffering because it is a contaminated aggregate.' This reasoning is correct because the reason used is a conclusive reason. It is qualified by the first mode because our body is a contaminated aggregate, it is qualified by the second mode because whatever is a contaminated aggregate is necessarily a true suffering, and it is qualified by the third mode because if something is not a true suffering it is necessarily not a contaminated aggregate.

Sometimes we might want to deepen our understanding by considering further one or other of the three modes. For example, if we are not sure whether or not our body is a contaminated aggregate we can use a separate line of reasoning to establish that this is the case. Thus, we can consider the syllogism, 'My body is a contaminated aggregate because it is produced from karma and delusion and because it is conducive to the development of delusions.'

DIVISIONS OF INFERENTIAL COGNIZER

There are three types of inferential cognizer from the point of view of the type of reason upon which they depend:

1 Inferential cognizers through the power of fact
2 Inferential cognizers through belief
3 Inferential cognizers through renown

Inferential cognizers through the power of fact realize slightly hidden objects. Examples are an inferential cognizer realizing that there is a fire in a house because there is smoke, and an inferential cognizer realizing that the body is impermanent because it disintegrates. Most of our inferential cognizers are of this type. We gain initial realizations of impermanence, emptiness, pervasive suffering, and so forth through such inferential cognizers.

Inferential cognizers through belief realize deeply hidden objects such as the specific law of karma that from giving comes wealth and from discipline comes happiness. Sentient beings cannot prove the existence of such deeply hidden objects through their own direct experience or through inferential cognizers through the power of fact. The only way we can know such objects incontrovertibly is by relying upon Buddha's scriptures, having already ascertained that Buddha is a thoroughly non-deceptive person.

For example, to realize that the scripture revealing 'From giving comes wealth, from discipline comes happiness' is a completely reliable scripture we need to use the following reasoning: 'This scripture is completely reliable because it is free from contradiction by direct perception, free from contradiction by inferential cognizers through the power of fact, and free from contradiction by inferential cognizers through belief.' In dependence upon this reasoning we can generate an inferential cognizer realizing that this scripture is completely reliable. Then we can generate an inferential cognizer that realizes that from giving comes wealth and from discipline comes happiness because the scripture that reveals this is completely reliable. This inferential cognizer is an inferential cognizer through belief.

Inferential cognizers through renown realize the suitability of terms on the basis of renown, or convention. In principle any object is suitable to be called by any name because the suitability of a particular name arises not from characteristics in the object but simply from convention. Thus the white orb we see in the night sky is suitable to be called 'the moon' because that is how it is commonly known, but it could just as easily be known by any other name. Similarly the term 'moon' could be used to designate any other object. Thus, for example, if we had grown used to referring to the white orb in the night sky as 'the sun' and the yellow orb in the day sky as 'the moon', these terms would be entirely suitable because they would have been established by convention.

Inferential cognizers through renown realize a terminological suitability – that an object is suitable to be called anything because it exists among objects of conception. There is no natural relationship between objects and sounds. Thus, we can call a person 'Patience' even though a person cannot be patience because patience is a state of mind, not a person. Even so, it is suitable to call a person 'Patience' simply because that name is established by common usage. Moreover, since countless different languages exist, any object of a conceptual mind can be an object of any language, and so any object is suitable to be called anything.

In *Commentary to Valid Cognition* Dharmakirti says:

An expressive sound is dependent upon the wish of whoever expresses it.

One person may say 'John is good' because that is his experience of John, but someone else, with a different experience of John, may say 'John is bad.' Thus, our speech has no freedom because what we say depends upon our mind. In the same text Dharmakirti says 'Sound is everywhere', which means that we can express a sound for anything.

There is also a twofold division of inferential cognizer from the point of view of how they are generated:

1 Inferential cognizers arisen from listening
2 Inferential cognizers arisen from contemplation

An example of the first is an inferential cognizer realizing that the body is impermanent simply in dependence upon listening to the statement 'The body is impermanent because it will finally die.' If we generate an inferential cognizer realizing the impermanence of the body principally through the force of our contemplating the meaning of such a statement, this is an example of an inferential cognizer arisen from contemplation.

When we first realize subtle objects such as impermanence in dependence upon inferential cognizers, we attain an intellectual understanding of them, but we should not be satisfied with this. We need to deepen our experience of the object through meditation. In this way we shall gradually attain a profound experience induced by meditation, and finally a yogic direct perceiver that realizes the object directly. Inferential cognizers are seeds of yogic direct perceivers. Until we attain an actual yogic direct perceiver realizing a particular object we need to continue to meditate on the continuum of the inferential cognizer realizing that object.

GENERATION OF INFERENTIAL COGNIZERS

As mentioned before, we can generate an inferential cognizer either in dependence upon listening or in dependence upon contemplation, but either way it is necessary for us to realize fully the three modes. When it is said that a conclusive reason is qualified by the three modes, this means that for a reason to be conclusive for us we must realize all three modes. For example, if we simply think 'My body is impermanent because it will finally die', without realizing each of the three modes, this reason will not be a conclusive reason, and our understanding will not be an inferential cognizer. The reason will become conclusive and lead to an inferential cognizer only if we fully realize the three modes – that our body will finally die, that whatever finally dies is impermanent, and that whatever is not impermanent will not finally die.

APPLICATION OF INFERENTIAL COGNIZERS TO DHARMA PRACTICE

Most objects of meditation mentioned in the Sutras and Tantras are either slightly hidden objects or deeply hidden objects, and so we must realize them initially by generating inferential cognizers. This initial knowledge obtained through inferential cognizers is like a sprout that will later grow into an abundant crop of Dharma realizations. By repeatedly meditating on the continuum of these inferential cognizers, eventually we shall gain deep realizations of Sutra and Tantra, like a crop ripening into a rich harvest. Knowing this we should make a strong determination to generate these precious inferential cognizers in the way explained here, and then put this determination into practice.

Asanga

Re-cognizers

DEFINITION OF RE-COGNIZER

The definition of re-cognizer is a cognizer that realizes what has already been realized through the force of a previous valid cognizer.

The function of a re-cognizer is to maintain the continuum of an understanding initially gained by a valid cognizer. The first moment of an eye awareness apprehending a tree, for example, realizes its object freshly, through its own power. Subsequent moments of that eye awareness do not realize the tree through their own power but through the power of the first moment; hence they are re-cognizers. In a similar way, the first moment of an inferential cognizer realizing subtle impermanence is generated directly in dependence upon a conclusive reason and realizes its object through its own power. Subsequent moments of the same inferential cognizer realize subtle impermanence through the power of the first moment. Whereas the first moment of an inferential cognizer brings the mind from the state of correct belief to a state of incontrovertible realization, later moments merely prolong this initial realization. 'Moment' in this context means the shortest time it takes to notice or realize an object.

Although the second and third moments of omniscient mind realize what has already been realized by the first moment, they do so through their own power and are not mere continuations of the first moment. Every moment of Buddha's mind realizes all phenomena freshly through the force of having eliminated the two obstructions, and not simply through remembering the understanding gained by the first moment. Therefore, Buddhas have no re-cognizers.

The second moment of a Buddha's eye awareness, for example, is just as fresh as the first moment. By contrast, the second moment of our eye awareness realizing a particular object lacks the quality of freshness that is possessed by the first moment. It does not understand the object in a new way but merely maintains the original understanding.

Re-cognizers are necessarily valid cognizers. According to the Sautrantikas, however, this is not the case because they assert that all valid cognizers necessarily realize their objects freshly.

DIVISIONS OF RE-COGNIZER

Because there are two types of valid cognizer, there are two types of re-cognizer:

1 Non-conceptual re-cognizers
2 Conceptual re-cognizers

There are three types of non-conceptual re-cognizer:

1 Re-cognizers that are sense direct perceivers
2 Re-cognizers that are non-conceptual mental direct perceivers
3 Re-cognizers that are yogic direct perceivers

An example of the first is the second moment of an eye awareness realizing form, an example of the second is the second moment of clairvoyance, and an example of the third is the second moment of a direct realization of subtle impermanence.

When we look at an object, the first moment of that eye awareness apprehends the object through its own power, and later moments are re-cognizers that are sense direct perceivers. However, if we look away from the object and then look at it again, the first moment of the new eye awareness must engage the object freshly through its own power; it cannot rely upon the previous eye awareness because the continuum has been broken. The first moment of that new eye awareness is therefore not a re-cognizer even though it realizes an object that has already been realized. Similarly, during a meditation session all the moments of a Superior being's meditative equi-poise on emptiness after the first moment are re-cognizers, but when he or she begins a new session the first moment is not a re-cognizer.

There are two types of conceptual re-cognizer: those induced by direct perceivers and those induced by inferential cog-nizers. The former can further be divided into those induced by sense direct perceivers, those induced by mental direct perceivers, and those induced by yogic direct perceivers. An example of the first is a conceptual mind that thinks 'This is a flower' that occurs when we look at a flower. Examples of the second are remembering something that was previously seen with clairvoyance, and the last seven concentrations of mental abiding in tranquil abiding meditation. An example of the third is a Superior being's illusion-like subsequent attainment induced by his or her direct realization of empti-ness. Examples of conceptual re-cognizers induced by infer-ential cognizers are the second moment of an inferential cognizer and the second mental abiding.

GENERATION OF RE-COGNIZERS

We should maintain continually, without forgetting, any per-fect knowledge of Dharma subjects that we gain through sincere study by generating and maintaining re-cognizers, and the way to do this is to maintain mindfulness. The object of mindfulness is an object that has already been realized, the nature of mindfulness is not to forget its object, and the function of mindfulness is to prevent distraction. Maintain-ing mindfulness is the best method for improving our Dharma knowledge and experience, and it is the root of all meditation practices.

APPLICATION OF RE-COGNIZERS TO DHARMA PRACTICE

Those who wish to be liberated from suffering must under-stand the ultimate truth of phenomena. In Tibetan, ultimate truth is called 'dön dam denpa', in which 'dön' means 'object', 'dam' means 'holy', and 'denpa' means truth. Thus, ultimate truth is the supreme object of knowledge. All phenomena lack true existence, and this lack of true existence is ultimate truth. In *King of Concentration Sutra* Buddha says:

Magicians emanate various things
Such as horses, elephants, and chariots.
These things do not truly exist;
You should know all phenomena in the same way.

If we contemplate sincerely the conclusive reasons given in authentic commentaries such as *Ocean of Nectar* we shall generate an inferential cognizer realizing ultimate truth. This is the first step towards the attainment of tranquil abiding and superior seeing observing emptiness. We should then meditate on the continuum of this inferential cognizer, which is the nature of a re-cognizer, until we attain the union of tranquil abiding and superior seeing observing emptiness.

With respect to virtuous objects, the practice of re-cogniz-ers is of paramount importance because it is through this prac-tice that we maintain and increase all our spiritual experiences.

Correct Beliefs

The definition of correct belief is a non-valid cognizer that realizes its conceived object.

In general, conceptual minds apprehending chair, table, tree, and so on are correct beliefs; except that those that are induced by sense direct perceivers are not correct beliefs but re-cognizers. A mind that believes that future lives do not exist is not a correct belief but an incorrect belief because it is a wrong conceptual mind.

In the Sutras, Buddha explains a special meditation practice for abandoning attachment to samsaric environments in which we meditate on the whole earth covered with bone, marrow, pus, and blood. This meditation is a concentration that realizes its conceived object, which is an imaginary earth covered with imaginary bone, marrow, pus, and blood. This concentration can be a correct belief or a valid cognizer. The meditations on generation stage mentioned in the Tantric teachings can also be understood in the same way.

DIVISIONS OF CORRECT BELIEF

There are two types of correct belief:

1 Correct beliefs that do not depend upon a reason
2 Correct beliefs that depend upon a reason

An example of the first is a correct belief in impermanence that develops from just listening to instructions on it. An example of the second is a correct belief that develops from contemplating either a correct or an incorrect reason. Some people, who believe the same as the Vaibashikas, think that

65

the body is impermanent because it is first produced, then it remains, and finally it disintegrates. Contemplating these reasons they develop a conceptual mind conceiving the body to be impermanent. This conceptual mind is a correct belief developed from an incorrect reason.

Some people might think that the Vaibashika's view that functioning things are first produced, then remain, and finally disintegrate is correct. This indicates that they do not understand subtle impermanence. In reality, the production and disintegration of functioning things occur simultaneously. Since no functioning thing remains for one moment without changing, the reason mentioned above is incorrect. On the other hand, if we contemplate 'My body is impermanent because it will finally die', we can develop a rough understanding that our body is impermanent. This knowledge is a correct belief developed from contemplating a correct reason. This correct belief can later transform into an inferential cognizer that perfectly realizes the impermanence of the body.

GENERATION OF CORRECT BELIEFS

In general, a mind that simply believes something that exists is a correct belief. These are easy to generate because they can develop either from just listening or from contemplating. The most meaningful correct beliefs are those that cause living beings to be liberated from suffering, such as beliefs in karma, reincarnation, the six realms, the Three Jewels, and the four noble truths. These correct beliefs can be generated by developing strong faith in Buddha and his teachings. Believing that all living beings are our mothers is a very beneficial correct belief because it helps us to develop bodhichitta. The methods for generating such correct beliefs are explained in the Lamrim teachings.

The Tantric teachings explain a special practice of correct imagination, such as regarding oneself as a Deity and everything as completely pure. These kinds of correct imagination are special correct beliefs that we can generate once we have received an empowerment.

66

APPLICATION OF CORRECT BELIEFS TO DHARMA PRACTICE

In general, all objects of knowledge are objects of correct belief. Among these, the most meaningful are the objects of knowledge that are presented in the Lamrim and Tantric teachings. Through listening to and contemplating these teachings we shall first gain a rough understanding of their meaning. This understanding will have the nature of a correct belief. This is like a tangkha painter initially drawing a rough outline of a tangkha. Once we have gained a rough understanding of the Lamrim and Tantric teachings, if we continue to study and practise them sincerely we shall gain a deep knowledge and experience of the entire Lamrim and Tantra, and eventually we shall attain full enlightenment. This is like the tangkha painter completing the painting. Contemplating this, we should make a strong determination thinking 'I must accomplish both the initial knowledge and the final attainment', and then put this determination into practice.

Non-ascertaining Perceivers

DEFINITION OF NON-ASCERTAINING PERCEIVER

The definition of non-ascertaining perceiver is a cognizer to which a phenomenon that is its engaged object appears clearly without being ascertained.

An example is an eye awareness of a new-born baby that apprehends its father's face. Also, when we are in a big city we see many people, but we do not know who they are. Our minds that see these people are non-ascertaining perceivers because they clearly see something but do not realize it.

Non-ascertaining perceivers are necessarily direct perceivers. They apprehend their engaged object, but not strongly enough, and so they do not realize it. Non-ascertaining perceivers are always manifest within our mind, even during single-pointed meditation. All living beings have these minds – only Buddhas are completely free from them. Most sense awarenesses of new-born babies are non-ascertaining perceivers.

DIVISIONS OF NON-ASCERTAINING PERCEIVER

There are two types of non-ascertaining perceiver:

1 Non-ascertaining sense direct perceivers
2 Non-ascertaining mental direct perceivers

An example of the first is an ear awareness that occurs while we are engrossed in looking at an attractive form. Even though sounds appear to such an awareness they are not recognized or understood because most of our attention is directed towards the visual form. We might also develop a non-ascertaining ear awareness while we are listening to teachings given in a foreign language. The sounds appear to our ear awareness but since we do not understand the language we do not ascertain their meaning.

Examples of the second are mental direct perceivers induced by non-ascertaining sense direct perceivers. For example, when we are listening sincerely and single-pointedly to a beautiful teaching we may develop an eye awareness apprehending a form. Such an eye awareness, which is in nature a non-ascertaining sense direct perceiver, induces a conceptual mind apprehending the same object. This conceptual mind is a non-ascertaining mental direct perceiver. There are no non-ascertaining yogic direct perceivers.

GENERATION OF NON-ASCERTAINING PERCEIVERS

In general, a non-ascertaining perceiver develops when the conditions for a phenomenon to appear are assembled but the conditions for its nature to be realized are not. When looked at from the point of view of their causes we can distinguish five main types of non-ascertaining perceiver. These will now be explained.

The first type occurs when the mind is unable to ascertain the nature of its object due to external conditions. For example, an eye awareness may not be able to recognize what it sees because the light is too dim; because the object is too far away, too small, or moving too fast; or because it closely resembles another object. Similarly, an ear awareness might be unable to ascertain its object because the sound is too faint or because it is unclear. These conditions may also lead to doubts or wrong awarenesses. For example, we might not be able to tell whether a particular sound is the sound of a car or the sound of the wind. If we simply listen to the sound without being able to identify it, this is a non-ascertaining perceiver. If we then begin to wonder 'Is that a car or is it the wind?', this is doubt. If we incorrectly decide that it is the sound of a car when in fact it is the sound of the wind, this is a wrong awareness. Non-ascertaining perceivers often lead to doubts or wrong awarenesses.

The second type of non-ascertaining perceiver is related to the nature of the mind, or the power. Sometimes non-ascertaining perceivers develop because the gross consciousnesses are gathering inwards, as they do during the death process or when we fall asleep. As death advances, other minds such as valid direct perceivers, inferential cognizers, re-cognizers, and correct beliefs gradually cease, and non-ascertaining perceivers increase. Even before their eye sense powers have ceased to operate, dying people lose the ability to recognize the people gathered around them because their discrimination has become unclear. At present all our subtle minds are non-ascertaining perceivers because although subtle appearances such as white appearance or clear light appear to our subtle minds, we do not recognize them.

Alcohol and other drugs can also make our discrimination unclear and, while they might not cause us to hallucinate, they do often prevent us from recognizing what appears to us. Over-tiredness has a similar effect. Another example is a newborn baby seeing its mother. Although all the conditions for the eye awareness apprehending the mother have been met, the conditions for ascertaining or understanding the mother have not been assembled. Because the object, the eye sense power, and the eye awareness have come together, the baby apprehends its mother, but because the baby's discrimination is unclear it cannot understand what it perceives. As the baby grows, however, it will learn to recognize its mother as its mother.

The third type of non-ascertaining perceiver can develop because we have decided, or learned, to ignore a particular stimulus. People who live close to busy roads, for example, learn to ignore the noise of the traffic. This type of non-ascertaining perceiver can be very useful because it enables us to pay full attention to more meaningful objects. Thus, a mother living in a house near a busy road may be able to ignore the noise of the traffic while she reads a book, yet still be able to hear and ascertain the much fainter sound of her baby starting to cry. Her non-ascertaining perceiver with respect to the sound of the traffic arises through the power of her decision not to pay attention to it, and so even when that sound appears to her ear awareness it does not attract the attention of her mental awareness.

The fourth type is similar to the third in that a stimulus is shut out, but here it is because we have been distracted by an object of delusion. For example, when we are engrossed in an object of attachment or when we are very angry we become oblivious to many things that occur around us, even to our own physical pain. Car accidents often happen because the driver has been distracted by objects of attachment such as an attractive person on the pavement.

The fifth type of non-ascertaining perceiver occurs when we do not understand some part of the nature of an object. An example of this might occur when we are shopping in a foreign country. We see many strange fruits and vegetables but do not know what they are, whether they are tasty, or how to prepare them. Our eye awareness clearly perceives the items but it does not ascertain those aspects that are relevant to us. This type of non-ascertaining perceiver develops because we have not previously learnt to recognize that aspect of the object that we now wish to recognize. In general, whenever we clearly perceive an object but do not know what it is or what it is for we have developed this type of non-ascertaining perceiver.

APPLICATION OF NON-ASCERTAINING PERCEIVERS TO DHARMA PRACTICE

At the moment, when we meet an attractive object we usually pay considerable attention to it and try to gain as vivid a perception of it as possible. Similarly, when we meet an unattractive object we dwell on its bad qualities until anger develops. Instead of paying so much attention to objects of delusion it would be wiser to develop non-ascertaining perceivers with respect to them. Training in non-ascertaining perceivers with respect to objects of delusion is the practice of restraining the doors of the sense powers.

In *Guide to the Bodhisattva's Way of Life* Shantideva advises us to remain like a block of wood whenever we encounter an object that stimulates strong delusions. His meaning is that we should practise non-ascertaining perceivers towards these objects. When our attachment or anger towards these objects becomes less intense we can begin to practise other methods to overcome our delusions. If we are successful in overcoming our anger towards someone, then when we see them again they will no longer be an object of anger for us but an object of patience. Eventually they may even become an object of pure love or compassion!

For those who wish to attain tranquil abiding it is very important to restrain the doors of the sense powers by practising non-ascertaining perceivers towards distracting objects. During the meditation session it is necessary to practise non-ascertaining perceivers towards all the objects of the senses so that we can pay full attention to the internal object on which we are meditating.

To prevent too many unnecessary conceptual thoughts or distractions from arising it is better not to pay much attention to things that are not relevant to our spiritual practice, such as mundane business activities, the quality of our food, or the quality of our accommodation.

The five minds explained so far – direct perceivers, inferential cognizers, re-cognizers, correct beliefs, and non-ascertaining perceivers – are all correct minds. A correct mind is a mind that is not mistaken with respect to its engaged object. However, this does not mean that all correct minds are unmistaken awarenesses. Within the minds of sentient beings, only the exalted awareness of meditative equipoise of Superior beings observing emptiness is an unmistaken awareness. All other minds of sentient beings are mistaken awarenesses because their objects appear to be truly existent; and this appearance is a mistaken appearance that is by nature an obstruction to omniscience. Only Buddhas have abandoned this obstruction. These explanations are very different from those of the lower Buddhist schools such as the Sautrantikas.

Doubts

The definition of doubt is a mental factor that wavers with respect to its object.

When a primary mind is associated with doubt, the primary mind itself and all its other mental factors such as feeling, discrimination, and intention also take on the two-pointed quality of doubt. Doubts prevent us from engaging in either worldly or spiritual actions with confidence and resolve. There is a saying in Tibetan that just as we cannot sew with a two-pointed needle, so we cannot fulfil our wishes with a two-pointed mind. An essential prerequisite for success in our spiritual practices is unwavering faith and confidence. If we lack this we shall not be able to commit ourself whole-heartedly to a particular practice or maintain our effort long enough to accomplish any results. Therefore, it is essential to eliminate those doubts that interfere with the development of pure faith.

DIVISIONS OF DOUBT

There are two types of doubt:

1 Deluded doubts
2 Non-deluded doubts

Both types of doubt are characterized by an indecisive waver-ing with respect to their object, but whereas deluded doubts disturb our mind, non-deluded doubts do not. Non-deluded doubts often occur when we are studying profound Dharma topics such as emptiness. In the process of trying to under-stand a difficult point we wonder 'Does it mean this or does

73

it mean that?' This is doubt because it engages its object two-pointedly, but it does not disturb our peace of mind. On the contrary, this type of doubt can often arouse a strong interest in Dharma and lead to a thorough understanding of the subject. For example, it is said that just developing doubts about emptiness will damage samsara. Unfortunate beings do not even develop such doubts.

Deluded doubts, on the other hand, greatly disrupt our spiritual practice. They can shake our faith in Dharma, discourage us from study, and prevent us from succeeding in our meditations. Deluded doubts are the most common cause of abandoning Dharma practice. They also interfere with our worldly actions by rendering us incapable of making decisions, or of staying with a particular course of action. Since deluded doubts are so harmful it is important to recognize them as soon as they occur and to take steps to dispel them.

Foe Destroyers have abandoned all delusions but as they have not yet understood all objects of knowledge they still have non-deluded doubts. Even tenth-ground Bodhisattvas who are very close to attaining enlightenment do not fully understand the subtle good qualities of the body, speech, and mind of a Buddha, and have non-deluded doubts about the precise nature of these qualities.

There is also a threefold division of doubt:

1 Doubts tending towards the truth
2 Doubts tending away from the truth
3 Balanced doubts

An example of the first is thinking that past and future lives probably exist, an example of the second is thinking that past and future lives probably do not exist, and an example of the third is simply wondering whether or not they exist. Unless we meet unfavourable circumstances such as a bad teacher, doubts tending towards the truth will probably transform into correct beliefs, and for this reason they are regarded as correct awarenesses. Doubts tending away from the truth, on the other hand, are usually classed as wrong awarenesses.

There is another threefold division of doubt:

1 Virtuous doubts
2 Non-virtuous doubts
3 Neutral doubts

In general, any doubt that has a virtuous motivation is a virtuous doubt. Virtuous doubts arise when, out of faith and to increase our wisdom, we analyze hidden objects such as actions and their effects, subtle impermanence, or emptiness, and are unable to decide on the precise meaning of something. It is said that sentient beings remain in samsara because they do not question whether phenomena actually exist in the way that they appear. When we start to doubt that our I, our body, or our mind exist in the way that they appear, our self-grasping is weakened and samsara begins to crumble. If cultivated correctly, this doubt will transform into a correct belief in emptiness, and finally into a valid cognizer.

If we contemplate the same topics with a non-virtuous motivation we shall develop non-virtuous doubts. For example, we might investigate the teachings on karma with a wish to disprove them. Any doubts we develop as a result of such mistaken investigation are non-virtuous doubts, and are very dangerous. A neutral doubt is a doubt with a neutral motivation. An example is wondering what we should eat for breakfast.

GENERATION OF DOUBTS

In general, a doubt arises because due to ignorance or the imprints of ignorance we do not know an object with a valid cognizer. Non-ascertaining perceivers, correct beliefs, and wrong awarenesses can all lead to doubts. For example, if we see a vase of flowers but cannot tell whether the flowers are real or artificial, this non-ascertaining perceiver may cause us to develop the doubt 'Are these real flowers or artificial flowers?' Until we realize an object in a completely reliable way, that is with a valid cognizer, there is always the possibility of doubts occurring.

The most common causes of deluded doubts are wrong views or the imprints of wrong views. Two beginners might listen to a teaching on karma, and one might believe it while the other might develop many deluded doubts about it. This indicates that the first person has imprints of believing in karma, or already believes some similar doctrine, while the second person has imprints from denying the law of karma in previous lives, or cherishes views that are incompatible with a belief in karma. Another reason why someone might doubt the teachings on karma is that he or she has no faith in the Teacher or in Buddha. If we have strong faith in the Teacher or in Buddha we shall believe the teachings, even if we do not fully understand them.

Yet another cause of developing doubts is incorrect investigation and analysis. For example, people with scientific training may find it difficult to believe in hidden objects because their existence cannot be proved by ordinary scientific methods. If they try to establish the existence of karma or enlightened beings, for example, by means of a scientific experiment they will be unable to do so, and as a result they may develop deluded doubts. The laws of karma and the existence of enlightened beings are hidden objects that are beyond the scope of scientific observation. If we want to investigate these phenomena to prove that they exist, we must use correct methods, such as the logical reasons that are presented in Dharma.

The causes of virtuous doubts are often the opposite of the causes of deluded doubts. While listening to teachings on profound subjects such as the twelve dependent-related links, for example, an intelligent and faithful student may develop more doubts than a dull student with less faith. The less capable student may be satisfied with a very rough understanding, but the intelligent one will want to understand it precisely and validly. He or she will analyze the subject carefully and ask many questions. Although we may never lose conviction in the truth of Buddha's teachings, in the process of striving to understand them fully we may develop many doubts as to their exact meaning. If we have faith we shall yearn to penetrate the profound meaning of Dharma and not be content with a superficial understanding.

Thus, faith encourages us to study deeply and ask many questions. Skilful questioning based on an appreciation of the profundity of Buddha's teachings can increase faith, whereas unskilful questioning based on scepticism can destroy it.

APPLICATION OF OUR UNDERSTANDING OF DOUBTS TO DHARMA PRACTICE

As long as deluded doubts and hesitations remain in our mind our practice will not be very effective. If we are always wondering 'Should I practise like this or like that?' or 'Does this method really work?' we shall not be able to commit ourself wholeheartedly to our practice, and so we shall not accomplish great results. This is particularly true in the practice of Secret Mantra where faith is of supreme importance.

Even if we make some mistakes in our practice, such as mispronouncing mantras or visualizing incorrectly, we can still attain pure realizations if we practise with unwavering conviction. There is a story of an old woman who sustained herself through a famine by transforming stones into food through the power of mantras. She was able to do this because she had unshakeable faith in the mantra. Later her son, who was a monk, informed her that she was mispronouncing the mantra. This shook her faith, and even though she then learned to pronounce the mantra correctly it was no longer effective for her.

The way to overcome doubts about our spiritual practice is to gain a thorough understanding of our practice through study, discussion, and relying upon a qualified Spiritual Guide. In particular, we can speedily resolve doubts by developing quick wisdom. Quick wisdom is one of the seven types of wisdom. It enables us to answer our own questions as soon as they arise. If we possess quick wisdom we shall never become burdened with unanswered questions that gradually transform into deluded doubts and undermine our faith. Quick wisdom acts like a Spiritual Guide who is always there to answer our questions and give us good advice. When we read books, quick wisdom enables us immediately to understand the meaning. If, due to imprints of wrong views, deluded doubts start to arise, quick wisdom immediately recognizes them and averts them.

A powerful method for developing quick wisdom is to meditate on the seed-letter of Manjushri, the letter DHI. To do this we visualize at the root of our tongue an orange-coloured letter DHI, which is in essence the quick wisdom of Manjushri. We invite the quick wisdom of all the Buddhas in the aspect of many letter DHI's to dissolve into the DHI at the root of our tongue. Then light radiates from this DHI and fills our entire body. Each atom of this light is a letter DHI and so our whole body is filled with DHI's. We recite 'DHI' as many times as possible with one breath and then, together with a little saliva, we swallow the letter DHI at our tongue. This dissolves into our root mind at our heart and we imagine that our mind transforms into the quick wisdom of all the Buddhas. If we practise this with strong faith early in the morning each day, we shall definitely develop quick wisdom.

Special methods for accomplishing the seven types of wisdom are explained in the book *Heart Jewel*.

Wrong Awarenesses

DEFINITION OF WRONG AWARENESS

The definition of wrong awareness is a cognizer that is mistaken with respect to its engaged object.

An example of a wrong awareness is a mind that apprehends a toy snake as being a real snake. Since a toy snake is not a real snake, any mind that apprehends it as such is mistaken with respect to its engaged object. Whereas a mistaken awareness is mistaken with respect to its appearing object, a wrong awareness is mistaken with respect to its engaged object or its conceived object. If a mind is a wrong awareness it is necessarily a mistaken awareness, but if it is a mistaken awareness it is not necessarily a wrong awareness. As mentioned above, apart from the exalted awareness of meditative equipoise of a Superior being, all minds of sentient beings are mistaken awarenesses because their objects appear to them to be truly existent when in fact they are not. However, this does not mean that all these minds are also wrong awarenesses. A mind is a wrong awareness only if it is mistaken with respect to its engaged object or its conceived object.

There are two types of wrong awareness: non-conceptual wrong awarenesses and conceptual wrong awarenesses, and of these the latter are the more harmful. All delusions are conceptual wrong awarenesses. Whereas non-conceptual wrong awarenesses can cause temporary problems, leading to embarrassment, accidents, and sometimes even death, they are by no means as harmful as conceptual wrong awarenesses because they are not the main cause of engaging in negative actions. Conceptual wrong awarenesses, on the other hand, cause us to commit negative actions and so lead us into lower rebirths in future lives. Because the harmful results of these minds

Vasubandhu

extend beyond this life they are far more damaging than non-conceptual wrong awarenesses. Moreover, by obscuring the ultimate nature of phenomena, conceptual wrong awarenesses prevent us from attaining liberation and so cause us to remain trapped within samsara. We normally blame other people or external circumstances for our problems but in reality all our problems are caused by these wrong awarenesses.

All wrong awarenesses are objects to be abandoned. The entire spiritual path consists of eliminating wrong awarenesses and developing the correct awarenesses that are their opposites. When we have completely removed wrong awarenesses and their imprints from our mental continuum we shall be a Buddha. The only difference between a sentient being and a Buddha is that a sentient being has wrong awarenesses or their imprints and a Buddha does not.

DIVISIONS OF WRONG AWARENESS

As mentioned above, there are two types of wrong awareness:

1 Non-conceptual wrong awarenesses
2 Conceptual wrong awarenesses

Non-conceptual wrong awarenesses can be divided into wrong sense awarenesses and wrong non-conceptual mental awarenesses. A wrong sense awareness can be mistaken with respect to its object in any of seven different ways: being mistaken with respect to its object's shape, colour, activity, number, time, measurement, or entity.

A sense awareness can be mistaken with respect to shape when the shape of the object resembles the shape of another object. Examples are an eye awareness seeing a toy snake as a real snake, an eye awareness seeing artificial flowers as real flowers, and an eye awareness seeing the reflection of a face in the mirror as a real face.

Examples of sense awarenesses that are mistaken with respect to colour are an eye awareness seeing a white conch shell as yellow as a result of jaundice, or an eye awareness seeing a distant snow mountain as blue due to hazy atmospheric conditions.

An example of a sense awareness mistaken with respect to activity can occur when we are in a stationary train and a train next to us begins to move. Because at that time our eye awareness is deceived with respect to the activity of the other train, it seems as if it is our train that is moving. Another example of this type of wrong sense awareness is an eye awareness seeing trees moving past when we are travelling by train or car.

An example of a sense awareness mistaken with respect to number is an eye awareness seeing two moons in the sky when we are squinting at the moon.

An example of a sense awareness mistaken with respect to time is when we wake from an afternoon sleep and our eye awareness sees the light of morning, making us feel that it is morning.

Examples of sense awarenesses that are mistaken with respect to measurement are an eye awareness seeing a large object in the distance as smaller than a nearby small object, an eye awareness misjudging the distance of the car in front of us when we are driving, an eye awareness mistaking the position of a fish in the water because of refraction, and an eye awareness seeing a rainbow as having a fixed location.

All the above types of wrong sense awareness are mistaken with respect to an aspect of the object and therefore do not identify the object correctly, but they are not mistaken with respect to all aspects of the object. A person who sees two moons, for example, is mistaken with respect to number, but is not mistaken with respect to the shape of the object, nor with respect to its being the moon. On the other hand, a sense awareness that is mistaken with respect to the entity of the object is mistaken with respect to the whole object. Examples are an eye awareness seeing hairs floating in front of us when our eyes are tired or sore, an eye awareness seeing a mirage as actual water, or an ear awareness hearing an echo of a voice as the actual sound of a voice.

Examples of wrong non-conceptual mental awarenesses are a dream eye awareness apprehending a dream mountain as a real mountain, dream money as real money, and so on.

There are two types of conceptual wrong awareness: intellectually-formed wrong awarenesses and innate wrong awarenesses. Intellectually-formed wrong awarenesses are those that develop from incorrect philosophical views or incorrect reasons, and innate wrong awarenesses are those that develop naturally from imprints carried over from previous lives. Examples of the first are the twenty intellectually-formed views of the transitory collection listed on pages 212–3, and the sixteen wrong awarenesses, listed in the Sutras, that contradict the sixteen characteristics of the four noble truths. We can also develop intellectually-formed anger and attachment. Although most of our anger and attachment arise spontaneously, without our having to contemplate reasons, sometimes we develop anger as a result of strong adherence to particular views, attachment to a certain lifestyle, and so on. These are also intellectually-formed wrong awarenesses. All intellectually-formed wrong awarenesses are abandoned on the path of seeing. Examples of innate wrong awareness are innate self-grasping and all the other innate delusions.

It is important to note that not all wrong awarenesses are delusions. An eye awareness seeing an artificial flower as a real flower, for example, is a wrong awareness that arises from ignorance or the imprints of ignorance, but it is not a delusion.

GENERATION OF WRONG AWARENESSES

There are two causes of wrong awareness: ultimate causes and temporary causes. The ultimate cause of all wrong awarenesses is ignorance. As long as ignorance exists in our mind we shall develop many kinds of wrong awareness. Even after we have eliminated ignorance from our mind we shall still have the imprints of ignorance, and these can cause us to develop non-deluded wrong awarenesses. However, these are not so harmful. Only a Buddha is completely free from wrong awarenesses.

As for the temporary causes of wrong awareness, there are temporary causes of wrong sense awareness and temporary causes of wrong mental awareness. There are four temporary causes of wrong sense awareness:

1 A deceptive quality of the object
2 A deceptive situation
3 A defective sense power
4 A fault in the preceding awareness

The first two are external causes of error and the second two are internal causes of error. As for the first, objects can act as causes of wrong awareness when they closely resemble other objects. For example, artificial flowers can be mistaken for real flowers, or a toy snake for a real snake. Other ways that objects can deceive us are if they are small, camouflaged, or transparent. Sometimes railway lines seem to converge in the distance, which causes an eye awareness mistaken with respect to shape.

As for the second cause, certain situations make it difficult to identify objects clearly and so they often lead to mistakes. For example, when it is too dark to see properly, or too noisy or windy to hear properly, or when we are moving quickly, we can easily develop wrong awarenesses. Mirages and rainbows are both appearances arising from an interaction between special conditions – the light, moisture, and the position of the observer – but they seem to be real with a definite location and therefore often cause mistaken minds. When we look through a microscope tiny objects appear very large, and looking through binoculars makes distant objects appear close. A straight stick half submerged in water appears bent, and a white object seen through brown sunglasses looks brown. These are all examples of how a situation can lead to wrong awareness.

As for the third cause, certain diseases impair the sense powers and cause us to apprehend objects incorrectly. Jaundice, for example, can impair the eye sense power and make white objects appear yellow, tiredness of the eyes can give rise to the appearance of hairs floating in front of us, and a fever can impair the tactile sense power and cause a warm room to feel cold. When the inner winds mounted by the sense awarenesses begin to gather inwards during the death process, many wrong sense awarenesses occur. Alcohol and drugs can also affect our sense powers. Swallowing the drug dhatura, for example, can cause us to see the ground as golden in colour.

As for the fourth cause, when our mind is in a very disturbed or preoccupied state we often develop wrong sense awarenesses. It is said that sometimes violent anger makes everything appear red. Someone who is 'on edge' is much more likely than someone in a calm state of mind to make mistakes, such as seeing a piece of rope as a snake. We also tend to make mistakes when our attention is strongly directed towards another object. For example, if we are engrossed in a book and a stranger walks by, we may mistake him for someone we know. Sometimes when we are strongly expecting to see something we shall 'see' it, even if it is not there.

External causes of error do not always lead to the development of wrong awarenesses. For example, when we look into a mirror the reflection of our face looks like our face but we do not mistake it for our face, and so our eye awareness seeing the reflection is not a wrong awareness. The reason we are sometimes deceived by external causes of error is that we still have the ultimate cause of mistaken minds, ignorance. Buddhas have abandoned ignorance completely and so even when they meet a deceptive external condition they do not develop wrong awarenesses.

There are many temporary causes of wrong mental awareness. Usually a wrong sense awareness will induce a wrong conceptual mind. Seeing a rope as a snake for example will probably lead to a conceptual mind thinking 'This is a snake.' However, if we understand the object well a wrong sense awareness will not lead to a wrong conceptual mind. Although a rainbow appears to our eye awareness to have a definite location, if we understand the nature of rainbows we shall know that this appearance is deceptive and we shall not think that the rainbow exists where it appears to.

Another cause of wrong mental awareness is our winds gathering inwards during sleep or death. When the winds gather, the mind becomes more subtle, and as a result our mindfulness deteriorates and we are not able to use our mind in a reliable way. When we dream, we rarely realize that we are dreaming, so we regard the pleasant or frightening appearances of the dream as real, and consequently develop attachment or fear towards them. When advanced Bodhisattvas sleep, however, the power of their mindfulness does not decrease and so they do not develop wrong awarenesses. They are able to transform sleep and dreaming into the spiritual path.

As mentioned earlier, there are two types of conceptual wrong awareness – innate and intellectually-formed. Innate wrong awarenesses arise through the force of imprints of delusions. These delusions arise naturally because we have been familiar with delusions since beginningless time. Intellectually-formed wrong awarenesses arise either through being influenced by misleading teachings or through our own incorrect reasoning. Even if we have not formally studied mistaken philosophies we can acquire wrong views through the influence of our parents, friends, and so forth. For example, we may have been brought up to think that although it is wrong to kill human beings there is no fault in killing animals, or that the only purpose of a human life is to enjoy ourself as much as possible. To practise Dharma purely and wholeheartedly we must discard any such wrong views that we may have adopted.

We can also develop wrong awareness through our own illogical reasoning. For example, if we do not seem to be making much progress in our Dharma practice we may think that Dharma has little power, or that Buddhas and Bodhisattvas either do not exist or are not interested in helping us. False reasoning such as this arises very easily and can destroy our practice, so we must always be on our guard against it and counter it as soon as it occurs. If we are disappointed with our progress we should examine our mind to see what it is that is hindering us. In general, our greatest obstacle is that we do not have complete confidence in the practice we are doing, or in our Teacher, and this prevents us from committing ourself wholeheartedly to the practice. Instead of blaming Dharma for our slow progress we should blame our lack of faith.

There are two main purposes of Dharma practice – to eliminate wrong awarenesses and to cultivate correct awarenesses. Wrong awareness is the source of suffering, and correct awareness is the source of happiness. By clearly distinguishing these two we should strive to abandon wrong awarenesses in general, and self-grasping in particular.

To abandon minds such as anger and attachment we need to understand that their conceived objects do not exist but are merely fabrications of ignorance. The observed object of attachment, for example, is a contaminated phenomenon, but the mind of attachment views it as a source of true happiness. In reality there is no such thing as a contaminated phenomenon that is a source of true happiness because all contaminated phenomena are true sufferings. When through contemplating in this way we realize that the conceived object of attachment, or of any other delusion, is non-existent, we shall find it easy to abandon that delusion.

The root cause of all our suffering is the wrong awareness, self-grasping; but because it is so deeply ingrained in our mind it is difficult for us to understand that it is a wrong awareness. The objects of self-grasping – the truly existent I and so forth – appear so vividly to our mind that we find it difficult to believe that they do not actually exist. How can something appear so clearly if it does not exist? The main reason we study all the different types of non-conceptual wrong awareness listed above is to help us to overcome such doubts. By considering these examples, which are part of our everyday experience, we can see that just because something appears in a certain way to our mind it does not follow that it actually exists in that way. For example, when we press our eyeball and look at the moon, two moons appear vividly to our eye awareness. Though two moons appear, we know that two moons do not exist. Similarly, just because a truly existent I appears vividly to our mind it does not mean that a truly existent I actually exists.

Every spiritual realization has a wrong awareness that is its opposite and that must be removed by that particular realization. To eliminate these wrong thoughts we must first identify them, understand how they arise, and recognize their faults. In the preparatory practices of the stages of the path we offer a mandala to the Buddhas and Bodhisattvas and request the attainment of the three great purposes. The first purpose is to overcome wrong awarenesses quickly, the second is to develop correct awarenesses quickly, and the third is to be free from external and internal obstacles. Internal obstacles are our delusions. Specifically, we pray to be able to overcome the sixteen wrong thoughts and attitudes and replace them with the sixteen correct thoughts and attitudes. These were listed previously (pages 27–8). We should memorize this list so that we can identify the wrong thoughts and attitudes as soon as they arise. If we can do this we can immediately apply the appropriate opponent, and then that wrong awareness will not harm us greatly; but if we fail to recognize them they will grow stronger and may even destroy our spiritual practice. Each of these wrong thoughts can be overcome temporarily by refuting its object and then familiarizing our mind with the opposite correct awareness. To eliminate them completely, however, we must eradicate the root of all wrong awarenesses, self-grasping ignorance, by attaining a yogic direct perceiver realizing emptiness.

We have now completed the presentation of the sevenfold division of mind. The main purpose of explaining this is to show how we gain authentic Dharma realizations, and in particular to show the stages involved in attaining a direct realization of emptiness. Before we meet Dharma teachings we do not have any correct minds with respect to emptiness, or even any doubts. We have only innate self-grasping, and sometimes also intellectually-formed self-grasping, both of which are wrong awarenesses. When we hear teachings on emptiness we begin to consider the possibility that phenomena lack inherent existence. At first we shall generate a doubt, thinking 'Probably phenomena exist in the way that they appear, but it is possible that they do not.' By continuing to think correctly about emptiness we shall pass through balanced doubt and doubt tending towards the truth, and gradually our doubt will transform into a correct belief in emptiness.

At this point we do not yet understand emptiness precisely, but we nevertheless have conviction about the truth of emptiness. We should not be satisfied with this correct belief but should continue to study, contemplate, and meditate on emptiness until we gain a valid cognizer realizing emptiness. The first valid cognizer of emptiness we gain will be an inferential valid cognizer.

At this stage, even though we now have a valid understanding of emptiness, we still need to meditate on emptiness for a long time using re-cognizers to deepen our experience. This is because an inferential cognizer realizing emptiness is only an intellectual understanding, which does not have the power to eliminate self-grasping. Now we must strive to attain a direct realization of emptiness that actually has the power to eradicate self-grasping. To do this we must first attain the union of tranquil abiding and superior seeing observing emptiness, and then meditate on this until it transforms into a yogic direct perceiver realizing emptiness. When we attain this mind we shall have attained the path of seeing and passed beyond the level of ordinary beings. We shall have become a Superior being who can no longer fall to lower rebirths, and we shall definitely attain liberation from samsara or great enlightenment.

Until we attain an inferential cognizer realizing emptiness there is always a danger that we shall develop doubts or wrong awarenesses with respect to emptiness, and so we must always be on guard against them; but once we have attained an inferential cognizer realizing emptiness our understanding of emptiness can no longer be shaken by doubts. However, there is still a danger that our meditation on emptiness can be impeded by distractions. To overcome these we must cultivate non-ascertaining perceivers towards the objects of distraction. If we restrain our sense doors in this way we shall easily attain strong concentration that will enable us to transform our inferential cognizer of emptiness into a direct perceiver realizing emptiness directly.

To summarize, the main obstacles to attaining a realization of emptiness are deluded doubts and wrong awareness with respect to emptiness. Our initial knowledge of emptiness is a correct belief, and this acts as the substantial cause of an inferential cognizer, which is our first valid cognizer of emptiness. The method for transforming this valid cognizer into a direct realization of emptiness is to meditate on emptiness with a re-cognizer. While we are meditating we must eliminate distractions by developing non-ascertaining perceivers towards the objects of delusion. By practising in this way we shall eventually attain the fruit, a yogic direct perceiver realizing emptiness directly, and thereby attain the path of seeing. As Dharmakirti said:

> If all the causes and conditions are assembled, nothing can prevent the effect from arising.

If we sow seeds in a field that is free from obstacles and that has all the necessary conditions such as moisture and warmth, a crop will appear even if we pray for it not to. In the same way, if we follow sincerely the path of mental development explained here, we shall definitely attain the fruit of a direct realization of emptiness and go on to experience the taste of true liberation from suffering.

Valid and Non-valid Cognizers

VALID COGNIZERS

In general 'valid' means 'non-deceptive' or 'completely reliable'. There are three ways in which the term can be applied:

1 Valid Teachers
2 Valid teachings
3 Valid cognizers

If we rely upon valid Teachers, valid teachings, and valid cognizers they will never lead us astray because they will not cause us to develop non-virtuous states of mind or to commit non-virtuous actions. Instead they will lead us in the direction of purity and happiness. To attain liberation we need to develop valid cognizers with respect to the two truths, and to do this we need to rely upon valid teachings given by valid Teachers.

In the second chapter of *Commentary to Valid Cognition* Dharmakirti defines a valid Teacher as a Teacher who knows fully and without error what objects are to be abandoned and what objects are to be practised, and who, out of compassion, reveals this knowledge to others.

A valid Teacher, therefore, must have five qualities:

(1) Unmistaken knowledge of all objects to be abandoned
(2) Complete knowledge of the methods for abandoning them
(3) Unmistaken knowledge of all objects to be practised
(4) Complete knowledge of the methods for practising them
(5) Revealing all this to others with the motivation of compassion

If we meet a Teacher who has these five qualities we can place our complete and unreserved trust in him or her. The supreme example of a valid Teacher is Buddha. His mind perfectly accords with the way things are, he is free from the two obstructions, and he sees clearly what binds sentient beings to samsara and how to release them. Since he has completely fulfilled his own purpose he has nothing to gain from deceiving sentient beings – his only motivation for teaching is great compassion. Just as a valid mind can never lead us into error because its nature is non-deceptive, so Buddha can never deceive us or disappoint us because his nature is non-deceptive. Merely by looking at Buddha or his image we receive immense benefits, and because he is such a pure and powerful being any virtuous action that we do with respect to him is a cause of attaining enlightenment.

The definition of valid teaching is an instruction that principally explains without error the objects to be abandoned and how to abandon them, and the objects to be practised and how to practise them. All the eighty-four thousand teachings of Buddha are included within these two types of instruction.

Buddha Shakyamuni skilfully included all spiritual practices within the practice of the four noble truths. All objects to be abandoned are included within true sufferings and true origins, and all objects to be practised are included within true cessations and true paths. From this we can see that even though they seem to be very concise, the four noble truths have a very extensive meaning. The four noble truths can be practised according to any of the four schools, but the most profound way of practising them is according to the Madhyamika-Prasangika school. The sixteen characteristics of the four noble truths can be understood at a gross, subtle, and very subtle level; and someone who is skilled at presenting these various levels of explanation is indeed a valid Teacher. As Dharmakirti says in *Commentary to Valid Cognition*, if we wish to attain liberation we do not need a Teacher who has clairvoyance and miracle powers; we need only a Teacher who has a clear understanding of the four noble truths and the ability to explain them well.

In essence, Dharma practice consists of gaining valid cognizers of all the objects of the stages of the path, and in this way eradicating all our wrong awarenesses. Every valid cognizer has a wrong awareness to which it is the opponent. The valid cognizer realizing the faults of samsara, for example, is the opponent of the wrong awareness that views samsara as pleasant, and the wisdom realizing emptiness is the opponent of self-grasping.

We need valid cognizers realizing both the objects to be abandoned and the objects to be practised. Without realizing these with valid cognizers our experience of Dharma will not be stable, and may even degenerate. Therefore, it is most important to know the defining characteristics of valid cognizers so that we can distinguish them from less reliable states of mind. It was principally to explain these characteristics that Dignaga wrote *Compendium of Valid Cognition* and Dharmakirti composed a commentary to it entitled *Commentary to Valid Cognition*. These two texts are quite technical and difficult to understand, and in the past many scholars have thought that they were of no practical value. Je Tsongkhapa, however, saw the great importance of these texts and showed how they are an indispensable prerequisite for a deep understanding of Sutra and Tantra. By explaining valid cognizers, these texts show exactly what types of mind we need to cultivate if we wish to attain true and lasting experience of Dharma.

Dignaga developed the wish to compose *Compendium of Valid Cognition* while he was in retreat in a forest cave. He composed the first stanza, praising Buddha Shakyamuni as a valid Teacher, wrote it on a slate, and left it in a high place inside his cave while he went out to collect some food. When he returned he noticed that the verse had been erased, and so he rewrote it. The next day he left the cave again to collect food and, once again when he returned, the verse had been erased. Determined to find out who was interfering with his work Dignaga wrote a message on the slate, 'I wish to compose this text for the benefit of all living beings, but you are obstructing me. If you have some objection you should remain here until I return and discuss it with me.' The following day he went out as usual and, when he returned, a non-Buddhist teacher called Tubgyal Nagpo was waiting there. 'Is it you who have been interfering with my composition?' he asked. 'Yes', replied Tubgyal Nagpo. 'Then we must debate the issue', Dignaga continued, 'and the view of whoever wins the debate will prevail.' Tubgyal Nagpo agreed, and they proceeded to debate the merits of composing such a special text. Dignaga won the debate outright, but Tubgyal Nagpo refused to abide by the terms of the debate and tried to destroy Dignaga. Using his mundane miracle powers he blew fire at Dignaga from his mouth, but he was unable to harm him. Dignaga was so upset by the evil and treachery of Tubgyal Nagpo that he despaired of his work ever benefiting living beings. Seizing the slate, he threw it into the air saying 'As soon as this slate lands on the ground I will stop working on this text', but to his amazement the slate did not come down again! When he looked up to see what had happened, Dignaga beheld the Wisdom Buddha Manjushri above him. 'Do not be discouraged, my Son', Manjushri said, 'This work will benefit many living beings in the future; it will be like their eyes guiding them in the darkness of their ignorance and leading them to liberation. You must complete this text.' Inspired by this, Dignaga immediately set about completing his composition, and as a result many living beings have subsequently benefited from *Compendium of Valid Cognition*.

Later, many Tibetan Geshes came to believe that Dignaga's slate finally landed in central Tibet, in a small town called Jang, near Lhasa. They believed that if Dignaga's text was studied in that town their understanding would develop very quickly, and so every year many monks from Sera, Drepung, and Ganden monasteries would go to Jang for three months at a time to study Dharmakirti's commentary to *Compendium of Valid Cognition*. They felt that three months' study in that town was equal to three years' study in other places. It was believed that the slate moved about, so at night, when their classes had finished, the monks would make many prostrations in different places hoping to place their head on the slate!

If we do not understand with valid cognizers the objects to be practised and the objects to be abandoned our Dharma practice will be inconsistent. For example, some people are inspired by their first Dharma teachings and then apply themselves with great enthusiasm to meditation for a few months, but when they find that they have not made much progress they become discouraged and give up their practice. This kind of thing happens because we do not realize the meaning of the teachings with valid cognizers, and so our understanding remains unstable and vulnerable to doubts and wrong awarenesses. If we realize a Dharma subject with a valid cognizer, however, we shall never be disturbed by doubts or wrong awarenesses, and we shall never feel that we want to abandon our efforts to attain liberation.

Correct beliefs are useful but they are not completely reliable. If we meet a famous Teacher from another tradition, or if we meet with unfavourable circumstances, our correct beliefs may easily turn into doubts and eventually be lost altogether. Therefore, we should not be satisfied with correct beliefs alone, but strive continuously to transform them into valid cognizers.

The supreme valid cognizer is omniscient wisdom. Because Buddhas validly understand all objects of knowledge simultaneously, they are able to help all living beings. Although we have only a few valid cognizers of Dharma subjects, these are extremely important because they are the seeds of omniscient wisdom.

Valid cognizers will now be explained under three headings:

(1) Definition of valid cognizer
(2) Function of valid cognizers
(3) Divisions of valid cognizer

DEFINITION OF VALID COGNIZER

The definition of valid cognizer is a cognizer that is non-deceptive with respect to its engaged object.

Correct beliefs, non-ascertaining perceivers, doubts, and wrong awarenesses are all deceptive cognizers. It is not difficult to understand why wrong awarenesses are deceptive. For example, the wrong awareness that sees worldly pleasures as true happiness and regards them as the essence of human life deceives us by preventing us from seeking release from samsara; the wrong awareness of a moth seeing a flame as an attractive abode encourages the moth to fly into the flame and die; and the wrong awareness of our self-grasping mind conceiving our I to be truly existent encourages us to commit heavy non-virtuous actions that cause us to be reborn in the hell realms and experience unbearable pain for a long time. Wrong awarenesses cloud our judgement and make us see the impure as pure, the pure as impure, the existent as non-existent, and the non-existent as existent. When we are under the influence of wrong awareness the causes of hell can seem reliable and the causes of enlightenment meaningless!

It is also not difficult to see why doubts and non-ascertaining perceivers are deceptive or unreliable states of mind. Doubts are unreliable because they prevent certainty about correct objects, and non-ascertaining perceivers are unreliable because they do not realize their object.

It is a little more difficult to understand why correct beliefs are deceptive. After all, for as long as we have a correct belief in an object we do not have doubts or wrong awarenesses about that object. However, correct beliefs do not penetrate their object in sufficient depth to eliminate all misconceptions about the object, and therefore they leave us vulnerable to doubts and wrong awarenesses. This is why they are deceptive. At present, most of our Dharma understanding consists of correct beliefs. Unless we have learned to distinguish correct beliefs from valid cognizers, we may mistake these correct beliefs for firm realizations, and this may lead to complacency. After listening to an inspiring teaching on renunciation, for example, we may develop a correct belief and feel that samsara has no good qualities, but this alone will not change our mind. On the other hand, if we realize this with a valid cognizer our mind will definitely change.

FUNCTION OF VALID COGNIZERS

The special function of valid cognizers is to act as the opponent to wrong awarenesses. Each valid cognizer counteracts a specific wrong awareness. The valid cognizer realizing that the body is impermanent, for example, counteracts the wrong awareness believing the body to be permanent, and the valid cognizer realizing the faults of samsara counteracts the wrong awareness that sees good qualities in samsara. Even a valid cognizer realizing a book counteracts the wrong awareness thinking that it is not a book. Whenever a valid cognizer manifests it is impossible for the particular wrong awareness that it opposes to manifest. For example, for as long as we have a manifest valid cognizer realizing selflessness of persons, self-grasping will not be able to function in our mind. Je Tsongkhapa said that to check whether or not we have developed a valid cognizer realizing emptiness we should watch our mind of self-grasping. If as a result of our meditation our self-grasping is reduced, this indicates that we have a valid cognizer realizing emptiness and that we are meditating correctly; but if our self-grasping is not reduced, this indicates that we have not yet attained a valid cognizer realizing emptiness. A valid cognizer realizing emptiness is the direct antidote not only to self-grasping but also to all the other delusions.

All our suffering is caused by our negative actions of body, speech, and mind, which in turn are caused by our wrong awarenesses. We can see, therefore, the importance of opposing wrong awarenesses with valid cognizers. First we need to weaken specific delusions by developing valid cognizers realizing their faults and by familiarizing our mind with the opposing virtue. Then we need to attack the root of all delusions by meditating on emptiness. Through continued meditation we shall attain the exalted awareness of meditative equipoise of a Superior being, and by improving this wisdom we shall eventually attain the ultimate valid cognizer, omniscient wisdom.

DIVISIONS OF VALID COGNIZER

There are two types of valid cognizer:

1 Direct valid cognizers
2 Inferential valid cognizers

Some texts list four types, adding valid cognizers through belief and valid cognizers through analogy, but these are not separate divisions because they are included within inferential valid cognizers. The twofold division is definite in number because more than two types of valid cognizer would be superfluous and fewer than two would be insufficient. This is because there are definitely two types of object of knowledge – manifest objects and hidden objects – and so there are definitely two types of valid cognizer – direct valid cognizers (which realize manifest objects) and inferential valid cognizers (which realize hidden objects).

The definition of manifest object is an object whose initial realization by a valid cognizer does not depend upon logical reasons. In general, any object that can be realized by an ordinary being by means of a direct valid cognizer, without their first gaining an inferential cognizer of that object, is a manifest object. From this point of view all sense objects are manifest objects. However, from the point of view of particular persons an object can be a manifest object for one person and a hidden object for another. For example, a fire in a house is a manifest object for the people sitting by the fireplace but a hidden object for people outside the house. Similarly, hell is a manifest object for hell beings but a hidden object for humans, and vice versa.

The definition of hidden object is an object whose initial realization by a valid cognizer depends upon correct logical reasons. In general, there are certain objects that it is impossible for anyone to realize directly without their first realizing them inferentially. These include subtle impermanence, emptiness, and the laws of karma. The only way that these objects can become manifest objects is if we first realize them with an inferential cognizer and then go on to generate a re-cognizer and eventually a yogic direct perceiver of them. There are other objects, however, that are hidden to some beings but manifest to others who live in different places or at different times, or who have different karma. These objects can become manifest simply through a change in external circumstances – they do not necessarily have to be realized first by an inferential cognizer.

The definition of direct valid cognizer is a non-deceptive cognizer that apprehends its manifest object. There are three types of direct valid cognizer: valid sense direct cognizers, valid mental direct cognizers, and valid yogic direct cognizers. These have already been explained in the section on direct perceivers.

Although manifest objects do not exist from their own side they do nevertheless exist because they are objects of direct valid cognizers. By relying upon direct valid cognizers we can avoid falling into the extreme view of nothingness. The main reason Dharmakirti explained direct valid cognizers in great detail in the third chapter of *Commentary to Valid Cognition* was to establish the existence of manifest objects.

The definition of inferential valid cognizer is a non-deceptive cognizer that realizes its hidden object by depending upon a conclusive reason. There are three types of inferential valid cognizer: inferential valid cognizers through the power of fact, inferential valid cognizers through belief, and inferential valid cognizers through renown. These have already been explained.

If four types of valid cognizer are listed, as mentioned above, valid cognizer through analogy is defined as an inferential cognizer that realizes its hidden object principally through analogy.

NON-VALID COGNIZERS

The definition of non-valid cognizer is a cognizer that is deceptive with respect to its engaged object.

There are two types of non-valid cognizer: non-conceptual non-valid cognizers and conceptual non-valid cognizers. All wrong

sense awarenesses and non-ascertaining sense direct perceivers are examples of the first, and all wrong mental awarenesses, such as delusions, and all correct beliefs and doubts,
are examples of the second. Non-valid cognizers are called
'deceptive' because they are not perfect knowledge and so
are unreliable.

PART TWO

Primary Minds and Mental Factors

Dignaga

Primary Minds and Mental Factors

From the point of view of function, mind can be divided into primary minds and mental factors. Primary mind, mentality, and consciousness are synonyms. The definition of primary mind is a cognizer that principally apprehends the mere entity of an object. The definition of mental factor is a cognizer that principally apprehends a particular attribute of an object. These definitions were given by Maitreya.

In the case of a pot for example, the pot itself is the mere entity of the pot, and the base, sides, shape, colour, size, and so forth are particular attributes of the pot. Because a distinction exists within the object, there is a corresponding distinction on the part of the mind that cognizes that object. Thus, the function of a primary mind is to apprehend the mere entity of the object, while the function of mental factors is to apprehend particular attributes of the object. As each object has only one general entity but many particular attributes, any one object has only one primary mind but many mental factors observing it. Thus, when an eye awareness perceives a pot, for example, the primary mind principally apprehends the general entity of the pot – the pot itself – and the mental factors associated with that primary mind principally apprehend the particular attributes of the pot – its various parts.

There are six types of primary mind: eye consciousness, ear consciousness, nose consciousness, tongue consciousness, body consciousness, and mental consciousness. The Chittamatrins posit two more primary minds: a consciousness-basis-of-all and a deluded mentality. According to them the consciousness-basis-of-all is a stable consciousness that does not cease at death but maintains the continuity of the person from one life to the next. It is the repository of karmic potentials and the source of all other consciousnesses. The deluded mentality observes the consciousness-basis-of-all and mistakenly apprehends it as a self-supporting, substantially existent self. The Madhyamika-Prasangikas conclusively refute both the consciousness-basis-of-all and the deluded mentality. There are only six types of primary mind because there are only six types of object – forms, sounds, smells, tastes, tactile objects, and phenomena. Here, 'phenomena' means phenomena that appear only to mental awareness.

The quality of a primary mind depends upon the mental factors that accompany it. If the mental factors are virtuous the primary mind is virtuous, but if the mental factors are non-virtuous or neutral the primary mind is non-virtuous or neutral. Non-virtuous mental factors cause suffering and virtuous mental factors cause peace and happiness. Thus, if we wish to experience lasting peace of mind we must make a determined effort to eliminate non-virtuous mental factors and cultivate virtuous ones.

Each primary mind is accompanied by at least five mental factors, without which it would be unable to function. These are feeling, discrimination, intention, contact, and attention. They are known as the 'five all-accompanying mental factors'. Just as a car cannot function if any of its wheels is missing, so a primary mind cannot function if any of these five mental factors is absent. For example, all physical objects are composed of eight substances – the four elements (earth, water, fire, and wind) and the four transformed elements (forms, smells, tastes, and tactile objects) – and just as even the simplest physical object must have all eight substances, so even the most basic primary mind must have all five all-accompanying mental factors. Even very subtle primary minds have these five mental factors.

We should not think of a primary mind and its mental factors as being separate entities, like a leader and his subjects, because each mental factor is a part of a primary mind. However, although a mental factor is a part of a primary mind, it is not a primary mind, just as a hand is a part of the body but not the body.

The Tibetan word for mental factor is 'sem jung', which literally means 'arisen from mind'. Thus, a primary mind can be likened to a candle flame and its mental factors to the rays of that flame. Just as a candle flame has many rays of light, so one primary mind has many mental factors; just as the rays of light come from the flame and exist simultaneously with it, so mental factors come from the primary mind and exist simultaneously with it; and just as the flame illuminates objects by depending upon the rays of light that emanate from it, so a primary mind knows its object by depending upon its mental factors.

A primary mind and its mental factors are the same entity and possess five similarities:

1 Basis – they have the same dominant condition
2 Object – their observed object is the same
3 Aspect – their engaged object is the same
4 Time – they arise, abide, and cease simultaneously
5 Substance – one primary mind has only one of
   each type of mental factor

For example, when a tongue awareness tastes tea, both the primary mind and the mental factor feeling associated with it develop from the same uncommon dominant condition, the tongue sense power, and so their basis is the same. Their observed objects are the same because they both focus on the same object – the taste of the tea; their engaged objects are the same because they both apprehend the taste of the tea; and their time, or duration, is the same because they both arise, abide, and cease simultaneously. They possess the fifth similarity, similarity of substance, because one primary mind can have only one mental factor feeling, one mental factor discrimination, one mental factor intention, and so forth. Similarly, one specific mental factor can be associated with only one primary mind. Sometimes we say that we have mixed feelings about something, and it may seem that in this case one primary mind has several feelings observing the same object, but this is impossible. Ordinary beings cannot have two different manifest minds observing one object at the same time. What actually happens is that we have several primary minds, each with only one feeling. For example, if we have 'mixed feelings' about a house it can either be that at one time we like the house and at another time we dislike it, or that we simultaneously have two different minds relating to the house, each focusing on a different aspect of the house.

There are fifty-one mental factors, which are divided into six groups:

1 The five all-accompanying mental factors
2 The five object-ascertaining mental factors
3 The eleven virtuous mental factors
4 The six root delusions
5 The twenty secondary delusions
6 The four changeable mental factors

Each mental factor will now be explained under three headings: definition, function, and divisions. The first identifies the mental factor, the second shows the results of generating it, and the third deepens our understanding of it. Some of the fifty-one mental factors are quite similar, and so we need to study them carefully and discuss them with others until we have a clear generic image of each one. Although we develop these mental factors within our own mind, we still need to try to identify them precisely so that we know which ones to abandon and which ones to cultivate. Abandoning non-virtuous mental factors and cultivating virtuous ones is the essence of Dharma practice. Deluded mental factors are the cause of all negative actions and the source of all suffering and danger. By identifying them and eradicating them we solve all our problems. When I studied this subject in Tibet I was very young and, although I understood the subject intellectually, I did not fully appreciate how useful it is for training the mind. Now I understand this very clearly.

The Five All-accompanying Mental Factors

The five all-accompanying mental factors are so called because they accompany every primary mind. If just one of them were missing, the primary mind would not be able to cognize its object. The five all-accompanying mental factors are:

1 Feeling
2 Discrimination
3 Intention
4 Contact
5 Attention

Feeling experiences an object as pleasant, unpleasant, or neutral; discrimination functions to distinguish an object from other objects and thereby to identify it; intention enables the mind to move towards its object and become involved with it; contact perceives an object as pleasant, unpleasant, or neutral and thereby serves as the basis for the development of feelings; and attention functions to focus the mind on a particular attribute of an object.

The need for all five of these mental factors to be present can be illustrated by considering a tongue consciousness tasting tea. Without the mental factor feeling, the tongue consciousness would not experience the taste of the tea as pleasant, unpleasant, or neutral. Without discrimination, it would not be able to distinguish the taste of the tea from other objects and so would not be able to recognize it. Without intention, an internal tongue consciousness could not become involved with the taste of the tea, which is an external object. Without contact, it could not perceive the taste of the tea as pleasant, unpleasant, or neutral and so there would be no basis for developing pleasant, unpleasant, or neutral feelings. Without attention, it would not be able to focus on the taste of the tea.

FEELING

DEFINITION OF FEELING

The definition of feeling is a mental factor that functions to experience pleasant, unpleasant, or neutral objects.

Because there are three types of object – pleasant, unpleasant, and neutral – there are three types of feeling that experience these objects – pleasant feelings, unpleasant feelings, and neutral feelings. It is impossible to cognize an object without experiencing it as pleasant, unpleasant, or neutral.

Buddhas have only pleasant feelings; the gods of the form realm and the formless realm have pleasant and neutral feelings but do not have unpleasant feelings; and beings living in the desire realm experience all three types of feeling. During sleep most of our feelings are neutral feelings, but when we are dreaming we may also experience unpleasant and pleasant feelings. Correct meditation will induce peaceful and pleasant feelings, or at least neutral feelings; it can never induce unpleasant feelings.

FUNCTION OF FEELING

The general function of feeling is to experience the effects of previous actions, or karma. In the Sutras, Buddha says:

> The fully ripened effects of actions ripen not on soil or stones, but only on consciousness.

This is because only consciousness has feelings, and only with feelings can we experience the ripened effects of actions. Virtuous actions result in pleasant feelings, non-virtuous actions in unpleasant feelings, and neutral actions in neutral feelings. We tend to think that pleasantness and unpleasantness are characteristics that exist from the side of the object, but in reality whether we experience an object as pleasant or unpleasant depends entirely upon our karma. Two people might eat the same food and one find it delicious while the other thinks it is revolting. If this happens it is because the first person has good karma ripening with respect to that food and the other has bad karma ripening.

More specifically, the function of contaminated feelings is to act as the basis for the three poisons – attachment, hatred, and ignorance. Contaminated pleasant feelings induce attachment, contaminated unpleasant feelings induce hatred, and contaminated neutral feelings induce ignorance. In *Guide to the Bodhisattva's Way of Life* Shantideva says:

Because of feeling, craving develops.

When ordinary beings develop pleasant feelings they develop craving, or attachment. Similarly, their unpleasant feelings induce anger, and their neutral feelings induce ignorance. By closely watching our mind we can observe these automatic reactions occurring almost continuously. Contaminated feelings are like moisture germinating the seeds of delusion that we have carried from previous lives. Foe Destroyers have eradicated the seeds of delusion from their mental continuum and so even when they develop intensely pleasant feelings they do not develop desirous attachment. Being free from self-grasping, their feelings are uncontaminated and so they cannot be the cause of delusions.

All contaminated feelings are objects to be abandoned. It is easy to generate a wish to abandon unpleasant feelings, but to generate a wish to abandon contaminated pleasant and neutral feelings we need a very good understanding of the nature of samsara. Both contaminated feelings and contaminated discriminations are key links in the chain that binds us to samsara. Contaminated discriminations identify objects as pleasant, unpleasant, or neutral; and contaminated feelings experience them in these ways. Contaminated feelings then give rise to the three poisons, which in turn lead us to perform contaminated actions, the principal causes of rebirth in samsara. As mentioned earlier, it is because feelings and discriminations are so important that when Buddha explained the five aggregates he selected them from among the fifty-one mental factors and designated them each as a separate aggregate.

There are several ways of dividing feeling, including the threefold division already discussed:

1 Pleasant feelings
2 Unpleasant feelings
3 Neutral feelings

There is also a twofold division from the point of view of their uncommon dominant condition:

1 Bodily feelings
2 Mental feelings

Bodily feelings are feelings associated with the five sense consciousnesses. They are generated in dependence upon a sense power possessing form. Mental feelings are feelings associated with mental consciousness, which arise in dependence upon a mental power.

There is another twofold division from the point of view of their nature:

1 Contaminated feelings
2 Uncontaminated feelings

Contaminated feelings are feelings conjoined with self-grasping, and uncontaminated feelings are feelings conjoined with wisdom directly realizing emptiness. Until we attain the path of seeing, most of our feelings are contaminated feelings.

DISCRIMINATION

DEFINITION OF DISCRIMINATION

The definition of discrimination is a mental factor that functions to apprehend the uncommon sign of an object.

Every object has features that distinguish it from other objects and enable us to recognize it. The function of the mental factor discrimination is to apprehend these uncommon features. When we look at a tree, for example, our eye consciousness knows the tree because it discerns, or discriminates, the uncommon signs of the tree. If our eye consciousness lacked the mental factor discrimination it would not be able to distinguish the tree from other objects, and so it would not be able to recognize it. To recognize an object we need to understand what are its uncommon signs, or defining characteristics. For example, a newborn baby does not understand the uncommon signs of a wristwatch, and so it cannot recognize a watch as such.

FUNCTION OF DISCRIMINATION

The function of discrimination is to distinguish an object from other objects and to identify the object as 'this' and not 'that'. Discrimination associated with conceptual minds also functions to impute, label, or name objects. There are two ways of imputing: imputing by sound and imputing by thought. The former is the same as naming and the latter is the same as conceiving.

The defining characteristics of an object do not exist from the side of the object but are merely imputed by the mind that apprehends them. We can understand this by considering how different people view one object. For example, observing a particular person called John, one person may identify an enemy while another identifies a friend. If the characteristics of enemy and friend existed from the side of the person there would be a contradiction here, but since these characteristics are merely imputed onto the person by different minds there is no contradiction. From his own side John does not have a fixed set of defining characteristics waiting to be discovered by various minds; what he is depends solely upon how he is identified by the minds that apprehend him. We can choose how we discriminate objects. As Dharma practitioners we should choose to discriminate only in constructive ways, in ways that are conducive to virtue.

DIVISIONS OF DISCRIMINATION

There are three ways of dividing discrimination. First, from the point of view of uncommon dominant condition there are six types of discrimination:

1 Discriminations associated with eye consciousness
2 Discriminations associated with ear consciousness
3 Discriminations associated with nose consciousness
4 Discriminations associated with tongue consciousness
5 Discriminations associated with body consciousness
6 Discriminations associated with mental consciousness

If any of the six consciousnesses lacked the mental factor discrimination it would not be able to understand its object. Discrimination associated with eye consciousness is eye awareness but not eye consciousness, because consciousness is synonymous with primary mind.

There is also a twofold division of discrimination:

1 Mistaken discriminations
2 Non-mistaken discriminations

All wrong awarenesses have mistaken discrimination, and all unskilful actions of body, speech, and mind result from mistaken discrimination. We act destructively because we are under the influence of delusions, and all delusions are based upon mistaken discrimination. Anger, for example, has a discrimination of its object as inherently unpleasant, while attachment has a discrimination of its object as inherently attractive. In both cases the discrimination is mistaken because attractiveness and unattractiveness depend upon the mind and do not exist from the side of the object.

If the mental factor discrimination is mistaken, the primary mind and all the other mental factors that it accompanies are wrong awarenesses. It is precisely because self-grasping and wrong views have mistaken discrimination that they apprehend wrong objects. The sixteen wrong thoughts explained in the Lamrim teachings and listed on pages 27–8 are all based on mistaken discriminations. For example, the second of these, not wishing to take the essence of our precious human life, involves the mistaken discrimination that the only meaning of this life is worldly pleasure. Dharma practitioners should make prayers to be free from all these mistaken discriminations because they severely hinder our attainment of the realizations of the stages of the path. Lamrim realizations are attained by eliminating these mistaken discriminations and developing the opposite, non-mistaken discriminations.

There are many causes of mistaken discriminations, such as previous imprints, familiarity, listening to wrong teachings or advice, and contemplating wrong reasons. We all have the seeds of mistaken discriminations but whether or not they ripen and influence our life depends to a large extent upon our lifestyle. If we lead a negative, or non-virtuous, life we shall tend to develop wrong thoughts as a way of justifying our behaviour; but if we lead a positive, or virtuous, life we shall be much more likely to adopt correct thoughts.

The imprints of ignorance cause mistaken discriminations that apprehend an inherently existent self, even though such a self does not exist. Moreover, because of our familiarity with delusions we discriminate some people as our friends, some as enemies, and some as strangers; but all these discriminations are mistaken discriminations because in reality all sentient beings are our mothers.

There is another twofold division of discrimination:

1 Clear discriminations
2 Unclear discriminations

If our discrimination is clear we shall be able to learn easily and quickly. Clear and correct discrimination is a basis for improving our understanding, and it helps us to avoid unskilful actions of body, speech, and mind.

As we fall asleep our discrimination becomes unclear, and so we are liable to make mistakes. To begin with, our senses are still working so that, for example, we can still hear sounds such as others talking, but we cannot clearly understand the meaning of what they are saying. People on their deathbed also have unclear discrimination and so it is difficult for them to understand instructions quickly, which is why they make many mistakes. Mental handicap is also often caused by unclear discrimination.

Sometimes when we listen to teachings or read Dharma books we find them confusing and feel that they are not presented very clearly, but in reality it is our discrimination that is unclear. If our discrimination were completely clear we could understand teachings just through hand gestures!

Realizing that our feelings and discriminations stimulate delusions, some practitioners try to abandon feelings and discriminations completely by withdrawing their mind inwards through the force of concentration and thereby becoming absorbed in a subtle state where disturbing mental activity is no longer manifest. This state is known as the 'absorption without discrimination'. It is a state in which the mind is single-pointedly absorbed in nothingness, with no gross feelings or discriminations. When these practitioners die they may be reborn as non-discrimination gods of the form realm, commonly known as the 'long-life gods', where they remain in absorption without discrimination for very long periods of time.

By preventing discrimination of gross objects these meditators make it impossible for gross delusions to manifest. However, they do not actually eradicate delusions in this way and so they do not attain liberation from samsara. Although it is possible to suppress gross feelings and discriminations associated with gross levels of consciousness, and thereby temporarily to avoid all the problems that they create, it is not possible to abandon the subtle feelings and discriminations associated with the subtle mind. When we fall into a deep sleep all the mental activity of which we are normally aware ceases and it seems as if we have become mindless, like an inanimate object, but what has actually happened is that our mind has become very subtle. Some practitioners attain a similar effect through the force of meditation and mistake it for liberation. In reality, however, they are merely temporarily absorbed in a state that resembles a long, deep, sleep. Eventually, when their karma to remain in that state ends, their gross mental activity will resume and they will 'wake up'.

At the time of the third Buddha, Buddha Kashyapa, two Hinayana meditators entered into absorption without discrimination, and through the power of their concentration remained in that state for millions of years without dying. It was not until after the fourth Buddha, Buddha Shakyamuni, had passed into paranirvana that these meditators were discovered beneath the ground near Varanasi. As they rose from their subtle level of consciousness and developed gross feelings and discriminations again, they asked where Buddha Kashyapa was, and Buddha Shakyamuni's disciples had to explain that Buddha Kashyapa was no longer in this world, and that even Buddha Shakyamuni had appeared and passed away! After hearing this, both meditators died. Through the force of their concentration they had managed to isolate themselves for a long time from the problems of samsara, but they had not had any opportunity to make progress in their Dharma realizations while they were absorbed. Thus, when they finally rose from meditation they had received no benefit from their prolonged absorption.

Instead of trying to stop all discriminations it is more useful to try to develop correct discriminations. If we wish to overcome delusions completely, instead of just withdrawing our mind from the objects of delusion we should clearly identify the object of self-grasping, refute it with logical reasoning, and then meditate on actual emptiness. We also need to cultivate many correct discriminations with respect to the method side of spiritual practice.

As followers of the Mahayana we should not become too interested in meditation on the absorption of feelings and discriminations because it has no long-term benefit. It does not help us to develop renunciation, compassion, bodhichitta, the correct view of emptiness, or the realizations of the two Tantric stages. Sometimes it may be helpful to practise this absorption for a short time when our mind is very disturbed or anxious, but we should not regard it as our principal meditation.

INTENTION

DEFINITION OF INTENTION

The definition of intention is a mental factor that functions to move its primary mind to the object.

It is only through the mental factor intention that our primary mind is able to move towards an object; without it our mind would be motionless. Although our body remains in our room, our mind can travel wherever it wishes because it has the mental factor intention. Just as the movement of a candle flame depends upon wind, so the movement of the mind depends upon the mental factor intention. Our mind moves to an object by connecting with it, or becoming involved in it. For example, when we think of a distant city our mind 'moves' to that city by taking the city as its object.

FUNCTION OF INTENTION

The principal function of intention is to create karma. Of the three types of karma, or action – bodily actions, verbal actions, and mental actions – intention itself is mental action. However, it is also the cause of bodily and verbal actions, because all our bodily and verbal actions are preceded by mental actions.

If a tree falls down and kills someone it does not accumulate the karma of killing because it lacks the mental factor intention. All the karma created by sentient beings depends upon intention. If our intention is virtuous we create virtuous karma, if our intention is non-virtuous we create non-virtuous karma, and if our intention is neutral we create neutral karma. Intention plans the actions that we undertake, directing our action towards a particular goal. Since the quality of our experiences depends upon the quality of our actions, and the quality of an action depends upon the quality of the intention with which it is performed, ultimately all our happiness and unhappiness depend upon the mental factor intention. Even if someone is a great scholar, if he has bad intentions his knowledge will have little value and he will experience many problems.

According to the Sautrantikas and the Chittamatrins, only the mental factor intention is karma, but according to the Madhyamika-Prasangikas and the Vaibashikas, bodily and verbal actions are also karma. However, whether these actions are virtuous, non-virtuous, or neutral depends upon the intention that motivates them.

DIVISIONS OF INTENTION

There are three types of intention:

1 Non-virtuous intentions
2 Virtuous intentions
3 Neutral intentions

There are three types of non-virtuous action – non-virtuous bodily actions, non-virtuous verbal actions, and non-virtuous mental actions – and most are included within the ten non-virtuous actions. Of these, the first two are easy to recognize, but the third, non-virtuous mental actions, are more subtle and therefore more difficult to identify. The mental action covetousness, for example, is a type of desirous attachment that wishes to obtain the friends or possessions of others. Whereas desirous attachment in general may be a neutral mind, covetousness is necessarily non-virtuous. As with all complete actions, covetousness must have four conditions: the basis, intention, preparation, and completion. The basis of covetousness might be someone else's partner; the intention, the wish to obtain that person motivated by desirous attachment; the preparation, planning how to obtain that person for ourself; and the completion of the action, making a definite decision to obtain that person through our chosen method. This decision is the actual non-virtuous mental action of covetousness.

The four conditions must also be present to commit the actual non-virtuous actions of harmful thought and holding wrong views. Thus, the basis of harmful thought is another person whom we see as our enemy; the intention, the wish to harm them motivated by anger; the preparation, planning

117

how to inflict harm on them; and the completion, making a firm decision to harm them. The basis of holding wrong views is any object, such as the existence of past and future lives, that must be understood to attain liberation; the intention, the wish to deny it motivated by ignorance; the preparation, thinking of reasons to prove that it does not exist; and the completion, making a firm decision that it does not exist. It is quite difficult for Dharma practitioners to create the actual karma of holding wrong views, but we still have many imprints or tendencies of wrong views and these often function to obstruct the development of pure faith.

There are many virtuous mental actions. Meditating on compassion is both a virtuous mental action and the mental factor intention, as is meditation on love. Whenever we listen to Dharma teachings, contemplate Dharma, or meditate on Dharma, we are accumulating virtuous mental karma. There are many times when we cannot accumulate bodily and verbal virtuous karma, but we can always accumulate virtuous mental karma, even while we are relaxing, eating, enjoying ourself, or sleeping. Mental karma is more important than bodily or verbal karma because it is our mental intention that determines whether a bodily or verbal action is virtuous or non-virtuous. If we do not have a virtuous intention, then even if we perform positive bodily actions they will not necessarily be virtuous karma because virtuous actions must have a virtuous motivation.

There are many intentions that are neutral mental actions, such as deciding what to eat for breakfast or deciding what to wear.

Intention can also be divided from the point of view of its effect:

1 Meritorious actions
2 Non-meritorious actions
3 Unfluctuating actions

Meritorious and non-meritorious intentions can each be subdivided into those that are throwing karma, those that are completing karma, and those that are karma whose results are experienced in the same life. These three types of action are explained in detail in *Joyful Path of Good Fortune*.

CONTACT

DEFINITION OF CONTACT

The definition of contact is a mental factor that functions to perceive its object as pleasant, unpleasant, or neutral.

Whenever our mind cognizes an object, it perceives it as pleasant, unpleasant, or neutral. This is the function of the mental factor contact. If contact perceives an object as pleasant, pleasant feelings will develop, and if contact perceives the object as unpleasant, unpleasant feelings will develop. Thus, contact makes the development of feelings possible, which is why it precedes feeling in the serial order of the twelve dependent-related links.

FUNCTION OF CONTACT

Besides perceiving objects as pleasant, unpleasant, or neutral, contact also functions to give rise to feelings. For example, if in the first moment of a tongue consciousness tasting tea the mental factor contact associated with that consciousness perceives the tea as pleasant, we shall subsequently develop a pleasant feeling.

DIVISIONS OF CONTACT

There are six types of contact:

1 Contact associated with eye consciousness
2 Contact associated with ear consciousness
3 Contact associated with nose consciousness
4 Contact associated with tongue consciousness
5 Contact associated with body consciousness
6 Contact associated with mental consciousness

ATTENTION

DEFINITION OF ATTENTION

The definition of attention is a mental factor that functions to focus the mind on a particular attribute of an object.

An eye consciousness, for example, is moved towards the general entity of an object by the mental factor intention, but it is the mental factor attention which focuses that consciousness on a particular attribute of that object. Intention is said to be like a horse travelling along a road, while attention is said to be like the reins that direct the horse. Thus, a primary mind focuses on the general entity of its object through the power of the mental factor intention, and on particular attributes of the object through the power of attention.

FUNCTION OF ATTENTION

Attention has four functions: (1) to focus the mind on a particular object, (2) to fix the mind on that object, (3) to prevent the mind from moving from the object, and (4) to serve as a basis for mindfulness and concentration. Without the mind being focused and fixed on an object through the power of attention there is no possibility of developing mindfulness and concentration. Every mind has a certain degree of attention, though some minds, such as non-ascertaining perceivers, have very weak attention, whereas others, such as those that occur when we are in an agitated state, have unstable attention that flits from one object to another. To develop concentration we need both strong and stable attention.

DIVISIONS OF ATTENTION

There are two types of attention:

1 Correct attention
2 Incorrect attention

Correct attention is an attention whose engaged object exists, and incorrect attention is an attention whose engaged object does not exist. All wrong awarenesses have incorrect attention.

There is another twofold division of attention:

1 Appropriate attention
2 Inappropriate attention

The former is the same as correct attention and the latter is the same as incorrect attention.

The Five Object-ascertaining Mental Factors

The five object-ascertaining mental factors are:

1 Aspiration
2 Firm apprehension
3 Mindfulness
4 Concentration
5 Wisdom

They are called 'object-ascertaining' mental factors because they each realize a particular object.

ASPIRATION

DEFINITION OF ASPIRATION

The definition of aspiration is a mental factor that focuses on a desired object and takes an interest in it.

Aspiration, desire, and wish are synonyms. Thus, we are reading this book because we developed an aspiration, a desire, or a wish to do so.

FUNCTION OF ASPIRATION

The main function of aspiration is to induce effort. For example, if we lack the aspiration to receive teachings or to meditate we shall put no effort into these activities. All tasks, whether worldly or spiritual, must be preceded by aspiration if we are to apply ourself to them. The success of our actions depends upon how much effort we put into them; and the stronger our aspiration, the stronger our effort will be. If our aspiration is weak our effort will also be weak; and if we completely lack aspiration we shall do nothing at all.

It is most important to cultivate appropriate aspirations. For example, at the beginning of each meditation in the Lamrim teachings there is an explanation of the benefits of doing that meditation and the disadvantages of not doing it. The purpose of these explanations is to help us to develop the aspiration to engage in the meditation.

DIVISIONS OF ASPIRATION

There are four types of aspiration:

1 Wishing to meet an object
2 Wishing not to be separated from an object
3 Wishing to obtain an object
4 Wishing to be released from an object

Each of these can be virtuous, non-virtuous, or neutral, depending upon its motivation. Examples of the first are wishing to meet Spiritual Guides, Buddhas, or Bodhisattvas; or wishing to meet our family and friends. Examples of the second are wishing not to be separated from our Spiritual Guides or our Dharma practice; or wishing not to be separated from our friends, our possessions, or our home. Examples of the third are wishing to attain Dharma realizations such as renunciation, bodhichitta, and wisdom; or wishing to obtain material possessions, high status, good reputation, or other worldly achievements. Examples of the fourth are wishing to be free from samsara, the two obstructions, or self-cherishing and other non-virtuous minds; or wishing to escape from people or situations we dislike.

Every sentient being develops many aspirations each day, but they are all included within either the aspiration to obtain happiness or the aspiration to be free from unhappiness. There is no one who does not have these two aspirations; they are our basic wishes from which all our other wishes arise. Even tiny insects have these two wishes and strive to fulfil them. Unfortunately ordinary beings do not know the real causes of happiness and suffering, and so in their pursuit of happiness they often bring suffering upon themselves, and in striving to avoid suffering they often increase it.

There is also a twofold division of aspiration:

1 Mistaken aspirations
2 Non-mistaken aspirations

A mistaken aspiration is any wish that is not consistent with our basic aspirations to experience happiness and avoid suffering, and a non-mistaken aspiration is one that is consistent with these basic aspirations. The difference between a wise person and a foolish person is his or her aspirations. Even if we have not studied extensively, if our aspiration is good and unmistaken we shall naturally engage in virtuous actions, which will result in happiness; but if our aspirations are mistaken we shall not succeed in finding happiness no matter how great our worldly intelligence. Often criminals are highly intelligent and clever but because their aspirations are mistaken they commit crimes for which they are sent to prison.

If our wishes are not good, this is a sign that we do not possess true wisdom. Some people study Dharma for many years but receive little benefit, and their understanding remains only intellectual. The main reason for this is that their aspirations are not pure. Although superficially they have some interest in Dharma, deep down their real interest is in worldly things. Other people whose aspiration is pure receive genuine experience of Dharma even though they have not studied extensively. Their correct aspirations encourage them to engage in pure, virtuous actions, and these result in pure effects. What we accomplish depends primarily upon what we wish for, and so if our wishes are pure we shall obtain pure results from our practice. The most important thing, therefore, is to develop and maintain correct aspirations. The supreme aspiration is bodhichitta, the wish to attain Buddhahood for the benefit of all sentient beings. With this aspiration all our actions become causes of attaining Buddhahood.

Basically Dharma practice is quite simple because all we need to do is to receive correct Dharma teachings by listening to qualified Teachers or by reading authentic books, and then mix our mind with these teachings by meditating on them. Whenever we listen to teachings or read Dharma books we should develop a correct aspiration, or motivation, concerning each subject, and maintain this aspiration with single-pointed focus. We need to cultivate virtuous aspirations such as the wish to seize the essence of our human life, renunciation, and bodhichitta. If we meditate on these aspirations continuously, eventually they will arise spontaneously in our mind. Training in this way is the very essence of Dharma practice.

FIRM APPREHENSION

DEFINITION OF FIRM APPREHENSION

The definition of firm apprehension is a mental factor that makes its primary mind apprehend its object firmly.

This mental factor is present in all realizations. If a correct awareness holds its object firmly through the force of this mental factor it necessarily realizes its object. Although some wrong awarenesses hold their objects firmly, they are not realizations because their objects do not exist and so there is no actual understanding. The reason non-ascertaining direct perceivers do not realize their objects is that they lack this mental factor.

FUNCTION OF FIRM APPREHENSION

The main function of firm apprehension is to make its primary mind apprehend its object firmly and thereby to realize that object. It also acts as a cause of mindfulness and concentration. Unless we understand an object firmly, with certainty, it is very difficult to keep our mind on it for long. Without firm apprehension our mind is like flowing water or a leaf in the wind. The reason we find it more difficult to keep our mind on a subtle object such as emptiness than on a gross object such as our breath is that we do not yet have firm apprehension of subtle objects.

There are three special types of firm apprehension observing emptiness that are attained during our spiritual development:

one on the patience level of the path of preparation, one on the path of seeing, and one on the eighth ground. These are explained in teachings on the perfection of wisdom.

DIVISIONS OF FIRM APPREHENSION

There are two types of firm apprehension:

1 Correct firm apprehensions
2 Mistaken firm apprehensions

The first includes all firm apprehensions whose engaged object exists. An example of the second is grasping very tightly to a wrong view – for example, believing with strong conviction that this world is created by Ishvara. Even if we have wrong views, if we do not hold them very strongly they will not be very harmful because they can quickly be dispelled by listening to correct teachings; but if our wrong views are made firm by mistaken firm apprehension it will be very difficult for us to overcome them.

MINDFULNESS

DEFINITION OF MINDFULNESS

The definition of mindfulness is a mental factor that functions not to forget the object realized by the primary mind.

Mindfulness can focus only on an object that has already been realized; it is not present in the first moment of realizing an object. Mindfulness maintains the continuum of the original cognition by not forgetting the object. The reason an object is not forgotten is that the primary mind does not forget it, and the reason the primary mind does not forget the object is that it possesses the mental factor mindfulness. If a primary mind lacks mindfulness it will immediately forget its object. Without mindfulness our mind is like a leaky vessel – no matter how much we study we shall not be able to retain anything.

Mindfulness is essential whenever we are listening to, contemplating, or meditating on Dharma teachings. It is the life-force of Dharma practice. If our mindfulness declines, our knowledge and realizations will be lost. In *Friendly Letter* Nagarjuna says:

If mindfulness degenerates, all Dharmas degenerate.

FUNCTION OF MINDFULNESS

The function of mindfulness is to prevent distractions. The more stable our mindfulness, the fewer distracting thoughts we shall have. If we meditate with strong mindfulness our mind will remain on its object without distraction and we shall naturally develop stable concentration. At the moment the only type of mindfulness we can use is the conceptual mindfulness associated with gross levels of consciousness. We cannot yet use subtle mindfulness associated with subtle levels of consciousness, which is why we are unable to think clearly or meditate while we are asleep. When through meditation we learn to use subtle mindfulness we shall be able to meditate even during sleep.

Dharma practitioners need to make a continuous effort to improve their mindfulness, both in and out of meditation. There are some teachers, such as the twelfth-century Chinese monk Hashang, who teach that the way to meditate is simply to relax and let the mind go blank. This is very harmful advice because if we emphasize this practice our mindfulness will deteriorate and we shall forget all we have learnt. Our Dharma realizations will degenerate and we shall become dull and stupid.

DIVISIONS OF MINDFULNESS

In the Mahamudra teachings, mindfulness is divided into:

1 New mindfulness
2 Old mindfulness

Mindfulness functions both to keep the mind on an object that has not been forgotten, and to bring back to mind an object that has been forgotten. Until we attain the fourth mental abiding we sometimes forget the object of meditation and have to make an effort to remember it. To do this we need to rely upon new mindfulness. On the fourth mental abiding the power of mindfulness is complete and we never forget the object during the meditation session. From this point onwards all our mindfulness has to do is to keep a hold of the object. This is called 'old mindfulness'.

There is another twofold division of mindfulness:

1 Mindfulness with movements of mental sinking and mental excitement
2 Mindfulness without movements of mental sinking and mental excitement

Although the power of mindfulness is completed on the fourth mental abiding, there still remain subtle mental sinking and subtle mental excitement within that state of non-forgetfulness. It is not until the eighth mental abiding that all movements of mental sinking and mental excitement cease.

Dharma texts advise us that if we wish to attain tranquil abiding we should try to do so while we are young because as we get older our powers decline and the power of our mindfulness decreases. Compared with old people, young people have clear and stable mindfulness. With stable mindfulness it is easier to develop concentration and eventually to attain tranquil abiding.

CONCENTRATION

DEFINITION OF CONCENTRATION

The definition of concentration is a mental factor that makes its primary mind remain on its object single-pointedly.

Concentration serves to focus our mind on one object. It can develop only when the object is held firmly by mindfulness. Most primary minds have a degree of concentration, but simply possessing good concentration does not mean that we have attained Dharma realizations. The concentrations that are mentioned in the Lamrim teachings are necessarily virtuous, but not all concentrations are virtuous. Sometimes concentration is neutral and sometimes it is non-virtuous. For example, when a black magician forms a curse he has strong concentration but this concentration is non-virtuous. Non-virtuous concentration should be avoided, but we need both virtuous and neutral concentration. Neutral concentration is necessary to prevent our mind from becoming distracted during mundane tasks, such as driving, sewing, and cooking. For example, if we are distracted while we are driving we may have an accident, and if we are distracted while we are working we shall be inefficient and make many mistakes. Without at least some concentration we could not even make a cup of tea.

Concentration is particularly important for our spiritual practice. Practices such as reciting mantras, listening, contemplating, and meditating are effective only if they are done with a concentrated mind. Actions done with a distracted mind do not have much power and are subject to many errors. As Shantideva says in *Guide to the Bodhisattva's Way of Life*:

Buddha, the All Knowing One, has said
That reciting mantras and prayers, and enduring
    spiritual hardships,
Even for a long time,
Are to no avail if the mind is distracted elsewhere.

Pure concentration has four qualities: lucidity, clarity, strength, and stability. When the mind is free from the clouds of distracting conceptions it becomes bright and clear, like a cloudless sky; this is known as 'lucidity'. 'Clarity' means that the object appears clearly and vividly to the mind, 'strength' that the object is held firmly by strong mindfulness, and 'stability' that the mind abides single-pointedly on its object.

FUNCTION OF CONCENTRATION

The main function of virtuous concentration is to make the mind peaceful. In *Precious Garland* Nagarjuna says:

From giving comes wealth,
From discipline comes happiness,
From patience come attractive forms,
From effort comes the fulfilment of wishes,
From concentration comes peace,
And from wisdom comes freedom from obstructions.

When our mind is free from the turbulence of distracting conceptions it becomes calm and smooth. When we are enjoying internal peace and happiness our craving for external sources of pleasure naturally declines and it is easy to remain content.

Pure concentration also helps to make our body and mind comfortable, flexible, and easy to use in the practice of Dharma. This serviceability of the mind, which is called 'suppleness', is one of the main benefits that come from concentration. Although at present we have a certain degree of concentration when we meditate, it is relatively weak and short-lived, and so the suppleness it produces is subtle and difficult to recognize; but as our concentration becomes stronger and more stable our suppleness will also improve.

It is not just the intensity of suppleness that is important, for suppleness must also be firm and long-lasting. If we have suppleness that lasts for twenty-four hours a day we shall always find it easy to engage in virtuous actions because we shall never become physically or mentally tired; and we shall always be delighted to listen to, contemplate, and meditate on Dharma teachings. With this joy in Dharma practice we shall find no difficulty in accomplishing the five paths, the ten grounds, and the realizations of the two stages of Tantra.

Suppleness is the real opponent of laziness. According to Dharma, laziness is not just attachment to sleep and physical ease – it is any mind that is disinclined to engage in virtuous activities. There is no more important spiritual task than to eliminate laziness. With suppleness, virtuous activities such as contemplation or meditation become a pleasure and there is no reluctance to engage in them. The attainment of suppleness depends upon concentration, concentration depends upon effort, effort depends upon aspiration, and aspiration depends upon recognizing the benefits of concentration. Ordinary people regard samsaric enjoyments, possessions, and money as beneficial and so they put all their effort into acquiring these; but Dharma practitioners see the great benefits of concentration and strive earnestly to attain it.

Concentration gives us the freedom to accomplish whatever we wish for. Without concentration our mind has no freedom but is forced to go wherever it is led by attachment, hatred, or other delusions. A person who has good, virtuous concentration has control over his mind, and his mind does what he wants it to do, like a well-trained horse that obeys its rider. By improving our concentration we can attain tranquil abiding, superior seeing, clairvoyance, and miracle powers, and eventually complete all the paths to enlightenment; but if we lack concentration we shall not be able to make any progress on the paths and grounds of the Mahayana, and so we shall not be able to attain Buddhahood. Therefore, all mundane and supramundane attainments depend upon concentration.

We need concentration not only during formal meditation but also when we are listening to teachings or reading Dharma books. For example, if we read a book with a distracted mind we shall not understand the meaning clearly. We may think that the fault lies in the book but in reality it lies in our distracted mind.

DIVISIONS OF CONCENTRATION

There are three ways of dividing virtuous concentration: from the point of view of realm, from the point of view of their effect, and from the point of view of their object. There are nine levels of concentration from the point of view of realm:

1 Concentration of the desire realm
2 Concentration of the first form realm
3 Concentration of the second form realm
4 Concentration of the third form realm
5 Concentration of the fourth form realm
6 Concentration of infinite space

7 Concentration of infinite consciousness
8 Concentration of nothingness
9 Concentration of peak of samsara

In samsara there are nine realms in which sentient beings can take rebirth: the desire realm, the four form realms, and the four formless realms. The desire realm has two levels: happy migrations, which include the realms of humans and gods, and unhappy migrations, which include the realms of hungry ghosts, animals, and hell beings.

There are nine levels of desire realm concentration:

1 Placing the mind
2 Continual placement
3 Replacement
4 Close placement
5 Controlling
6 Pacifying
7 Completely pacifying
8 Single-pointedness
9 Placement in equipoise

After we attain the ninth level, placement in equipoise, we go on to attain tranquil abiding, which marks the beginning of the concentration of the first form realm. There are four form realms: the first form realm, second form realm, third form realm, and fourth form realm. There are also four formless realms: infinite space, infinite consciousness, nothingness, and peak of samsara. Peak of samsara is the highest of the nine realms, and the desire realm is the lowest.

Corresponding to the nine realms there are nine levels of being, nine levels of mind, and nine levels of concentration. The grossest mind is that of a desire realm being. The mind of a being of the first form realm is slightly more subtle, and so on, until the concentration of peak of samsara, which is the most subtle mind within the nine realms.

To attain a mind of the first form realm it is not necessary to take rebirth in the form realm because we can attain tranquil abiding without abandoning our human body. Compared with the minds of the desire realm, form realm minds are more subtle, peaceful, and concentrated. Although form realm beings still experience attachment to inner peace they have no anger and no attachment to external objects. Desire realm minds, on the other hand, are very gross and rough, and easily give rise to strong delusions. Without training in meditation it is difficult for beings in the desire realm to develop pure, virtuous concentration because their minds are so gross and distracted. However, if we train in meditation over a long period of time our mind will gradually become more subtle, our distractions less intense, and our meditation deeper. Eventually we shall attain tranquil abiding and become free from the problems of desire realm beings.

There are two types of concentration from the point of view of their effect:

1 Mundane concentrations
2 Supramundane concentrations

Mundane concentrations are concentrations that are not motivated by at least renunciation and therefore cause only samsaric happiness. If our motivation for attaining tranquil abiding is to take rebirth in the form realm, for example, our concentration will be a mundane concentration because it will cause rebirth in samsara. Concentrations that are motivated by renunciation or bodhichitta are supramundane concentrations because they lead us beyond samsara, to liberation or enlightenment.

There is another twofold division of concentration from the point of view of their object:

1 Concentrations observing conventional objects
2 Concentrations observing ultimate objects

Since there are many different types of conventional object, there are many different concentrations observing conventional objects; but since there are not different ultimate objects, from the point of view of their object there are not different concentrations observing ultimate objects.

It is also possible to divide concentrations from the point of view of their duration. Concentrations can range from a few moments of single-pointedness to an absorption that lasts forever. Once we attain tranquil abiding our concentration will be capable of remaining on an object for as long as we wish. The concentration of a Buddha never weakens but remains focused on its object forever. Foe Destroyers are also able to remain in concentration on the same object for very long periods.

WISDOM

DEFINITION OF WISDOM

The definition of wisdom is a virtuous, intelligent mind that makes its primary mind realize its object thoroughly.

Many texts liken wisdom to an inner eye because to understand profound Dharma topics such as the four noble truths or the two truths we need wisdom eyes. To follow an external path we need to see it with our physical eyes, but to progress along the inner paths to liberation and enlightenment we need the eyes of wisdom. Wisdom is also likened to a light that enables us to see the jewels that lie within the treasure house of Buddha's scriptures.

FUNCTION OF WISDOM

In general, wisdom functions to eliminate doubts and misunderstandings, and in particular it functions to dispel ignorance. If we understand the benefits of developing wisdom we shall naturally strive to attain it. The opposite of wisdom is ignorance. Nothing harms us more than ignorance – it is the source of all our problems and the root cause of all our negative actions of body, speech, and mind. There is no better way to use our precious human life than to strive to overcome our ignorance, and the way to do this is to develop wisdom.

To attain enlightenment we need to eliminate ignorance and its imprints from our mind. The Tibetan word for 'Buddha' is 'sang gyä', in which 'sang' means 'purified' and 'gyä' means 'accomplished'. A Buddha, therefore, is someone who has completely purified his or her mind of ignorance and its imprints. At present our mind is like a clear sky obscured by clouds. The only reason we do not realize all phenomena is that our mind is obscured by the delusions and their imprints. Once these are eradicated our mind will naturally become the omniscient mind of a Buddha, realizing all phenomena directly and simultaneously. The way to dispel the clouds of ignorance from our mind is to cultivate wisdom; therefore there is no more important task than to increase our wisdom.

DIVISIONS OF WISDOM

There are three types of wisdom:

1 Wisdom arisen from listening
2 Wisdom arisen from contemplation
3 Wisdom arisen from meditation

Wisdom arisen from listening is a wisdom that arises when we develop a thorough understanding of a virtuous object principally through listening to conclusive reasons spoken by others. Wisdom arisen from contemplation is a wisdom that arises when we develop a thorough understanding of a virtuous object principally through our own contemplation of conclusive reasons. Wisdom arisen from meditation is a thorough understanding of a virtuous object that arises through the power of meditation. This is the most profound type of wisdom. All three wisdoms are necessarily valid cognizers. The most important wisdom is superior seeing, which is the means by which we completely eradicate ignorance and its imprints.

In the *Vinaya Sutras* Buddha says:

> You should generate wisdom in dependence upon concentration, which itself depends upon moral discipline.

This means that to develop the wisdom of superior seeing we first need to attain the concentration of tranquil abiding, and to attain tranquil abiding we need to practise pure moral discipline.

There is also a sevenfold division of wisdom:

1 Great wisdom
2 Clear wisdom
3 Quick wisdom
4 Profound wisdom
5 The wisdom of expounding Dharma
6 The wisdom of spiritual debate
7 The wisdom of composing Dharma books

A method for developing quick wisdom is explained on page 78. All these wisdoms and how to accomplish them are explained in detail in the book *Heart Jewel*.

The Eleven Virtuous Mental Factors

The eleven virtuous mental factors are all naturally virtuous, which means that they are virtuous through their own nature and not through the force of a specific motivation. If a spoonful of sugar is stirred into a cup of tea, all the tea becomes sweet because sugar is by nature sweet. Similarly, when a virtuous mental factor is present in the mind, that entire primary mind and all its attendant mental factors also become virtuous.

The eleven virtuous mental factors are:

1 Faith
2 Sense of shame
3 Consideration for others
4 Non-attachment
5 Non-hatred
6 Non-ignorance
7 Effort
8 Mental suppleness
9 Conscientiousness
10 Equanimity
11 Non-harmfulness

FAITH

DEFINITION OF FAITH

The definition of faith is a mental factor that functions principally to eliminate non-faith.

Without understanding non-faith we cannot understand faith. There are three types of non-faith: non-faith of disbelief, non-faith of non-admiration, and non-faith of not-wishing.

Dharmakirti

Non-faith of disbelief is disbelief in any correct object in which it is necessary to believe to make spiritual progress, such as the objects explained in Dharma teachings. If someone correctly explains Buddha's teachings on actions and their effects and we do not believe what they are saying, this is because the mental factor non-faith of disbelief is present in our mind. Non-faith of non-admiration is a mental factor that causes us to see faults in virtuous objects such as Dharma Teachers, the Three Jewels, and other holy beings. It makes our mind unclear and confused. Non-faith of not-wishing is a mind that does not desire virtuous attainments. It prevents us from developing a wish to engage in the paths to liberation or enlightenment.

These three types of non-faith are very harmful. Disbelief prevents us from engaging in spiritual practices and attaining Dharma realizations. It is harmful even for those who are not interested in Dharma. For example, there are many diseases that doctors call cancer but which are in fact caused by spirits or by previous karma. Although these cannot be cured by ordinary medical practices, they can be cured by the healing rituals and purification practices taught by Buddha. However, for these methods to be effective we need to have faith in them. Unfortunately few people in the West have sufficient faith in these methods and so we do not have many opportunities to witness their beneficial effects.

Non-faith of non-admiration robs us of our mental peace and makes our mind turbulent and defiled. As a result, our virtuous minds decrease and we are unable to develop pure experience of Dharma. Non-faith of not-wishing harms us by preventing us from practising Dharma purely. At present, our desire to enjoy the pleasures of samsara is much stronger than our desire for spiritual attainments, and this prevents us from practising Dharma purely, undistracted by worldly concerns. The mental factor faith overcomes all three types of non-faith.

FUNCTION OF FAITH

The special function of faith is to induce virtuous aspirations. Without faith in a particular practice we shall have no wish to engage in it; and without such a wish we shall not put any effort into the practice and so we shall not accomplish any results. Faith is the root of all virtuous attainments. If we have faith in Buddha we shall develop the aspiration to become a Buddha, which will encourage us to practise the Mahayana paths continuously and joyfully.

Faith is particularly important in the practice of Secret Mantra. An essential aspect of Tantric practice is the recitation of mantras, but success in mantra recitation depends largely upon the strength of our faith. A person who lacks faith may recite the mantra of his or her Deity for many years but fail to receive any attainments, whereas someone with pure faith may receive attainments after reciting the mantra for only a short time.

In *Lamp of the Jewel Sutra* (Skt. *Ratnalokanamadharani Sutra*) Buddha says:

Faith precedes all virtuous activities, like a mother.
It protects and increases all beneficial qualities,
Dispels hesitation, and rescues us from the four rivers.
Faith is the source of the siddhi of happiness.
It dispels mental defilements and turbulence, makes
    the mind clear,
Eliminates pride, and is the root of respect.
Faith is the supreme wealth, treasure, and legs;
And is like hands with which to gather virtues.

Just as a mother gives birth to children, so faith is the source of all virtuous activities because without faith we shall not engage in pure, virtuous practices. Faith prevents virtuous qualities from degenerating and causes them to increase. Believing faith dispels doubts and hesitations concerning Dharma practices. We have doubts and hesitations about Dharma because we lack faith, but when faith manifests, doubts cannot remain. Wishing faith causes us to strive to attain liberation from samsara and thereby rescues us from the 'four rivers' of birth, sickness, ageing, and death. Some types of faith act as a direct antidote to the delusion-obstructions and the obstructions to omniscience. For example, it is because the vajra-like concentration of the path of meditation is conjoined with believing faith in emptiness that it can act as the direct antidote to the most subtle obstructions to omniscience.

Faith is the source of the siddhi, or attainment, of happiness, because happiness is the result of virtuous actions, and all virtuous actions are motivated by faith. Admiring faith dispels mental defilements such as bad motivations or seeing faults in holy beings such as our Spiritual Guide. By pacifying the mental turbulence caused by disturbing conceptions faith makes our mind lucid and clear. Faith overcomes our pride and is the foundation of respect for the Three Jewels and our Spiritual Guides. It is the supreme wealth because, unlike material wealth, it never deceives us. To accumulate material possessions we frequently have to endure physical and mental hardship, and even commit negative actions, and yet even if we succeed in becoming rich we still do not experience pure peace and happiness. Moreover, material wealth can be lost or stolen and can even endanger our life. Thus, external wealth is the source of much anxiety and discontent. The inner wealth of faith, on the other hand, brings only happiness. If we strengthen our faith we perform only virtuous actions, and when we are rich in faith we experience pure, lasting happiness. The wealth of faith cannot be destroyed by fire or stolen by thieves; even death cannot take it from us. Ultimately the wealth of faith leads us to liberation and great enlightenment, and so it is far superior to external wealth.

Faith is like a treasure because it is the source of inexhaustible benefit and good fortune. It is called 'supreme legs' because it enables us to traverse the ten Bodhisattva grounds and finally to reach the city of great enlightenment. Ordinary legs can take us only to samsaric places but the legs of faith can take us to Dakini Land, where we shall meet Heruka and Vajrayogini, or to Sukhavati, the Pure Land of Buddha Amitabha. Faith is also like hands because it enables us to gather virtuous qualities. Just as we need hands to collect physical objects, so we need the hands of faith to gather the internal wealth of virtue.

DIVISIONS OF FAITH

There are three types of faith:

1 Believing faith
2 Admiring faith
3 Wishing faith

Believing faith is a belief in any object that is conducive to our spiritual development, such as the two basic objects (the two truths), the two paths (method and wisdom), and the three resultant bodies of a Buddha.

Admiring faith is a tranquil, lucid state of mind, free from negative conceptions, that arises when we contemplate the good qualities of virtuous objects or holy beings such as our Spiritual Guide. It is likened to a magical jewel that has the power to purify dirty water. When our mind is disturbed by negative conceptions it is like dirty water, but admiring faith causes these impure thoughts to subside and allows our primary mind to become lucid and pure, like clean, fresh water.

Wishing faith is a wish to follow any Dharma path, based on a recognition of its good qualities. All virtuous aspirations are wishing faith. An example is the wish to become a Buddha based on a recognition of a Buddha's good qualities. Although bodhichitta is a primary mind, not a mental factor, it has two aspirations – the aspiration to attain enlightenment and the aspiration to benefit others, both of which are wishing faith. Renunciation is also wishing faith.

Believing faith is based on admiring faith, but is much stronger and more definite. Even animals occasionally develop admiring faith, but believing faith involves consciously holding a special view. Faith pervades all virtuous minds just as space pervades all places. Every virtuous mind is mixed with faith.

SENSE OF SHAME

DEFINITION OF SENSE OF SHAME

The definition of sense of shame is a mental factor that functions to avoid inappropriate actions for reasons that concern oneself.

Sense of shame prevents us from committing negative actions by reminding us that it is not suitable for us to engage in such actions because we are a Dharma practitioner, an ordained person, a Teacher, an adult, and so on. For example, if we stop ourself from squashing a mosquito that is about to bite us by thinking 'It is not right for me to kill this insect because I am a Buddhist', this motivation is sense of shame.

FUNCTION OF SENSE OF SHAME

The function of sense of shame is to serve as the foundation of moral discipline, particularly the moral discipline of restraint. If we are unable to generate sense of shame we shall find it extremely difficult to practise moral discipline. Sense of shame guards us against committing negative actions by appealing to our conscience and to the standards of behaviour that we feel to be appropriate.

DIVISIONS OF SENSE OF SHAME

There are three types of sense of shame:

1 Sense of shame that restrains us from inappropriate bodily actions
2 Sense of shame that restrains us from inappropriate verbal actions
3 Sense of shame that restrains us from inappropriate mental actions

There is also a twofold division of sense of shame based on the reasons for restraint:

1 Sense of shame that restrains us from inappropriate actions out of concern simply for ourself

143

2 Sense of shame that restrains us from inappropriate actions out of concern for the specific undesirable results for ourself

Examples of the first type are thinking 'I should not do this because I am a Buddhist', or 'I should not do this because I am a Dharma practitioner', or 'I should not commit this action because I am a nun.' Examples of the second type are thinking 'I should not do this because it will damage my Dharma practice', or 'I should not do this because it will cause me to take rebirth in the lower realms', or 'It is inappropriate for me to commit this action because it transgresses my commitments.'

CONSIDERATION FOR OTHERS

DEFINITION OF CONSIDERATION FOR OTHERS

The definition of consideration for others is a mental factor that functions to avoid inappropriate actions for reasons that concern others.

Examples of consideration are holding back from saying something unpleasant because it will upset another person, or giving up fishing because of the suffering it causes the fish. We need to practise consideration whenever we are with other people by being mindful of how our behaviour might disturb them or harm them. Our desires are endless, and some of them would cause other people much distress if we acted them out. Therefore, before we act on a wish we should consider whether it will disturb or harm others, and if we think that it will we should not do it. If we are concerned for the welfare of others we shall naturally practise consideration.

FUNCTION OF CONSIDERATION FOR OTHERS

The main function of consideration is the same as that of sense of shame – to serve as the foundation of the moral discipline of restraint. Consideration is important for Dharma practitioners and non-practitioners alike. If we are considerate, others will like us and respect us, and our relationships with our family and friends will be harmonious and long-lasting. Without consideration, however, relationships quickly deteriorate. Consideration prevents others from losing faith in us and is the basis for developing a mind of rejoicing.

Consideration for others is the foundation of the spiritual path. One of the commitments of going for refuge is not to cause harm to others, and this is the essence of the practice of consideration. If we do not practise consideration our experience of advanced practices such as tummo meditation and vajra recitation will quickly degenerate; and our aim should be to progress in our spiritual practice, not to regress.

Whether we are a good person or a bad person depends upon whether or not we have sense of shame and consideration. Without these two mental factors our daily behaviour will soon become negative and cause others to turn away from us. Sense of shame and consideration are like beautiful clothes that cause others to be attracted to us. Without them we are like a naked person whom everyone tries to avoid.

DIVISIONS OF CONSIDERATION FOR OTHERS

There are three types of consideration for others:

1 Consideration for others that restrains us from inappropriate bodily actions
2 Consideration for others that restrains us from inappropriate verbal actions
3 Consideration for others that restrains us from inappropriate mental actions

There is also a twofold division of consideration for others based on the reasons for restraint:

1 Consideration for others that restrains us from inappropriate actions out of concern simply for others
2 Consideration for others that restrains us from inappropriate actions out of concern for the specific undesirable results for others

NON-ATTACHMENT

DEFINITION OF NON-ATTACHMENT

The definition of non-attachment is a mental factor that functions as the direct opponent of attachment.

Non-attachment is not simply freedom from attachment but a mental factor that directly opposes attachment. Attachment harms us greatly by preventing us from developing the wish to escape from samsara. As long as we are attached to samsaric places, enjoyments, and bodies we shall not be able to develop the wish to abandon samsara, and so we shall continue to accumulate contaminated karma that throws us into samsaric rebirths. To attain liberation we must first overcome attachment to this life by practising the stages of the path of initial scope, and then overcome attachment to samsara in general by practising the stages of the path of intermediate scope. In this way we develop renunciation, which is a type of non-attachment.

FUNCTION OF NON-ATTACHMENT

Non-attachment is the gateway to liberation. Attachment is like a rope that ties us to samsara. As long as we have strong attachment we have no mental freedom but are controlled by circumstances, like a puppet on a string. As soon as a pleasant object presents itself to our mind we automatically develop attachment, which causes us more problems and binds us even more tightly to samsara. To overcome this attachment and develop a genuine interest in attaining liberation from samsara we need to train in non-attachment.

To practise non-attachment it is not necessary to avoid all objects of attachment. In fact, this is impossible in our present circumstances because wherever we go we find objects of attachment. If we try to avoid places or people to whom we are attached by going elsewhere, we shall soon find ourself developing attachment to new places and new friends; and if we try to abstain from all the things we presently enjoy, such as food, drink, and clothing, we shall find it difficult to survive. Rather than trying to avoid objects of attachment, the way to practise non-attachment is to recognize the faults of the mind of attachment and then to try to abandon that mind. The faults of attachment are explained below in the section on attachment.

DIVISIONS OF NON-ATTACHMENT

There are three types of non-attachment:

1 Non-attachment to samsaric places
2 Non-attachment to samsaric enjoyments
3 Non-attachment to samsaric bodies

There is another threefold division:

1 Non-attachment to this life
2 Non-attachment to samsara
3 Non-attachment to solitary peace

Ordinary beings have attachment to this life and attachment to samsara, but only those who have attained tranquil abiding can develop attachment to solitary peace. Some Hinayana Foe Destroyers, for example, remain in the peace of concentration for thousands of years, during which time they do nothing to help other sentient beings. Although their attachment to peace is not an actual delusion, it is called 'attachment' to emphasize the fact that it is a major obstacle to the Bodhisattva's way of life. Bodhisattvas consider attachment to solitary peace to be more harmful than ordinary attachment. If a Bodhisattva generates attachment towards his or her family this will not necessarily cause his compassion or his wish to benefit others to diminish, but if he develops attachment to solitary peace his compassion and bodhichitta will definitely degenerate. Moreover, if he remains too long in a state of solitary peace he will transgress his commitment to benefit others. Bodhisattvas on the first and second grounds experience ordinary attachment, but this does not disturb their spiritual practice, and they are able to use it as a means of benefiting others. Just as farmers use unpleasant things such as manure to create favourable conditions for growing crops, so Bodhisattvas use their attachment as a means of helping others. The main objects to be abandoned by Bodhisattvas are attachment to solitary peace and concern for their own welfare.

We overcome these three types of attachment by training in the stages of the path of the three scopes. By practising the stages of the path of initial scope we overcome attachment to this life, by practising the stages of the path of intermediate scope we overcome attachment to samsara in general, and by practising the stages of the path of great scope we overcome attachment to solitary peace.

NON-HATRED

DEFINITION OF NON-HATRED

The definition of non-hatred is a mental factor that functions as the direct opponent of hatred.

In *Guide to the Bodhisattva's Way of Life* Shantideva says:

> There is no evil greater than anger,
> And no virtue greater than patience.

Hatred, or anger, is the most destructive of all non-virtuous minds. It has the power to destroy our Dharma experiences and the merit we have accumulated in the past. Unless we make an effort to practise non-hatred we shall find it difficult to control our anger; and if our mind is filled with anger we shall not experience peace or happiness. When we are angry we cannot enjoy life, even if we live in a luxurious house and eat the most expensive food. It is difficult to fall asleep with an angry mind, and when we do sleep we have unpleasant, disturbing dreams. When anger controls our mind we develop the intention to harm others, and we may even wish to kill ourself. We usually cherish ourself dearly, but hatred can so disturb our mind that we consider committing suicide. Shantideva said that for as long as we harbour painful thoughts of anger our mind will not experience peace.

Unless we have some experience of Dharma we shall think that our enemies are other people who cause us harm, but according to Dharma our real enemies are the delusions in our mind, such as anger and attachment. If we regard other people as our enemies we shall try to harm them, and this will only make the situation worse. Our relationships will deteriorate, and we shall gradually accumulate more and more enemies. On the other hand, if we practise love, regarding all living beings as our kind mothers, our relationships will improve and our problems will gradually disappear. If we are going to retaliate we should do so against our delusions, for they are the source of all the harm we experience. If we succeed in destroying these inner enemies we shall bring an end to all our suffering and problems, but if we show them patience and understanding they will continue to betray and harm us.

The mental factor non-hatred opposes our internal enemy of hatred. If we are about to develop hatred towards someone but counter it by thinking 'It is inappropriate for me to hate this person because hatred is like poison', we are practising non-hatred. It is most important to practise non-hatred as soon as we detect signs of anger or hatred arising in our mind. Anger is like fire. If we detect a fire as soon as it starts it will be easy to extinguish, but if we wait until it has taken hold it will be very difficult to control. In the same way, if we catch anger as soon as it arises in our mind we can easily counter it with non-hatred, but if we leave it to develop fully we shall find it very difficult to stop. Therefore, as soon as we become aware that anger is about to manifest we should prevent it by reflecting on its many disadvantages. These are explained extensively in the chapter on patience in Shanti-deva's *Guide to the Bodhisattva's Way of Life* and in the commentary *Meaningful to Behold*.

FUNCTION OF NON-HATRED

Non-hatred has many functions. It overcomes irritation and frustration and enables us to respond to adverse conditions with a calm and positive mind. It frees us from the inner pain of hatred, and makes our mind smooth and comfortable at all times. It is the basis for generating affectionate love and all the other Mahayana realizations. When our mind is filled with non-hatred we have no enemies because everyone appears to us as kind and agreeable. As a result, we do not engage in negative actions such as fighting or killing, and so we do not have to suffer the consequences of such actions. Affectionate love, cherishing love, wishing love, compassion, and patience are all the nature of non-hatred.

DIVISIONS OF NON-HATRED

There are three types of non-hatred:

1 Non-hatred towards those who harm us
2 Non-hatred towards inanimate objects that cause us suffering
3 Non-hatred towards resultant suffering

The first type is the same as the patience of not-retaliating. If someone attacks us, insults us, or causes us harm in some other way, and we manage to stop ourself getting angry with them, it is the first type of non-hatred that prevents the anger from arising.

There are many inanimate objects with which we get angry. For example, we may get angry with the weather if it is too hot or too cold, with our car if it will not start, or with a piece of furniture if it falls on our foot. Some people are angered by the existence of nuclear weapons or pollution, while others become upset if their food is not to their liking. Whenever we encounter inanimate objects that cause us suffering we should remember the futility of getting angry with such things and prevent anger by practising the second type of non-hatred.

The third type of non-hatred, non-hatred towards resultant suffering, is the patience of voluntarily enduring suffering. When we are unhappy or sick we are much more prone to anger than when we are happy and healthy. People who are usually patient when they are well often develop a bad temper when they are sick. This indicates that they lack the patience of voluntarily enduring suffering. All our suffering, both physical and mental, is the result of our own negative karma. Therefore, when we are about to become angry with our suffering we should think:

This pain is the result of my own non-virtuous actions. Since I committed these negative actions I must experience their resultant suffering. Therefore, I must accept this suffering patiently.

If we are able to think like this we shall not get angry or upset but shall be able to endure our suffering with a peaceful mind. If our pain becomes unbearable we should try to ease it with medicines or, if our mind is strong enough, use our pain to enhance our experience of the two bodhichittas by meditating on compassion and emptiness. With a direct realization of emptiness we shall not experience pain even if our limbs are cut off, because when we have seen emptiness directly we experience only peace. Even a relatively superficial experience of emptiness can ease our pain and restore our body and mind to health. We should use whatever methods we can to cure our sickness but even if these fail there is no point in becoming angry with our pain, for this will just add mental suffering to our physical suffering.

NON-IGNORANCE

DEFINITION OF NON-IGNORANCE

The definition of non-ignorance is a mental factor that functions as the direct opponent of ignorance.

Non-ignorance is a special type of wisdom that acts as the antidote to ignorance. Examples are wisdom realizing selflessness of persons and wisdom realizing selflessness of phenomena.

FUNCTION OF NON-IGNORANCE

The function of non-ignorance is to enable us to understand emptiness, the ultimate nature of phenomena. As our understanding of emptiness grows, our ignorance gradually becomes weaker, and is eventually eradicated altogether. The temporary benefit of non-ignorance is that it helps us to overcome daily problems that are caused by attachment, anger, and other delusions; its long-term benefit is that it leads us to liberation and enlightenment. Our friends and family cannot solve our internal problems for us, and even our Spiritual Guides cannot remove them directly. The only way to eliminate our mental problems is to rely upon our own wisdom. Those who possess wisdom realizing emptiness can solve all their internal problems by meditating on emptiness. It is because we lack this wisdom that we need to ask others for advice when we are confronted with problems. If we had wisdom we would be able to solve all our own problems.

The benefits of wisdom realizing emptiness are inconceivable. If we had a million pounds in our pocket it would cause us much anxiety and possibly even endanger our life, but if instead of money we possessed wisdom realizing emptiness we would have no worries or problems. We would be able to use our wisdom all the time, and it would be a constant source of guidance and comfort to us. Therefore, wisdom realizing emptiness is the supreme friend and the supreme wealth.

DIVISIONS OF NON-IGNORANCE

There are four types of non-ignorance:

1 Non-ignorance arisen from listening
2 Non-ignorance arisen from contemplation
3 Non-ignorance arisen from meditation
4 Non-ignorance arisen from imprints

The first three types of non-ignorance can be understood from the three wisdoms – wisdom arisen from listening, wisdom arisen from contemplation, and wisdom arisen from meditation – explained previously in the section on wisdom. However, whereas the three wisdoms as presented in the previous explanation are not necessarily wisdom realizing emptiness, here, because non-ignorance is the direct opponent of ignorance, they are. The fourth type of non-ignorance is a wisdom realizing emptiness that arises naturally from imprints from past lives without the need to study emptiness in this life. It is also known as the 'wisdom attained just through the power of birth'. Some people who have meditated deeply and for a long time on emptiness in a previous life are able to carry this understanding into this present life, and as a result they are able to understand emptiness very easily without having to study or contemplate for a long time. When we eventually attain the concentration of the Dharma continuum on the path of accumulation we shall not forget any Dharma that we study but shall carry all our knowledge with us into the next life.

In *Training the Mind in Seven Points* Geshe Chekhawa says:

> The three objects, three poisons, and three virtuous
> roots
> Are the brief instruction for the subsequent
> attainment.

The three objects are attractive objects, unattractive objects, and neutral objects; the three poisons are attachment, hatred, and ignorance; and the three virtuous roots are non-attachment, non-hatred, and non-ignorance. When ordinary beings encounter the three objects they automatically develop the three poisons. The essential aim of Dharma practice is to reverse this so that we automatically develop the three virtuous roots instead. When someone who has thoroughly trained their mind in Dharma meets an attractive object they develop not attachment but non-attachment; when they meet an unattractive object they develop not hatred but non-hatred; and when they meet a neutral object they develop not ignorance but non-ignorance. Since all objects are included within the three objects, those who have mastered the three virtuous roots are able to transform all their experiences into the path to enlightenment. This is why the three virtuous roots are called the 'essence of Buddhadharma'.

EFFORT

DEFINITION OF EFFORT

The definition of effort is a mental factor that makes its primary mind delight in virtue.

Effort functions to make our mind happy to engage in virtue – delighting in actions such as giving, helping others, making prostrations, making offerings, reciting prayers, reading Dharma books, and listening to Dharma teachings. Effort is necessarily virtuous. Minds that strive for ordinary goals, such as business achievements, and minds that delight in non-virtue, are not effort.

The opposite of effort is laziness. There are three types of laziness: laziness arising from attachment to worldly pleasures, laziness arising from attachment to distracting activities, and laziness arising from discouragement. In general, fondness for sleep is a type of laziness, but if we are able to practise the yoga of sleeping and transform sleep into a virtuous action, then the mind that enjoys sleep is effort. Similarly, if we transform other neutral actions such as eating, cooking, and playing into virtuous actions by performing them with a good motivation, our enjoyment of them is also the mental factor effort.

FUNCTION OF EFFORT

The function of effort is to instigate virtue, protect virtue from degenerating, facilitate the increase of virtuous qualities, and bring virtuous practices to completion. In *Ornament for Mahayana Sutras* Maitreya lists many benefits of effort:

Among virtuous collections, effort is supreme.
With effort we can accomplish all virtuous qualities,
With effort we can accomplish a peaceful body and
    mind,
With effort we can accomplish mundane and
    supramundane attainments,
With effort we can obtain the pleasures of samsara,

With effort we can take rebirth in a Pure Land,
With effort we can be freed from delusions such as
    the view of the transitory collection, and attain
    liberation,
With effort we can attain great enlightenment.

Effort is the supreme virtue because all virtuous qualities are
attained through the power of effort. Effort makes both body
and mind peaceful, comfortable, and healthy by inducing
physical and mental suppleness. When we have attained
physical suppleness we do not need physical exercise to keep
our body flexible and healthy. By relying upon effort we can
attain both mundane and supramundane attainments, such
as the Highest Yoga Tantra realizations of Deities like Heruka
and Vajrayogini. Even the happiness of humans or gods
depends solely upon our own effort because if we do not
make an effort to practise virtuous actions we shall not be
able to take such rebirths in the future. Similarly, as Dharma
practitioners we have the opportunity to attain rebirth in a
Pure Land, but whether we succeed in doing so depends
upon our own effort. If we joyfully and continually engage
in the methods for attaining rebirth in a Pure Land our
wishes will definitely be fulfilled.

We may be aware of the faults of delusions such as the
view of the transitory collection, and we may have heard
teachings on how to eliminate them and attain liberation, but
we shall succeed in this only if we apply strenuous effort. If
we do not apply ourself to our Dharma practice no one can
grant us liberation from suffering – not our spiritual friends,
our Spiritual Guide, nor even all the Buddhas. We all have
the seed of Buddhahood within our mental continuum, and
we have the opportunity to practise the methods for ripening
this seed, but our attainment of Buddhahood depends upon
our own efforts. An intellectual understanding of Dharma is
not sufficient to carry us to Buddhahood – we must also
overcome our laziness and put our knowledge into practice.
All those who have already become Buddhas have attained
enlightenment through their own effort, and all those who

will become Buddhas in the future will do so through their effort. In the Sutras, Buddha says:

If you have only effort you have all Dharmas,
But if you have only laziness you do not know any
  Dharmas.

A person who has no great knowledge of Dharma but who nevertheless applies effort consistently will gradually attain all virtuous qualities; but a person who knows a great deal and has only one fault – laziness – will not be able to increase his or her good qualities and gain experience of Dharma. Many other benefits of effort are mentioned in Shantideva's *Guide to the Bodhisattva's Way of Life* and Chandrakirti's *Guide to the Middle Way*.

DIVISIONS OF EFFORT

In *Guide to the Bodhisattva's Way of Life* Shantideva presents four types of effort:

1 Armour-like effort
2 Effort of non-discouragement
3 Effort of application
4 Effort of non-satisfaction

All four types of effort are very important for Dharma practitioners. The first two overcome conditions unfavourable to the practice of Dharma, the third actually engages in Dharma practice, and the fourth enables us to complete our practice.

Armour-like effort is a courageous mind that helps us to persevere in our Dharma practice no matter what hardships are involved. We can generate this effort by thinking:

I will continue to practise Dharma even if it takes me many aeons to attain great enlightenment. I will never give up my Dharma practice, no matter what difficulties I might encounter.

If we have armour-like effort we shall have a long-term perspective that prevents us from being discouraged by unfavourable external conditions, and we shall joyfully persevere with our practice even if it takes a long time to attain Dharma realizations. In the past when soldiers went to war they wore armour to protect their bodies; similarly when Dharma practitioners wage war against their delusions they need to wear armour-like effort to protect their minds against difficult external conditions.

We need armour-like effort at the outset because without it we may soon become discouraged by the length of time it takes to attain realizations, and as a result we may abandon our Dharma practice. Sometimes, when we find it difficult to fulfil our spiritual expectations, encounter others who are trying to dissuade us from practising, or have difficulty in finding the resources to support our practice, we may consider giving up Dharma. If this happens it indicates that we lack armour-like effort. At such times we need to recall our initial enthusiasm, and strengthen our resolve by reminding ourself of the benefits of our practice.

Whereas armour-like effort protects our practice against external obstacles, the effort of non-discouragement protects us against the internal obstacle of discouragement. We may wonder 'How is it possible for someone like me who has so many delusions and so little time to practise Dharma to realize emptiness, develop bodhichitta, and attain liberation and enlightenment?' By indulging in such thoughts we may conclude that we are incapable of attaining realizations. To counteract this kind of discouragement we need to generate the effort of non-discouragement by contemplating correct reasons. For example, we can contemplate:

Sometimes my delusions are strong and sometimes they are weak. This indicates that they are impermanent. If they can be reduced temporarily, they can be eradicated altogether; so why can I not attain liberation? Buddha said that everyone has Buddha nature. If I rely sincerely upon my Spiritual Guide and practise sincerely what he or she teaches me there is no reason why I cannot attain enlightenment. With my mind empowered by my Guru's blessings I can accomplish anything.

The effort of application is a mind that engages in the practice of Dharma with delight. This effort inspires us to listen to, contemplate, and meditate on Dharma teachings. It is the source of all our understanding and experience of Dharma. This effort can be either forceful or steady. Some-times it is appropriate to use forceful effort to reach a specific goal or to overcome a particular obstacle, but it is difficult to sustain this kind of effort and it may soon lead to tiredness or discouragement. For the most part we should practise with steady effort, like a broad river flowing constantly. We should adjust our expectations and not hope for quick results, but practise steadily and constantly over a long period.

The effort of non-satisfaction encourages us continually to deepen our understanding and experience of Dharma by not being satisfied with a merely superficial experience or under-standing. After having studied Dharma for two or three years we may feel contented with our understanding and feel that we have no need to listen to more teachings or to continue to meditate. Such a complacent attitude prevents us from developing deep experience and understanding. We cannot expect great results after only a few years' practice. Until we have reached the final realizations of great enlightenment we need continuously to listen to teachings and meditate on their meaning.

Bodhisattvas on the first ground are not satisfied with their realizations, even though compared to ordinary beings they have attained exalted states of mind. Spurred on by the effort of non-satisfaction they ascend to the second ground, where again the same effort prevents them from becoming complacent and urges them to strive for higher goals. In this way they progress through all ten grounds to the final goal of great enlightenment.

Great enlightenment is called the 'Path of No More Learn-ing' because it is the only state of complete fulfilment. Before we reach this stage we still have things to learn and so our Dharma practice is not yet complete. We should not be dis-couraged by the fact that we shall have to practise Dharma for a long time. If we abandon the path to liberation or enlightenment we shall never find a better path. All other paths will lead us into samsara; and no matter how much effort we put into following samsaric paths we shall never experience true happiness. In our previous lives we put great effort into accumulating material wealth, but now everything we owned has vanished; our effort was in vain. In the past we have enjoyed every conceivable samsaric pleasure, but now we have nothing to show for it. All that remain are the imprints of the negative actions we committed in fulfilling our desires. Now that we have the opportunity to follow a perfect path that definitely leads to ultimate happiness it would be a great shame if we were to abandon it for a worldly path.

In summary, at the outset of our practice we should generate armour-like effort and arm ourself with a strong determination to complete our practice, no matter how long it may take or how many external obstacles we may have to overcome. Armed with this effort we should then generate the effort of application and apply ourself steadily and confidently to our practice. To prevent ourself from becoming discouraged by the extent and duration of our practice we should develop the effort of non-discouragement; and to prevent complacency and ensure that we bring our practice to completion we should rely upon the effort of non-satisfaction.

In *Compendium of Abhidharma* Asanga presents a fivefold division of effort:

1 Armour-like effort
2 Effort of non-discouragement
3 Effort of application
4 Effort of non-satisfaction
5 Effort of irreversibility

The first four are the same as the four just explained. The fifth, the effort of irreversibility, is a type of effort that prevents harmful conditions, such as wrong advice or bad friends, from diverting us from our virtuous activities. It is called 'irreversibility' because it ensures that we continue until our goal is reached with no lessening or diversion of our energy.

If we have armour-like effort and the effort of non-discouragement we shall automatically have the effort of irreversibility.

In the Lamrim teachings, three types of effort are explained:

1 Armour-like effort
2 Effort of gathering virtuous Dharmas
3 Effort of benefiting others

In this classification armour-like effort is the same as that
previously explained, and the other two are included within
the effort of application. Because there are two types of virtuous action – gathering virtuous Dharmas and benefiting
others – there are two types of effort of application that
correspond to these.

Effort does not arise naturally but is generated by using special
methods. In *Guide to the Bodhisattva's Way of Life* Shantideva
explains four powers that are the methods for sustaining and
increasing effort: the power of aspiration, the power of steadfastness, the power of joy, and the power of rejection.

The power of aspiration is a strong wish to practise Dharma.
This is cultivated by contemplating both the benefits of training in Dharma and the disadvantages of not training in
Dharma. All our problems are the result of taking rebirth in
samsara, and the reason we continue to take uncontrolled
rebirth is that we do not have sufficient experience of Dharma.
Since experience of Dharma depends upon training in Dharma
we can say that all our problems are the result of not training
in Dharma.

If we do not train in Dharma we shall never find real inner
peace, and we shall remain ignorant of profound and important truths such as the hidden objects that are explained in
Dharma. We shall not be able even to identify the self-grasping mind that imprisons us in samsara, let alone abandon it.
Even though many of the fifty-one mental factors manifest
in our mind, if we do not train in Dharma we shall not be able
to recognize them, and so we shall not be able to distinguish
those that should be cultivated from those that should be
rejected.

One of the main benefits of training in Dharma is that day by day our wisdom grows sharper and our ignorance becomes weaker. The more wisdom we have, the more peaceful our mind will be. Through training in Dharma we gradually attain all the spiritual realizations that directly protect us from suffering. All our problems are caused by desirous attachment, anger, jealousy, and other negative minds. By gaining experience of virtuous minds such as love, compassion, patience, and wisdom we shall overcome these negative minds. These virtuous minds are our real refuge. Thus, by training in Dharma we build a refuge within our own mind. Eventually we shall become a refuge for all beings, a Buddha Jewel. By contemplating these benefits of training in Dharma we develop the aspiration to practise Dharma and this makes our effort more powerful. For this reason the aspiration to practise Dharma is called a 'power'.

Having developed the power of aspiration we should practise the power of steadfastness, which means that we should make our effort in Dharma practice stable and unchangeable by developing a strong determination. In the chapter on effort in *Guide to the Bodhisattva's Way of Life* Shantideva advises us that before we commit ourself to engaging in a practice we should investigate it carefully to see whether it is suitable and whether we can sustain it; but once we have committed ourself to it we should never turn back but continue until we attain the final result. Switching from one practice to another unrelated practice not only prevents us from fulfilling our wishes in this life, but also makes it difficult for us to accomplish our goals in future lives. Moreover, it is often the cause of breaking our commitments and severing precious relationships, such as those that exist between Guru and disciple, and between spiritual friends.

We must be careful not to misunderstand the effort of non-satisfaction. Practising this effort does not mean that we should become dissatisfied with our tradition or with our main practice, and try to follow many different traditions or mix together many different practices. Every Teacher and every tradition has a slightly different approach and employs different methods. The practices taught by one Teacher will differ from those taught by another, and if we try to combine them we shall become confused, develop doubts, and lose direction. If we try to create a synthesis of different traditions we shall destroy the special power of each and be left only with a mishmash of our own making that will be a source of confusion and doubt. Having chosen our tradition and our daily practices we should rely upon them single-pointedly, never allowing dissatisfaction to arise. At the same time as cherishing our own tradition we should respect all other traditions and the right of each individual to follow the tradition of their choosing. This approach leads to harmony and tolerance. It is mixing different religious traditions that causes sectarianism. This is why it is said that studying non-religious subjects is less of an obstacle to our spiritual progress than studying religions of different traditions.

Once we have decided which tradition to follow and which practices to do, we should engage in them wholeheartedly with a joyful mind. This is the power of joy. Whether we are listening to Dharma teachings, reading Dharma books, reciting prayers, contemplating, or meditating, we should do so with a light and happy mind, like a child at play. If we enjoy a practice we shall naturally have enthusiasm for it.

We may think that renunciation, for example, is a joyless state of mind because it is so keenly aware of the suffering nature of samsara, but in fact renunciation is a light and peaceful mind that is bound for freedom. Renunciation is induced by wisdom, and wisdom never gives rise to unhappiness. Joy is called a 'power' because it sustains our effort in practising Dharma. If Dharma practice brings us no pleasure we shall soon become exhausted.

The fourth power, the power of rejection, means to reject, or eliminate, tiredness. Sometimes as a result of studying, meditating, or other virtuous activities, we become physically or mentally tired. If our body becomes tired, our mind can easily become unbalanced. If instead of resting we push ourself beyond our capacity, this can cause problems such as physical illness or a disinclination to practise. It is better to relax for a while and resume our practice when our body and mind are fresh and comfortable. This is particularly important when we are doing a lot of formal meditation. Knowing when to exert ourself and when to rest is essential for successful practice.

Besides the ability to know when to stop and relax, the power of rejection also includes the ability to postpone taking on more advanced practices until we have built a suitable foundation for them, and the ability to leave behind a particular stage of development and progress to higher stages.

These four powers are explained in detail in *Meaningful to Behold* and *Joyful Path of Good Fortune*.

MENTAL SUPPLENESS

DEFINITION OF MENTAL SUPPLENESS

The definition of mental suppleness is a flexibility of mind induced by virtuous concentration.

In general, concentration induces two types of suppleness – physical suppleness and mental suppleness – but only the latter is the mental factor suppleness. Physical suppleness is a flexible and light tactile object within our body that develops when meditation causes a pure wind to pervade the body. It purifies defiled winds and makes our body flexible and light, and this in turn induces mental suppleness.

FUNCTION OF MENTAL SUPPLENESS

Physical suppleness functions to overcome stiffness and inflexibility of the body, and makes our body feel light, comfortable, and easy to use in virtuous actions. Mental suppleness removes the inflexibility, slowness, and heaviness of the mind and makes it light and easy to use in virtuous actions. The mental rigidity that is dispelled by suppleness is the basis of many delusions, and is a principal cause of resistance to and dislike of virtuous activities. By removing rigidity, suppleness overcomes laziness and other obstacles. However, only strong suppleness can do this effectively; weak, short-lived suppleness does not have the strength to overcome many obstacles.

Both physical and mental suppleness develop initially through meditation, and then function to refine and improve our concentration. Mental suppleness enables us to direct our mind wherever we wish and thus helps both analytical meditation and placement meditation. Through attaining full, authentic physical and mental suppleness we shall continuously experience the physical and mental bliss of suppleness, and as a result we shall feel little need to seek external sources of pleasure.

There are two types of mental suppleness:

1 Subtle mental suppleness
2 Gross mental suppleness

Mental suppleness exists whenever we experience pure, virtuous concentration. However, on the first and second mental abidings the mental suppleness is so subtle that it goes unnoticed. Therefore this suppleness is called 'subtle mental suppleness'. Gross mental suppleness first develops on the third mental abiding. From then on it gradually becomes stronger and stronger until we attain tranquil abiding, at which point our suppleness is fully developed. At this stage suppleness pervades our body and mind, and we experience the bliss of suppleness without interruption. When we have attained this unchangeable suppleness we no longer experience the physical and mental discomfort that make virtuous actions difficult, and so we become completely free from laziness. With suppleness, spiritual practice is very easy because when it arises our mind naturally becomes tranquil and positive.

Initially, mental suppleness is developed through the force of concentration, but there is also a type of suppleness that is induced by wisdom. This is accomplished as a result of analytical meditation combined with tranquil abiding. The development of this type of suppleness marks the attainment of superior seeing. With superior seeing, our wisdom and concentration become mutually beneficial, and we attain the union of tranquil abiding and superior seeing.

CONSCIENTIOUSNESS

DEFINITION OF CONSCIENTIOUSNESS

The definition of conscientiousness is a mental factor that, in dependence upon effort, cherishes what is virtuous and guards the mind from delusion and non-virtue.

Conscientiousness prevents the mind from being influenced by a delusion. There are two ways to rely upon conscientiousness. The first is to keep our mind free from a delusion by preventing our mind from meeting the objects of that delusion. We can, for example, prevent ourself from getting angry with someone with whom we have had a disagreement by avoiding them and not thinking about them. The second way is to prevent our mind from developing inappropriate attention when it meets with objects of delusion. Inappropriate attention causes delusions to arise by exaggerating the good or bad qualities of an object. If we prevent inappropriate attention it is impossible for delusions to arise, even if we are directly confronted with an object of delusion. Thus, for example, if we unexpectedly meet someone with whom we normally get angry we can avoid inappropriate attention, and so prevent anger, by focusing on his or her good qualities or by remembering the faults of anger.

In *Guide to the Bodhisattva's Way of Life* Shantideva says that there is no practice more important than keeping our mind free from negativity. Normally we take great care to protect our body from injury, but it is much more important to protect our mind. For example, if we are crossing a busy street we take great care to avoid being run over, but if we were to be run over the worst that could happen would be that we would lose this one life. By contrast, if we do not take care to protect our mind from negativity when we are surrounded by so many objects of delusion there is great danger of our mind being overrun by delusions, which will inflict harm on us for many future lives. Therefore, the practice of conscientiousness is of paramount importance.

Conscientiousness should be practised in conjunction with mindfulness and alertness. With mindfulness we tie our mind to a virtuous object. A virtuous object is any object that has a positive effect on our mind, such as the twenty-one objects of meditation presented in *The Meditation Handbook*. We should try to keep our mind on virtuous objects all the time. Alertness is a type of wisdom that understands the faults of delusions and keeps watch over our mind to check whether or not we are beginning to develop inappropriate attention. If through alertness we discover that a delusion is about to arise we should immediately prevent it by recalling the faults of delusions. This is the practice of conscientiousness. Shantideva said that when an elephant runs amok it can cause a great deal of harm, but this is nothing compared to the harm caused by the crazy elephant of an unconscientious mind, which can drag us into the deepest hell. By binding our mind to the pillar of virtuous objects with the rope of mindfulness we protect ourself from delusions, the source of all danger, and find it easy to make progress in our spiritual practice.

FUNCTION OF CONSCIENTIOUSNESS

The main function of conscientiousness is to enable us to keep pure moral discipline and to improve our concentration. Conscientiousness is so important that in *Guide to the Bodhisattva's Way of Life* Shantideva devotes an entire chapter to it.

Through practising conscientiousness we can reduce our delusions and thereby stop committing negative actions of body, speech, and mind. As a result we shall naturally possess pure moral discipline. If our delusions are diminished and our life becomes more disciplined we shall develop far fewer distractions, and as a result we shall find it easy to make progress in meditation.

If our meditation is not proceeding well we do not need to seek special advice on how to improve it – we need only to practise conscientiousness. As mentioned before, in the *Vinaya Sutras* Buddha says that through moral discipline we shall attain concentration and through concentration we shall attain wisdom. Since conscientiousness is the root of moral discipline it follows that concentration and wisdom also depend upon conscientiousness. By practising conscientiousness we keep our mind pure and harnessed to virtuous objects, and so our energy is not dissipated by external or internal distractions. As a result our mind becomes settled and gathered within, making it easy for us to develop virtuous concentration. Virtuous concentration makes our mind lucid and powerful, which in turn enables us to improve our wisdom.

If we plan to do long meditation retreats in the future, we need to understand conscientiousness fully and begin to train in it now. To prepare our mind for advanced levels of meditation we need to cultivate favourable internal conditions and gradually eliminate conditions that interfere with meditation. The main favourable condition is familiarity with virtuous objects, and the main obstacle is distraction. Even if we lead a busy life we can keep our mind on virtuous objects if we understand that what makes an object virtuous or non-virtuous is our attitude towards it. By applying the instructions mentioned above on generating the three virtuous roots we can transform every object we meet into a virtuous object for us.

DIVISIONS OF CONSCIENTIOUSNESS

There are two types of conscientiousness:

1 Conscientiousness that is a virtuous root of mundane paths
2 Conscientiousness that is a virtuous root of supramundane paths

Conscientiousness is necessarily virtuous and a cause of happiness. The first type of conscientiousness causes samsaric happiness and the second causes the happiness of liberation and enlightenment. The difference between them lies in their motivation. The first type is a conscientiousness motivated by the wish to obtain the happiness of gods or humans in future lives, and the second is a conscientiousness motivated by the wish to attain liberation or enlightenment.

EQUANIMITY

DEFINITION OF EQUANIMITY

The definition of equanimity is a mental factor that functions to keep the primary mind free from mental sinking and mental excitement.

In general there are three types of equanimity: equanimity of feeling, immeasurable equanimity, and compositional equanimity. Equanimity of feeling is any neutral feeling; immeasurable equanimity is the wish for all beings equally to be free from attachment and hatred, and is a form of compassion; and compositional equanimity is the mental factor explained here.

Compositional equanimity allows our mind to abide in a balanced state, free from mental sinking and mental excitement. Since mental sinking and mental excitement are the principal obstacles to concentration, equanimity is essential if we wish to perfect our concentration. When we are meditating we should examine our mind from time to time to see if our concentration is pure. Pure concentration has three characteristics: it remains on a virtuous object single-pointedly without moving towards any other object; it holds the object firmly; and it is clear, lucid, and alert. At the beginning we can sustain such pure concentration only for a moment or two, but by training we shall gradually be able to increase the duration of pure concentration until eventually we attain tranquil abiding. Until we reach the eighth mental abiding there is a danger of our developing mental sinking and mental excitement, and to remain free from these interferences we need to put effort into maintaining equanimity; but after the eighth mental abiding mental sinking and mental excitement can no longer occur and equanimity arises spontaneously.

FUNCTION OF EQUANIMITY

The function of equanimity is to keep the mind in a balanced state – tranquil, clear, and undisturbed by mental sinking or mental excitement. To understand the function of equanimity fully we need a clear understanding of mental sinking and mental excitement. These are explained in detail in *Joyful Path of Good Fortune* and *Meaningful to Behold*.

DIVISIONS OF EQUANIMITY

There are three types of equanimity:

1 Equanimity that requires gross effort
2 Equanimity that requires subtle effort
3 Equanimity that requires no effort

The fourth through to the sixth mental abidings have equanimity that depends upon gross effort. On the seventh and eighth mental abidings gross effort is no longer needed to eliminate mental sinking and mental excitement, but we still require subtle effort to maintain equanimity. On the ninth mental abiding no effort at all is required to maintain perfect concentration because at this stage equanimity is spontaneous. Just as we need no effort to fall asleep, so at this stage the practitioner needs only to focus on the meditation object and concentration develops effortlessly.

NON-HARMFULNESS

DEFINITION OF NON-HARMFULNESS

The definition of non-harmfulness is a mental factor that wishes sentient beings not to suffer.

According to *Compendium of Abhidharma* non-harmfulness is not simply not harming others, but compassion. We must be careful to distinguish compassion from desirous attachment. Compassion is necessarily a virtuous mind whereas attachment is never virtuous. Sometimes our wish to help others arises principally from attachment. For example, a rider may wish his sick horse to get well so that he will not have to miss a riding event. At other times our concern for others is a mixture of attachment and compassion. This is often the case when we develop the wish for our friends or relatives to be free from suffering. Pure compassion, however, is completely free from attachment and is exclusively concerned with the welfare of others.

It is said that because all living beings have some compassion all living beings have Buddha seed. By gradually improving and extending our compassion we shall eventually develop great compassion – the wish to protect all living beings from suffering. If we continue to improve our great compassion it will eventually transform into the omniscient wisdom of a Buddha, which has the power actually to protect all living beings. There is no better method for becoming a Buddha than to improve our compassion.

As human beings we have a perfect opportunity to develop and improve our compassion. Had we been born as gods of the form or formless realms we would not experience gross sufferings associated with a human body, and so we would find it difficult to develop concern for others who were experiencing these sufferings. Compassion is born of renunciation. If we can understand our own samsara and develop renunciation for that, we can understand the samsara of others and develop compassion for them. As humans we experience a great deal of suffering, and so it is relatively easy for us to see the faults of samsara and to develop the wish to be free from it. Then by looking around us we can see the countless sufferings experienced by other sentient beings and develop compassion for them.

FUNCTION OF NON-HARMFULNESS

The main function of non-harmfulness, or compassion, is to prevent us from harming sentient beings. A person whose

mind is filled with compassion can never wish to hurt anyone. It is only because we lack compassion that we sometimes
develop the intention to hurt others. Compassion and harmful intentions are like water and fire – completely incompatible. Refraining from harming others is one of the most
important practices for a Buddhist. If we always practise
non-harmfulness we shall always be practising Dharma, even
if we cannot do formal meditation.

Another function of compassion is to cause the attainment
of enlightenment. Compassion is the seed of Buddhahood,
and by developing and enhancing it we cause this seed to
ripen and draw us closer to full enlightenment.

DIVISIONS OF NON-HARMFULNESS

There are two types of non-harmfulness, or compassion:

1 Compassion wishing sentient beings to be free
   from suffering
2 Compassion wishing sentient beings to be free
   from the causes of suffering

The second type of compassion is a wish for sentient beings
to be separated from contaminated karma and delusions,
which are the actual causes of suffering. Only those who have
trained in Dharma can develop this type of compassion. When
an intelligent Dharma practitioner sees the suffering of sentient beings he or she thinks 'How wonderful it would be if
all sentient beings were free from delusions such as self-
grasping, and from karma committed under the influence of
delusions.'

There is another twofold division of compassion:

1 Mere compassion
2 Superior compassion

Wishing sentient beings to be free from suffering is mere
compassion. Thinking 'I myself will act to free them from
suffering' is superior compassion. Thus, the superior intention explained in the instructions on the sevenfold cause and
effect is a type of superior compassion.

171

In *Guide to the Middle Way* Chandrakirti presents a three-fold division of compassion: compassion observing sentient beings, compassion observing phenomena, and compassion observing the unobservable. These are explained in *Ocean of Nectar*.

Virtue, Non-virtue, and Delusion

VIRTUE

DEFINITION OF VIRTUE

The definition of virtue is a phenomenon that functions as a main cause of happiness.

DIVISIONS OF VIRTUE

There are five types of virtue:

1 Natural virtue
2 Virtue by association
3 Virtue by motivation
4 Virtue by subsequent relation
5 Ultimate virtue

The eleven virtuous mental factors are examples of natural virtue. A primary mind that has any one of the virtuous mental factors in its retinue is a virtue by association, as are all the other mental factors associated with that primary mind. They are virtuous because they are of the same substance as a virtuous mental factor. All virtuous actions are virtues by motivation because they are performed with a virtuous motivation. The imprints left on the mental continuum by virtuous minds and virtuous actions are virtues by subsequent relation. Since all sentient beings have performed virtuous actions at some time in the past, all sentient beings have virtuous imprints. Lower schools such as the Vaibashikas, however, assert that there are some sentient beings who have no virtuous imprints.

Gunaprabha

These four types of virtue can be understood from the following example. If we make prostrations out of faith, the mental factor faith is a natural virtue; the primary mind associated with it, as well as all its other attendant mental factors such as feeling and discrimination, are virtues by association; the bodily action of prostrating is a virtue by motivation; and the virtuous imprints left on the mental continuum by the mind of faith and the action of making prostrations are virtues by subsequent relation. The last type of virtue, ultimate virtue, refers principally to nirvana. Nirvana is ultimate virtue because when we attain nirvana we experience ultimate happiness.

NON-VIRTUE

DEFINITION OF NON-VIRTUE

The definition of non-virtue is a phenomenon that functions as a main cause of suffering.

DIVISIONS OF NON-VIRTUE

There are five types of non-virtue:

1 Natural non-virtue
2 Non-virtue by association
3 Non-virtue by motivation
4 Non-virtue by subsequent relation
5 Ultimate non-virtue

Anger, covetousness, harmful thought, and wrong views are all examples of natural non-virtues because they do not depend upon a non-virtuous motivation to be non-virtuous. Examples of non-virtues by association are a primary mind and other mental factors, such as feeling, associated with anger. Examples of non-virtues by motivation are actions done with a negative motivation. Examples of non-virtues by subsequent relation are the imprints left on our mental continuum by non-virtuous minds and non-virtuous actions. We have countless non-virtuous imprints on our mindstream.

Neither non-virtuous minds such as anger nor non-virtuous actions such as killing are permanent, but when they cease they leave imprints on our consciousness that, if not purified, will remain until they ripen as suffering. When we die our virtuous and non-virtuous imprints follow us like a shadow following a body.

These four types of non-virtue can be understood by considering the example of killing an insect out of anger. The mental factor anger is a natural non-virtue; the primary mind and the other mental factors associated with it, such as feeling, are non-virtues by association; the bodily action of killing is a non-virtue by motivation; and the imprints left on the mental continuum by the mind of anger and the action of killing are non-virtues by subsequent relation.

Ultimate non-virtue refers to samsara. What is samsara? According to Dharmakirti it is the five contaminated aggregates. It is because we have taken contaminated aggregates that we experience suffering continually. Human beings have to experience the suffering of humans because they have taken human aggregates, animals have to experience the suffering of animals because they have taken animal aggregates, and so on. All pain, fear, unhappiness, frustration, and all other forms of misery are experienced by the contaminated aggregate of feeling. If we did not have contaminated feelings we could not experience suffering. Our sufferings arise from our own aggregates like waves arising from the sea. If we had not taken samsaric aggregates we would have no basis for experiencing suffering. Buddha said that our contaminated aggregates are like a bundle of thorns that we carry on our back – until we abandon them we shall experience uninterrupted suffering.

All our delusions arise from our contaminated aggregates, and by acting under the influence of these delusions we create the cause to take new contaminated aggregates in the future. In this way samsara is perpetuated in a vicious circle of suffering from life to life. Because contaminated aggregates are the ultimate origin of all suffering they are known as 'ultimate non-virtue'.

DELUSION

DEFINITION OF DELUSION

The definition of delusion is a mental factor that arises from inappropriate attention and that functions to make the mind unpeaceful and uncontrolled.

If we did not have delusions we would experience only peace and contentment. When our delusions are not functioning strongly our mind is relatively tranquil and contented, but as soon as anger, jealousy, or desirous attachment arise they destroy our peace of mind like a sudden storm destroying the tranquillity of an ocean. Even if we are in good physical health, when delusions manifest our mind becomes ill at ease.

We should observe our mind for a day and see how often peaceful minds arise and how often deluded or neutral minds arise. If we are not well trained in Dharma it is likely that our deluded and neutral minds will far outnumber our peaceful minds. We should try gradually to increase the frequency of our peaceful minds until they remain with us all day long. When we are able to control our mind for one day we should try to control it for two days, and continue practising in this way until we can keep a peaceful mind continuously. Finally we shall attain the permanent peace of liberation. At this point we shall have completely abandoned delusions, and it will be impossible for our mind to be disturbed by anything.

The only way to attain the permanent peace of liberation is to cultivate and increase our present peaceful minds. Why is it so difficult to maintain a peaceful mind? The only reason is that we have so many delusions. External problems do not have the power to disturb our mind unless we respond to them by developing delusions. If we have no delusions, even our enemies cannot destroy our peace of mind. Because delusions are the main obstacles to our attaining liberation from samsara they are known as 'obstructions to liberation' or 'delusion-obstructions', and because they destroy our mental peace they are called 'inner enemies'.

177

FUNCTION OF DELUSIONS

Delusions function only to cause us harm. In *Guide to the Bodhisattva's Way of Life* Shantideva says:

> The inner enemies of hatred, attachment, and so forth
> Do not have arms and legs,
> Nor do they have courage or skill;
> So how have they made me their slave?

> While they remain within my mind
> They harm me at their pleasure,
> And yet, without anger, I patiently endure them.
> How shameful! This is no occasion for patience.

Normally we regard other people who harm us as our enemies, but our real enemies are the delusions such as hatred and attachment that dwell within our mind. Even though they do not have physical bodies and are not armed with weapons, nevertheless they are able to control us and inflict continuous misery. It is not suitable to be patient with delusions because if we are they will inflict even greater suffering on us. As Shantideva says:

> If all living beings, including the gods and demi-gods,
> Were to rise up against me as one enemy,
> They could not lead me to the fires of the deepest hell
> And throw me in;

> But this powerful enemy of the delusions
> In an instant can cast me into that fiery place
> Where even the ashes of Mount Meru
> Would be consumed without a trace.

The worst harm an external enemy can inflict on us is to take away this one life, he cannot harm us in future lives; but a single delusion such as anger can, in one short instant, cause us to take rebirth repeatedly in the deepest hells where the suffering is utterly unbearable. Moreover, external enemies are short-lived because sooner or later they will die of their own accord, but the enemies of the delusions have been with us since beginningless time, and will remain with us for ever if we do not take steps to destroy them. As Shantideva says:

No other kind of enemy
Can remain for as long a time
As can the enduring foes of my delusions,
For they have no beginning and no apparent end.

If another person is harming us and we practise patience to calm him down, he will stop harming us; but if we are patient with or tolerant towards our delusions they will simply grow stronger and continue to betray us and harm us. Thus, whereas other people who harm us can become our friends, delusions will always remain our enemies. As Shantideva says:

If I agree with external enemies and honour them,
They will eventually bring me benefit and happiness;
But if I entrust myself to delusions,
In the future they will bring me only more pain and
    suffering.

Realizing this, we should come to a very clear conclusion that all our delusions, no matter how appropriate or desirable they may seem, have only one function – to cause us harm – and we should make a firm decision not to rest until we have destroyed these inner enemies once and for all. In the words of Shantideva:

So how can I remain in samsara joyfully and without fear
While I readily reserve a place in my heart
For this interminable enemy of long duration
That alone is the cause of increasing all my suffering?

How can I ever be happy
While these guardians of the prison of samsara
That torture and torment me in the hells and elsewhere
Dwell like a net of iron in my mind?

Out of anger, worldly people who are filled with
    pride will not sleep
Until they have destroyed those who cause them
    even the slightest temporary harm.
In the same way, I will not abandon my efforts
Until this inner foe of mine is directly and definitely
    destroyed.

There was once a Tibetan Geshe called Geshe Ben Gungyal who used to spend all his time in his room, doing no meditation in the traditional posture, and reciting no prayers. His unorthodoxy attracted attention, and others asked him 'You do not recite prayers and you do not meditate in the usual way, so what do you do all day long in your room?' Geshe Ben Gungyal replied 'I have only one task – I am thrusting the spear of the opponents into the head of my delusions. When a delusion raises its ugly head I increase my alertness and with effort I plunge the spear straight into it. Then it leaves me in peace and I am happy. That is what I do all day long in my room.'

There are two types of opponent with which we can combat our delusions – the temporary opponents that are specific to each delusion, such as love (which is the opponent to hatred) and giving (which is the opponent to miserliness); and the ultimate opponent of wisdom realizing emptiness, which is the actual antidote to all delusions. Meditation on the specific opponents temporarily pacifies our delusions, and brings us a temporary inner peace with which we can develop the concentration and wisdom necessary to eradicate the delusions altogether by applying the ultimate opponent. To understand more fully how the different types of opponent work we first need to understand the causes of delusion.

There are six causes of delusion:

1 The seed
2 The object
3 Inappropriate attention
4 Familiarity
5 Distraction and being influenced by others
6 Bad habits

In *Treasury of Abhidharma* Vasubandhu explains that whenever the first three causes are assembled, delusion necessarily arises. The second three are conditions that encourage the development and increase of delusions.

THE SEED

The seed of a delusion is the potentiality for that delusion to arise; it is the substantial cause of the delusion. All ordinary beings have these potentialities in their mind, and they can be eradicated only by attaining wisdom directly realizing emptiness and meditating on this for a long time.

Until we have finally abandoned a delusion, the seed of that delusion will remain within our mind, even when the delusion itself is not manifest. Although the seed of a delusion is the substantial cause of that delusion and exists within us all the time, it will produce a manifest delusion only when the other necessary causes of delusion are present. For example, we have within us the seed of anger even when our mind is peaceful; but anger does not manifest in our mind until the other causes of anger, such as a disagreeable object and inappropriate attention, come together.

A Foe Destroyer has completely abandoned the seeds of all delusions. Thus, even if a Foe Destroyer meets with other causes of delusion, such as an attractive or disagreeable object, he or she will not be able to develop delusions. Foe Destroyers are so called because they have destroyed the inner foe of their delusions by eradicating their seeds. Delusions are the main obstructions to liberation because we cannot attain liberation from samsara until they are eradicated.

It is important to distinguish the seeds of delusions from the imprints of delusions. As already explained, the seeds of delusions are the substantial causes of delusions, and are obstructions to liberation. The imprints of delusions, on the other hand, are not causes of delusions but the effects of delusions. Even after we abandon the delusions by eradicating their seeds, the imprints of the delusions remain, rather as the smell of garlic lingers in a container long after the garlic has been removed from it. Because Hinayana Foe Destroyers have not abandoned the imprints of delusions, phenomena still appear to their minds as inherently existent, even though they no longer grasp at inherent existence. They are like a conjurer who can see an illusion he has created but is not taken in by it.

Because the imprints of delusions cause phenomena to appear as inherently existent they prevent us from directly realizing the two truths simultaneously, and so they prevent us from attaining an omniscient mind that can see all phenomena directly and simultaneously. For this reason they are known as 'obstructions to omniscience'. To remove these we must continue to meditate on emptiness on the Mahayana path of meditation. Thus, whereas the seeds of delusions, obstructions to liberation, are the principal object of abandonment for Hinayanists, the imprints of delusions, obstructions to omniscience, are the principal objects of abandonment for Mahayanists.

THE OBJECT

Delusions cannot arise without an object. For example, without seeing or recalling an attractive object we cannot develop attachment; and without seeing or recalling a disagreeable object we cannot develop anger. Thus, the fewer objects of delusion we encounter, the fewer delusions we shall develop.

To reduce the number of objects of delusion they encounter, some Dharma practitioners retire to isolated places to practise in solitude. Many texts praise solitude for those who wish to engage in retreat and other forms of concentrated practice. In *The Thirty-seven Practices of the Conquerors' Sons* Thogme Zangpo mentions three benefits of relying upon solitude:

> By avoiding non-virtuous objects, delusions gradually
>   diminish;
> With no distractions, virtuous actions naturally
>   increase;
> And through the clarity of mind, a definite
>   understanding of Dharma develops;
> Therefore, relying upon solitude is a practice of the
>   Conquerors' Sons.

Also, in *Guide to the Bodhisattva's Way of Life* Shantideva advises us that if we want to develop deep experience of Dharma we should abandon our attachment to worldly activities and abide in mental and physical solitude.

Although we may be able to avoid objects of delusion to some extent by retiring to an isolated place, we shall not be able to avoid such objects altogether. Even if we were to live in an isolated cave there would be some parts of the cave that would appear more attractive than other parts, and some kinds of weather that would seem more pleasant than others. We would soon find ourself preferring this sort of birdsong to that sort of birdsong, and we would still have the memories of other objects of delusion. Since we are so accustomed to finding plenty of objects of delusion wherever we go, the best way to avoid them is to practise restraining the doors of the sense powers. If we practise in this way, we shall be able to prevent delusions from arising wherever we are.

INAPPROPRIATE ATTENTION

Even if our mind meets an object of delusion, a delusion will arise in our mind only if we allow inappropriate attention to develop. Generally, inappropriate attention is a mind that dwells on a contaminated object and exaggerates its apparent qualities. There are many levels of inappropriate attention, from very subtle to very gross. Whenever ordinary beings see an object they naturally apprehend it as being inherently existent. This grasping mind is itself an exaggeration and a subtle form of inappropriate attention.

As a result of grasping things as being inherently existent we exaggerate their attractiveness or unattractiveness, and thus develop desirous attachment or anger. Whereas the initial development of self-grasping is subtle inappropriate attention, the subsequent exaggeration of the good or bad qualities of the object is gross inappropriate attention. Subtle inappropriate attention can be overcome only by a direct realization of emptiness. Gross inappropriate attention is overcome by applying mindfulness, alertness, and conscientiousness.

FAMILIARITY

The reason we develop delusions naturally, whereas we have to apply effort to cultivate virtuous minds, is that we are very familiar with delusions. Our minds have been acquainted with delusions since beginningless time and so deluded mental habits are very deeply ingrained. We can gradually reverse this situation by training in the various opponents of delusion and thereby becoming familiar with virtue instead of delusions. The more familiar we become with virtuous minds, the fewer delusions we shall develop. Eventually we shall reach the point where it is easier to develop virtuous minds than it is to develop delusions.

DISTRACTION AND BEING INFLUENCED BY OTHERS

We naturally imitate those with whom we associate. For example, if we have a close friendship with someone who disagrees with Dharma or who regularly engages in non-virtuous actions we shall gradually come under his influence and begin to adopt his view and his behaviour. If our friends are very fond of drinking, smoking, or engaging in reckless actions, we shall soon find ourself developing the same tendencies; and if they are thieves we may even follow their example and start stealing! If someone to whom we are close gives up his Dharma practice, this may leave an impression in our mind that will lead us to follow his example in the future. If we fall under the influence of bad friends our virtuous activities diminish in strength and our delusions increase. Good friends, on the other hand, have a beneficial influence on us. Thus, if we have a friend who is a pure Dharma practitioner we shall naturally find ourself adopting his or her view and behaviour, and thereby gradually developing the same good qualities.

Because we are so easily influenced by our friends it is important to choose good friends. In some ways our Dharma friends are more important than our Teacher because we are with our friends all the time but see our Teacher only occasionally. Good Dharma friends help us to reach liberation, while bad friends cause us to take rebirth in the lower realms.

There were once two friends who lived in an area of Tibet called Pembo. One of them drank heavily and often engaged in immoral actions, while the other led a blameless life. One day the good person moved to Lhasa where he took up work at an inn. Gradually he befriended the customers and as a result came under their influence. He started drinking and his general behaviour gradually deteriorated. At the same time his friend, who previously had set such a bad example, moved to Reting, a town with a famous monastery, where he became the assistant of a great Geshe. Through the influence and advice of the Geshe he finally gave up drinking and became a pure Dharma practitioner with impeccable conduct. Later when the two friends met up again they were surprised to see that their behaviour had completely reversed!

Listening to misguided teachings or advice also gives rise to delusions. Misguided teachings can cause us to develop negative thoughts towards the Three Jewels and to find fault with the Spiritual Guides in whom previously we had faith. They may even cause us to abandon Dharma. Such teachings confuse us by causing us to develop many conflicting views. For example, many teachers advocate attachment as a necessary ingredient of a healthy emotional life, or encourage us to express our anger freely, or to develop forms of self-confidence that are in fact types of deluded pride. Listening to such teachings seriously damages our Dharma practice and causes us to waste our precious human life. We must realize the danger of following such incorrect teachings and rely only upon authentic and pure teachings.

BAD HABITS

If we have bad physical habits, such as habits of killing, stealing, sexual misconduct, drinking, smoking, or taking drugs; or bad verbal habits, such as habits of lying, talking meaninglessly, or reading books that contradict Dharma, these will make our delusions stronger. Bad habits are the main cause of strong delusions arising in our mind.

If we think deeply about the six causes of delusions we shall see that there are many temporary measures we can take to reduce their intensity and frequency. However, to abandon them altogether we need to develop the wisdom directly realizing emptiness.

DIVISIONS OF DELUSION

There are three types of delusion from the point of view of realm:

1 Delusions of the desire realm
2 Delusions of the form realm
3 Delusions of the formless realm

Of these three, the delusions of the desire realm are the grossest, the delusions of the form realm are more subtle, and the delusions of the formless realm are the most subtle. All delusions that manifest before the attainment of tranquil abiding are delusions of the desire realm. These develop more quickly and more strongly than the delusions of the upper realms. There are three levels of desire realm delusion: big, middling, and small. A person with big anger, for example, will get very angry over insignificant incidents; a person with middling anger will get angry when confronted with major conditions for anger but not when encountering only slight conditions for anger; and a person with small anger will become only slightly irritated when faced with a major disturbance. The same applies to the other delusions of the desire realm. We can recognize these three levels of delusion from our own experience.

Each of the three levels of the desire realm delusions is further divided into big, middling, and small; and so altogether there are nine levels of each of the delusions of the desire realm, from big-big to small-small. We begin by eliminating the grossest level of each of the delusions, and then progressively eliminate the more subtle levels. This is like putting out a fire. We cannot extinguish a large fire all at once but must gradually reduce its intensity until finally we are left with only smouldering embers to extinguish.

The form realm has four levels, known as the first, second, third, and fourth form realms; and the formless realm also has four levels, called infinite space, infinite consciousness, nothingness, and peak of samsara. There are therefore nine realms in which sentient beings can take rebirth: the desire realm, the four form realms, and the four formless realms. Each of these nine realms has nine levels of delusion, from big-big to small-small, so altogether there are eighty-one levels of delusion. To attain liberation we need to identify and abandon all these delusions.

The grossest of the eighty-one delusions are the big-big delusions of the desire realm, and the most subtle are the small-small delusions of peak of samsara. When we have abandoned the small-small delusions of peak of samsara we have attained liberation. The first eighty levels of delusion can be abandoned temporarily, even by non-Buddhist practitioners or meditators, through the force of concentration alone; but to abandon the eighty-first level of delusion we need both authentic renunciation and the wisdom directly realizing emptiness.

There is a twofold division of delusion from the point of view of their cause:

1 Innate delusions
2 Intellectually-formed delusions

Innate delusions are delusions that arise naturally from imprints from previous lives – for example, all the delusions of animals and most of the delusions of humans, such as our normal self-grasping. Intellectually-formed delusions are delusions that arise as a result of relying upon incorrect philosophical systems or faulty reasoning. For example, some philosophical systems advocate animal sacrifice, claiming that this is a virtuous action that delights the gods. If we hold such a wrong view this is an intellectually-formed delusion. Another example of an intellectually-formed delusion is believing that war is good or spiritually justified. Buddhists are unlikely to be influenced by such wrong views but we can still develop intellectually-formed delusions through our own incorrect reasoning.

For example, after several years of trying to practise Dharma we may feel that we have made little progress and conclude that Dharma does not work, or we may decide that Buddhas do not exist because we cannot see them. The lower Buddhist schools teach that phenomena are inherently existent, and as a result adherents to these schools develop intellectually-formed self-grasping. Similarly there are many intellectually-formed delusions that result from adhering to non-Buddhist traditions.

When we attain the path of seeing we abandon all intellectually-formed delusions, but the innate delusions remain. We abandon these on the path of meditation. When we abandon the small-small delusions of peak of samsara we are liberated from samsara. However, if we want to attain full enlightenment, or Buddhahood, we still need to abandon the imprints of the eighty-one levels of delusion. We abandon these on the eighth, ninth, and tenth grounds of the Mahayana path of meditation. Finally, with the vajra-like concentration of the Mahayana path of meditation we eradicate the most subtle imprints of delusions, and simultaneously attain Buddhahood.

At present we develop desire realm delusions, and so it is these that we should strive to abandon first. After we have attained tranquil abiding we shall develop delusions of the form and formless realms. By gradually eliminating these, eventually we shall be liberated from samsara. Through understanding this process we shall gain confidence in the possibility of attaining liberation, and we shall see the great importance of sincere Dharma practice.

There is another twofold division of delusion from the point of view of entity:

1 Root delusions
2 Secondary delusions

These will now be explained in detail.

The Six Root Delusions

The six root delusions are the principal delusions from which all other delusions arise. They are:

1 Desirous attachment
2 Anger
3 Deluded pride
4 Ignorance
5 Deluded doubt
6 Deluded view

DESIROUS ATTACHMENT

DEFINITION OF DESIROUS ATTACHMENT

The definition of desirous attachment is a deluded mental factor that observes its contaminated object, regards it as a cause of happiness, and wishes for it.

Desirous attachment is not the same as desire. There are many non-deluded desires that it is suitable to cultivate, such as the desire to attain liberation and enlightenment, the desire to help others, or even the desire to abandon desirous attachment. Even Buddhas and Foe Destroyers have desires.

Desirous attachment develops as follows. First we perceive or remember a contaminated object and feel it to be attractive, then we focus our attention on its good qualities and exaggerate them. With an exaggerated sense of the attractiveness of the object we then hold it to be desirable and develop desire for it. Finally our desire attaches us to the object so that it feels as if we have become glued to it or absorbed into it. Only when all these stages are completed has desirous attachment occurred.

We must be careful to distinguish attachment from love. Love is a virtuous mind that creates only peace and happiness, whereas attachment is never virtuous and causes pain and problems.

DIVISIONS OF DESIROUS ATTACHMENT

There are three types of desirous attachment from the point of view of time:

1 Desirous attachment to past objects
2 Desirous attachment to present objects
3 Desirous attachment to future objects

An example of the first is recalling a friend and, out of attachment, longing to meet him or her again. We often develop this form of attachment when indulging in nostalgia, for example when remembering relatives who have died, possessions we once owned, places we used to live in, or good times we have enjoyed in the past. Examples of desirous attachment to present objects are, out of attachment, wishing for the pleasures we now enjoy to last forever, or wishing never to be separated from our present friends, possessions, and so forth. The anxiety we feel when we think of being separated from our partners or of losing our possessions comes from this type of desirous attachment. Examples of desirous attachment to future objects are, out of attachment, wishing to meet an attractive partner, to acquire wealth, or to own a bigger house. Even though we may never acquire such objects, nevertheless due to this type of attachment we spend much time planning or daydreaming about them. Attachment to future objects is the basis for most of our discontent and disappointment.

From the point of view of entity, desirous attachment can be divided into three – big, middling, and small – or into eighty-one – the nine levels of desirous attachment of each of the nine realms mentioned above. The grossest of these is the big-big desirous attachment of the desire realm, and the most subtle is the small-small desirous attachment of peak of samsara. These are all included within three:

1 Desire realm desirous attachment
2 Form realm desirous attachment
3 Formless realm desirous attachment

There is another threefold division from the point of view of its object:

1 Desirous attachment to samsaric places
2 Desirous attachment to samsaric enjoyments
3 Desirous attachment to samsaric bodies

HOW TO ABANDON DESIROUS ATTACHMENT

To eradicate attachment completely we need to develop renunciation and then meditate on emptiness until the seeds of attachment are removed from our mind. Temporarily we can abandon attachment by contemplating its faults and then applying appropriate opponents, such as meditation on impermanence or meditation on unattractiveness. The basis of all these practices is to understand why it is so important to abandon attachment, by contemplating its faults.

What are the faults of attachment? In the Sutras, Buddha says that living beings are bound within the prison of samsara by the rope of desirous attachment. The reason we experience suffering and problems is that we remain in samsara, the reason we remain in samsara is that we have made no effort to escape, the reason we have made no effort to escape is that we have no wish to escape, and the reason we have no wish to escape is that we are so strongly attached to the places, enjoyments, and bodies of samsara. Therefore, attachment is the root of all our suffering and problems.

When attachment arises in our mind it does not feel harmful; on the contrary, it usually feels beneficial. Therefore, it is important to contemplate repeatedly the faults of attachment and to recognize it as a delusion whose only function is to cause us harm. Why do criminals end up in prison? It is because they are led into committing crimes by their desirous attachment. Why do we suffer from illnesses such as heart disease? It is mostly because our attachment leads us to indulge in foods and drinks that are bad for us. Why do marriages and other relationships break up so often? It is because we are led by attachment to seek other partners. Attachment is the principal cause of dissatisfaction. It never causes contentment, only restlessness and discontent. Realizing this we should make a firm decision to abandon attachment and then apply the appropriate methods.

ANGER

DEFINITION OF ANGER

The definition of anger is a deluded mental factor that observes its contaminated object, exaggerates its bad qualities, considers it to be undesirable, and wishes to harm it.

Anger can be directed towards anyone, even towards our friends. We can also become angry with inanimate objects such as bad weather, poor food, or the non-fulfilment of our wishes.

DIVISIONS OF ANGER

From the point of view of entity there are nine types of anger, from big-big to small-small. However, since anger is exclusively a desire realm delusion there are not eighty-one levels of anger as there are for desirous attachment and self-grasping. Anger is a very gross and rough mind, and because beings in the form and the formless realms always have tranquil and refined minds they do not get angry.

There is another ninefold division of anger from the point of view of how it is generated:

1 Anger towards someone or something that harmed us in the past
2 Anger towards someone or something that is harming us now
3 Anger towards someone or something that might harm us in the future
4 Anger towards someone or something that harmed our friends or relatives in the past

5 Anger towards someone or something that is harming our friends or relatives now
6 Anger towards someone or something that might harm our friends or relatives in the future
7 Anger towards someone or something that helped our enemy in the past
8 Anger towards someone or something that is helping our enemy now
9 Anger towards someone or something that might help our enemy in the future

HOW TO ABANDON ANGER

As with attachment, anger can be finally eradicated only by gaining a direct realization of emptiness; but it can be temporarily abandoned by meditating on its opponents, patience and love. To practise patience we first need to contemplate the many faults of anger. Anger has no function other than to cause us harm; it is the most damaging and most destructive of all delusions. In *Tales of the Buddha* Master Vira says:

Due to the fire of anger, our beauty is lost.

Although we may have taken great pains to make ourself look attractive, as soon as we get angry our beauty disappears. When a friend whom we love is consumed with anger our love for them turns into fear. Anger prevents us from enjoying the things that normally give us pleasure. We might be lying on a soft mattress or eating delicious food but if we are angry our mind is in pain. Although our parents and Teachers have shown us nothing but kindness, if they do something we do not like we may get angry and treat them badly. Anger causes us to disregard many years of parental care, and can completely destroy our relationship with our parents.

If we constantly get angry we become unpopular and this makes it difficult for us to fulfil our wishes. When we are in a bad mood we become so unpleasant that even close friends avoid us. We use harsh and hurtful language and act in destructive, even violent, ways. When we are angry our wisdom declines and we lose our normal ability to discriminate right from wrong. Under the influence of anger we act reck-lessly, and even if our friends advise us to calm down we shun their advice. In short, anger makes our mind very rough and uncontrolled, robs us of our happiness, and dis-turbs others. Contemplating these points we should make a firm decision not to get angry.

When we wake in the morning we should remember the faults of anger and make a promise to ourself not to get angry that day. Whenever we experience misfortune or dis-appointment we should immediately remember our promise and calm our mind before anger develops. If we practise in this way every day, our anger will steadily decline in strength until finally nothing can make us angry. When we are free from anger others will appreciate us and respect us; and then we shall know the benefits of preventing anger from our own experience.

We do not need to be sitting on a meditation cushion to practise patience or love. We can practise these at any time, combining all our daily activities with them by applying mindfulness and alertness. As long as we remain in samsara we should expect problems and difficulties. In samsara it is not possible to remain in a state of peace forever; eternal peace can be found only by escaping from samsara. While we remain in samsara it is inevitable that we shall suffer because suffering is the very nature of samsara. Therefore, rather than becoming annoyed with suffering we should accept it as entirely natural. If we put our hand into a fire we would expect to be burned because it is the nature of fire to burn. In the same way, if we take rebirth in samsara we should not be surprised if we experience suffering because samsara is in the nature of suffering. Thinking like this helps us to prevent anger, even in the face of adversity. If we apply the teachings on training the mind, rather than getting angry when we experience difficulties we can use these situations to develop renunciation or compassion, to purify our nega-tivities, and to practise patience. As Shantideva explains in Guide to the Bodhisattva's Way of Life, we should consider ourself extremely lucky to meet with difficult circumstances or disagreeable people because they give us an opportunity to improve our patience, and without improving our patience we cannot attain enlightenment. If we have taken Bodhisattva vows or Tantric vows we have a commitment to practise patience, so when we find an opportunity to do so we should make the best use of it. The more our patience is tested the stronger it will become, and the more quickly we shall attain Buddhahood.

DELUDED PRIDE

DEFINITION OF DELUDED PRIDE

The definition of deluded pride is a deluded mental factor that, through considering and exaggerating one's own good qualities or possessions, feels arrogant.

Deluded pride is an inflated view of ourself that arises as a result of considering our own qualities such as our wealth, beauty, strength, education, knowledge, status, or race. Simply being aware that we have a particular quality or that we are in some respect better than other people is not necessarily deluded pride, for this may be a recognition of the truth. Deluded pride arises when our mind is 'puffed-up' with an exaggerated sense of our own importance.

There are non-deluded prides that we should cultivate, but these are not actual pride. Shantideva explains three types of non-deluded pride that are essential for completing the power of effort: pride with respect to our potential, pride in our actions, and pride in thinking we can destroy our delusions. The first is based on a recognition of our spiritual potential and leads us to think 'I can and will attain Buddhahood'. The second is a strong determination to perform virtuous actions, for example a mind of superior intention thinking 'I myself will free all sentient beings from suffering'. The third is the thought 'I can conquer all my delusions; they will never conquer me.' If we lack this self-confidence we shall easily be defeated by discouragement or by malevolent interferences.

Another type of non-deluded pride is the divine pride that is cultivated in Secret Mantra. This differs from ordinary pride in that the I it observes is imputed in dependence upon the pure aggregates of the Deity rather than upon ordinary, contaminated aggregates. All these types of non-deluded pride make our mind peaceful and virtuous.

DIVISIONS OF DELUDED PRIDE

There are seven types of deluded pride:

1 Pride over inferiors
2 Pride over equals
3 Pride over superiors
4 Pride in identity
5 Pretentious pride
6 Emulating pride
7 Wrong pride

The first type of pride is feeling superior to someone who is in some respect inferior to ourself; the second, feeling superior to someone equal to ourself; and the third, feeling superior to someone higher than ourself. The fourth type of pride, pride in identity, is an inflated sense of self-importance based simply on our identity, such as being proud of being an English person, proud of being white, proud of being a man, or proud of being a Tantric meditator. Pretentious pride is believing that we have qualities that we do not possess, such as thinking that the slightly peaceful mind we attain in meditation is actual tranquil abiding, or thinking that we are a pure Dharma practitioner when we are largely motivated by worldly concerns. Emulating pride is feeling equal or almost equal to someone who is vastly superior to us, such as Buddhas, Bodhisattvas, or our Spiritual Guide. Wrong pride is pride in inappropriate actions, such as pride at being a good marksman when shooting birds, feeling proud when we get away with shoplifting, or thinking that we are an excellent Teacher when the teachings we give are wrong.

HOW TO ABANDON PRIDE

As with all delusions, the first step in abandoning pride is to recognize its faults. The two main disadvantages of pride are that it causes us to disrespect others and that it is an obstacle to increasing our knowledge and good qualities. It is difficult for a proud person to receive much benefit from Dharma because he or she cannot listen to Dharma teachings with an open mind. This is particularly true for people who have studied other religious or philosophical traditions and who feel that they already understand certain topics. When such people hear a different view in Dharma teachings they conclude that Dharma is incorrect and of no relevance to them.

If we have been studying Dharma for a long time we may, when listening to teachings or reading a book, feel that we already know the subject and so pay only superficial attention to it. This is also a type of pride that prevents us from gaining deep experiences of Dharma. The only way to avoid such pride is to put the teachings into practice and thereby to gain some experience of their meaning. If we have a 'taste' of Dharma we shall find all teachings inspiring, no matter how many times we have heard them. As the Tibetans say:

An evil person can be tamed by Dharma, but a proud person cannot.

There are several methods for eliminating pride. For example, if we are proud of our knowledge we can investigate deep and subtle topics such as those presented in the ninth chapter of the *Guide to the Bodhisattva's Way of Life*. We shall soon discover that we still have much to learn, and our mind will be humbled. Another way to destroy our pride is to realize how vulnerable and unfree we are by meditating on all the unpleasant experiences we must suffer without choice, such as birth, sickness, ageing, and death. At present we might be beautiful, fit, intelligent, and successful, but we have no power to remain like this. Eventually, without any choice, we shall have to become old, decrepit, impoverished, handicapped, or senile. If we compare ourself to realized beings who have perfect freedom and whose happiness cannot be destroyed by external conditions we shall soon lose our pride.

IGNORANCE

DEFINITION OF IGNORANCE

There are two definitions of ignorance: a general definition given by Asanga and Vasubandhu, and a specific definition given by Chandrakirti and Dharmakirti. There is no contradiction between these two systems because the first gives a broad definition of ignorance in general, and the second gives a definition of a specific type of ignorance – the ignorance that is the root of samsara.

According to the first system, in *Compendium of Abhidharma* Asanga defines ignorance as:

A mental factor that is confused about the nature of an object and that functions to induce wrong awareness, doubt, and other delusions.

According to this definition, ignorance is a lack of knowing or understanding. For example, if we mistake a toy snake for a real snake we have an ignorance of the nature of that toy snake, and in dependence upon this we develop a wrong awareness that apprehends it as a real snake. Therefore, according to this system two distinct stages are involved in the development of wrong awarenesses. First we have ignorance, which does not understand the real nature of the object, and then, as a result of this unknowing, we develop a misapprehension of the object. Thus, in the example of the toy snake, first we simply fail to realize that the long thin object is a rubber toy, and then this non-understanding causes us to misapprehend the object as a real snake.

The fundamental ignorance is ignorance of the ultimate nature of phenomena. This is the very root of samsara and the basis of all mistakes and faults. According to Asanga, this ignorance also develops in two stages. Until we realize emptiness we are unaware of the ultimate nature of phenomena, and this unawareness is the fundamental ignorance. As a result of this unknowing we then develop actual wrong awareness – the self-grasping that misapprehends phenomena as truly existent.

Although a wrong awareness does not understand its object, it is not necessarily ignorance because ignorance is a mental factor and wrong awareness can be a primary mind. However, all wrong awarenesses possess the mental factor ignorance, and it is this that prevents the primary mind from understanding the nature of its object and makes it apprehend its object incorrectly. Asanga declared:

What is ignorance? All unknowing of the three realms.

The minds of all beings in the desire realm, form realm, and formless realm are completely pervaded by ignorance. There is never a time when ordinary beings do not develop ignorance.

Chandrakirti and Dharmakirti define ignorance as:

A mental factor that is the opposite of the wisdom apprehending selflessness.

According to this system, ignorance is necessarily self-grasping of persons or self-grasping of phenomena. Moreover, Chandrakirti and Dharmakirti do not accept the two-stage development presented by Asanga, but assert that ignorance just is self-grasping. Rather than being a mere unknowing of the real nature of phenomena, ignorance is an actual misconception that is the direct opposite of a realization of selflessness. Because of beginningless familiarity with ignorance, as soon as an object appears to the mind of an ordinary being it is apprehended as truly existent. This true-grasping mind itself obscures the real nature of phenomena.

There are many different types of self-grasping ignorance, such as self-grasping of persons, self-grasping of phenomena, innate self-grasping, and intellectually-formed self-grasping. The actual root of samsara is dependent-related ignorance, which is the first of the twelve dependent-related links. This is a particularly strong type of innate self-grasping that causes us to perform actions that throw us into samsara. It functions only in the minds of those who have not yet attained the path of seeing. When we gain a direct realization of emptiness on the path of seeing, this realization weakens the power of our self-grasping to such an extent that it can no longer cause us to create contaminated throwing karma, and thus cannot serve as the basis for samsaric rebirth.

DIVISIONS OF IGNORANCE

There are two types of ignorance:

1 Ignorance of conventional truths
2 Ignorance of ultimate truths

The first is confusion about any object other than emptiness, and the second is confusion about emptiness itself. All types of ignorance are included in these two categories.

There is another twofold division of ignorance:

1 Ignorance of actions and their effects
2 Ignorance of emptiness

Whereas the first is the cause of lower rebirth in particular, the second is the cause of rebirth in samsara in general. Because we do not understand the faults of non-virtuous actions or the benefits of virtuous actions, we behave in ways that result in rebirth in unhappy migrations. When we understand actions and their effects correctly we shall naturally strive to accumulate virtuous actions and abandon non-virtuous actions, and thereby protect ourself from lower rebirth. However, even if we understand the laws of karma and act accordingly, until we abandon ignorance of emptiness by realizing emptiness directly we shall still perform actions that throw us into samsara. Even virtuous actions motivated by self-grasping are true origins.

HOW TO ABANDON IGNORANCE

Since all mistakes, delusions, and incorrect actions arise from ignorance, we definitely need to abandon ignorance. There are three principal methods for eliminating ignorance: listening to, contemplating, and meditating on Dharma teachings. By developing the three wisdoms arisen from listening, contemplating, and meditating we can destroy our ignorance. Finally, it is a wisdom arisen from meditating – superior seeing – that eradicates ignorance; but before we can attain this wisdom we must first weaken our ignorance by listening to and contemplating Dharma teachings. In this context, 'listening' refers not only to receiving Dharma teachings directly from a Spiritual Guide but also to reading Dharma books and studying Dharma. Listening is the lamp that dispels the darkness of ignorance. Je Tsongkhapa said that without the light of listening we shall not be able to see the path to liberation. Through listening our wisdom will increase and our ignorance will diminish; and as a result we shall act appropriately and thereby experience fewer problems. When we are upset or worried our wisdom makes our mind happy, and when we are overexcited or distracted it helps to subdue our mind. Instead of relying upon others to solve our problems we should learn to rely upon our own wisdom. Without wisdom we are completely enveloped by the darkness of ignorance. In the diagram of the Wheel of Life ignorance is symbolized by a blind person. If we are ignorant, we are blind to the paths to liberation, whereas with wisdom we are like someone with perfect sight. The development of wisdom depends upon a calm mind and stable mindfulness, which in turn depend upon pure moral discipline.

Another method for overcoming ignorance is to rely upon the Wisdom Buddha Manjushri, or his emanation, Je Tsongkhapa. Visualizing Manjushri and Je Tsongkhapa, practising their sadhanas, and reciting their mantras are all powerful methods for developing wisdom.

DELUDED DOUBT

DEFINITION OF DELUDED DOUBT

The definition of deluded doubt is a two-pointedness of mind that interferes with the attainment of liberation or enlightenment.

In general, doubt is a mind of uncertainty that cannot decide between two alternatives. Although we have numerous doubts, not all doubts are deluded doubts. Simply being unable to decide whether to go out or to stay in, for example, is a doubt but it is not a delusion. Deluded doubt is an uncertainty about Dharma topics that causes our faith to decline and disturbs our peace of mind. For example, if our Spiritual Guide teaches us that virtuous actions lead to happiness and non-virtuous actions to suffering, and we feel this to be probably untrue, we have developed deluded doubt. This lack of conviction in actions and their effects prevents us from practising Dharma purely, and obstructs our progress on the path to liberation. If, although we cannot come to a definite decision, we are inclined to believe Buddha's teachings on actions and their effects, this is still doubt but it is not deluded doubt because it is a step towards developing a correct belief in the laws of karma.

DIVISIONS OF DELUDED DOUBT

As mentioned before, there are three types of doubt in general: doubts tending towards the truth, doubts tending away from the truth, and balanced doubts. Any doubt about spiritually significant objects that tends away from the truth is deluded doubt. Balanced doubts with respect to these objects may or may not be deluded. For example, if a person who previously believed that Buddha does not exist hears a teaching on Buddha, and as a result starts to doubt whether Buddha exists or not, this is not a deluded doubt because it is leading him or her towards a correct belief. On the other hand, a similar doubt in the mind of someone who once believed in Buddha but whose faith is now weakening is a deluded doubt.

Doubts about Dharma are not necessarily negative. For example, people who have not met Dharma have no doubts about emptiness because it is only through listening to teachings on emptiness that we begin to wonder whether or not phenomena lack inherent existence. Such doubts impel us to think more deeply about emptiness until finally we attain a valid cognizer that realizes emptiness with complete certainty. If we did not develop doubts about emptiness to start with, we would not subsequently gain such a deep understanding.

Although some doubts are helpful at certain stages of our development, eventually all doubts have to be abandoned. Doubts are completely abandoned only by Buddhas, whose perfect wisdom knows all phenomena exactly as they are, with no mistake or uncertainty. Hinayana Foe Destroyers have abandoned deluded doubts, but as they do not know all objects of knowledge they still have non-deluded doubts. Even tenth-ground Bodhisattvas do not fully understand the good qualities of a Buddha's body, speech, and mind, and still have some doubts about them. Superior beings do not have deluded doubts because they realize emptiness directly.

HOW TO ABANDON DELUDED DOUBT

We abandon doubt by developing valid cognizers. When we develop doubts about Dharma, rather than letting them remain in our mind we should take steps to resolve them. We should think carefully about the teachings and ask others to share their understanding. We can ask questions of Teachers and read relevant books to ascertain the true meaning of the instructions. In this way we shall eliminate our doubts. If we allow doubts about the teachings to remain in our mind, they will eventually turn into deluded doubts and hinder our practice. Conversely, if we are encouraged by our doubts to think more deeply about Dharma, they will help us to improve our understanding and eventually to attain valid cognizers.

The only way finally to eliminate a doubt is to understand the object with a valid cognizer. There are two ways of knowing an object correctly: through a correct belief and through a valid cognizer. The understanding of a correct belief is useful, but is not strong or stable; and if we later listen to incorrect instructions our understanding may change into doubt, or even into wrong awareness. Valid cognizers, on the other hand, know their object clearly and thoroughly, with complete certainty. Even if we hear clever arguments that try to deny an object we know with a valid cognizer, we shall not develop any doubts and our valid cognizer will be unshaken. For these reasons we should strive to understand Dharma with valid cognizers.

DELUDED VIEW

DEFINITION OF DELUDED VIEW

The definition of deluded view is a view that functions to obstruct the attainment of liberation.

In general there are three types of view: correct views, incorrect views, and neutral views. All deluded views are incorrect views. A correct view is a wisdom. A deluded view resembles a wisdom in that it discriminates its object thoroughly, but since its object does not exist it is not an actual wisdom.

DIVISIONS OF DELUDED VIEW

There are five types of deluded view:

1 View of the transitory collection
2 Extreme view
3 Holding false views as supreme
4 Holding wrong moral disciplines and conduct as supreme
5 Wrong view

Sometimes it is said that there are ten root delusions, the first five of the six root delusions being the 'five delusions that are non-views', and the five types of deluded view being the 'five deluded views'.

VIEW OF THE TRANSITORY COLLECTION

DEFINITION OF VIEW OF THE TRANSITORY COLLECTION

The definition of view of the transitory collection is a type of self-grasping of persons that grasps one's own I as being an inherently existent I.

The view of the transitory collection is the root of samsara and the source of all delusions. In *Guide to the Middle Way* Chandrakirti says:

Wisdom sees that all delusions and all faults
Arise from the view of the transitory collection.

Because we grasp strongly at an inherently existent I we develop self-cherishing, attachment, anger, and all other delusions; and these cause us to engage in contaminated actions that in turn cause us to experience the sufferings of samsara. The view of the transitory collection pervades all delusions because it functions whenever a delusion is manifest. If we wish to escape from samsara we need to eradicate this view, but before we can do this we must learn to identify it. Even though the view of the transitory collection is always manifest in the minds of ordinary beings it is not easy to recognize at first.

To recognize the view of the transitory collection we need to understand the difference between its observed object and its conceived object. For example, in the case of mistaking a toy snake for a real snake the observed object is a toy snake and the conceived object is this toy snake as a real snake. Similarly, in the case of the view of the transitory collection the observed object is the conventionally existent I, which is the I that is merely imputed in dependence upon the aggregates, and the conceived object is this conventionally existent I as an inherently existent I. The observed object of the view of the transitory collection, the mere I, exists, but the conceived object, the inherently existent I, does not.

When we think of ourself we apprehend not an I that is merely imputed upon our aggregates but an I that appears

Shakyaprabha

to be independent. For example, if we ask who is presently reading this book we do not think 'My body is reading this book', or 'My mind is reading this book'; we simply think 'I am reading this book', and this I appears to be independent of the body and mind. It is this independent I that is the conceived object of the view of the transitory collection, and that does not exist. Whatever exists does so in dependence upon other phenomena. The conventionally existent I, for example, exists in dependence upon the aggregates of body and mind. The conceived object of the view of the transitory collection, however, which is the I at which we habitually grasp and with which we usually identify, appears to be independent of the aggregates. Such an I could never exist.

What is the observed object of the view of the transitory collection, the conventionally existent I? Some non-Buddhist schools believe that the existent I is a permanent, indivisible entity that is a separate entity from the body and mind. Such a self is refuted by all Buddhist schools. Why is this? When our body is not healthy we say 'I am sick', and when our mind is not happy we say 'I am unhappy'; but if the I were a separate entity from the body and mind these statements would be nonsensical. If Peter becomes sick, John does not say 'I am sick', because John and Peter are separate entities. Similarly, if the I were a separate entity from the body and mind it would make no sense to say 'I am sick' just because our body was sick, or 'I am unhappy' just because our mind was unhappy.

Although no Buddhist school asserts an I that is a separate entity from the mental and physical aggregates, all the lower schools of Buddhism identify the I as existing somewhere within the aggregates. Some, such as the Vaibashikas and some Sautrantikas, assert that the collection of the five aggregates is the I, while other Sautrantikas identify the mental consciousness as the I. The Chittamatrins say that the I is the consciousness-basis-of-all, and the Madhyamika-Svatantrikas assert that it is the continuum of the subtle mental consciousness. However, according to the highest school of Buddhism, the Madhyamika-Prasangikas, all these assertions are incorrect.

The Madhyamika-Prasangikas deny that the I can be found either within the aggregates or outside them. No matter how carefully we search among the mental and physical aggregates we shall never find the I. The I is just a label that is imputed in dependence upon the five aggregates. The collection of the five aggregates is the basis for imputing the I, but it is not the I itself. If we are satisfied with the I as the mere term or label 'I' that is imputed in dependence upon the aggregates we shall be able to establish an I that exists and functions (the conventionally existent I); but if we search for a real I that exists 'behind' the label we shall find nothing.

It is very important to identify the view of the transitory collection from our own experience by identifying it within our own mind. At first the easiest way to do this is to cause the view of the transitory collection to manifest more strongly than usual by recalling or imagining situations in which we are falsely accused, afraid, praised, or embarrassed; and then to observe how the I appears at such times. We should direct most of our attention towards recreating or imagining the situation, but keep one part of our mind watching how the I appears. If we are not skilful and try to observe the I directly we shall probably fail. We need to practise watching the I out of the corner of our mind and try to catch a glimpse of it surreptitiously. This is an acquired skill that requires considerable practice. Eventually we shall see that the I is appearing independent of our body and mind. It seems as if our mind is 'this side' and the I is 'that side'. It is this independent I that is the conceived object of the view of the transitory collection.

By watching our mind in this way we shall gain a clear generic image of the inherently existent I. Even though this I does not exist we can nevertheless have a generic image of it. For example, unicorns do not exist but we can have an image of a unicorn in our mind. Once we are able to identify the view of the transitory collection operating in extreme circumstances, such as when we are afraid or embarrassed, we should then try to identify it in less extreme circumstances. For example, we can sit down to meditate and ask ourself 'Who is meditating?', and then try to observe the inherently existent I appearing as we think 'I am meditating.'

It is very helpful to understand the etymology of the view of the transitory collection. According to the lower Buddhist school, the Sautrantika school, the view of the transitory collection is a deluded view that observes the aggregates and apprehends a self-supporting and substantially existent I. Thus, they say that the observed object of this view is the five aggregates. According to them it is the aggregates themselves that are the 'transitory collection'. They are 'transitory' because they are impermanent, and a 'collection' because there are several of them. Thus, they assert that the view of the transitory collection observes the aggregates and mistakenly apprehends a self-supporting substantially existent I within them.

According to the Madhyamika-Prasangika explanation the term 'transitory collection' refers not only to the aggregates themselves but also to the I that is imputed upon them. Buddha called the I a 'transitory collection' to counteract non-Buddhists such as the Samkhyas who assert that the I is a permanent, indivisible, independent entity. The Samkhyas say that the I is permanent because it is not destroyed at death. They believe that the I has existed since beginningless time and that in each life it takes on a different body and mind, rather as an actor puts on a different mask each time he appears on stage. Just as the actor changes appearance but remains essentially the same, so the I changes appearance from one life to the next but remains the same entity.

The Samkhyas believe that if the I were not permanent, and independent of the body and mind, there would be no rebirth because the I would cease when the body dies. Thus, they believe that the I of our previous life, which created the karma that caused this life, still exists; and will continue to exist forever. This indicates that they do not understand subtle impermanence. In reality we do not remain the same for one moment without changing, let alone for one life. Without the I of the previous moment ceasing, the I of the next moment could not arise. The I of one moment is the cause of the I of the next moment, and a cause and its effect cannot exist at the same time. A sprout, for example, can develop only when its cause, the seed, disintegrates. It is precisely because the I disintegrates moment by moment that Buddha called the I 'transitory'. Since the I in one moment is a different entity from the I of the previous moment, it goes without saying that the I of one life is a different entity from the I of the previous life.

The Samkhyas also believe that the I is indivisible, or part-less. They say that if it were not partless it could be broken down into its component parts and would therefore not be indestructible and immortal. All Buddhist schools deny this, and the Madhyamikas in particular refute such things as partless objects. It is easy to see that the body has parts, such as the limbs, the head, and the trunk. The mind also has parts, such as feelings, discriminations, experiences, knowl-edge, and appearances, as well as having past, present, and future moments. Similarly, persons or selves have parts. One person may be a teacher, a father, and a Dharma practitioner. These are all different parts of the same person. Similarly, one person has parts that look, listen, taste, feel, think, and so forth. If we are looking at a crowd of a hundred people, for example, we have a hundred parts, each observing a different person. We can also divide a person into the past, present, and future moments. From this we can see that each person has many parts, and so, rather than being a single indivisible entity, each person is the nature of a collection. It is for this reason that Buddha called the I a 'collection'.

From this explanation we can see that the term 'transitory collection' in the phrase 'view of the transitory collection' refers not only to the aggregates but also to the I. The view of the transitory collection, therefore, is a deluded view that observes the I, the transitory collection that is merely imputed in dependence upon the aggregates, and conceives it to be an inherently existent I.

DIVISIONS OF VIEW OF THE TRANSITORY COLLECTION

There are two types of view of the transitory collection:

1 View of the transitory collection conceiving I
2 View of the transitory collection conceiving mine

The first observes only the I within our continuum and conceives it to be inherently existent, and the second observes both the I and mine within our continuum and conceives mine to be inherently existent. It is important to identify the observed object of the latter view. The view of the transitory collection is necessarily a self-grasping of persons that conceives one's own I to be inherently existent, and it necessarily takes the I within one's own continuum as its observed object. The view of the transitory collection conceiving mine, therefore, must observe our own I and conceive it to be inherently existent. When we see the aspect of other things, such as our clothes or our body, we develop a sense of 'mine'. At such times we are observing our I as a possessor, as 'mine', and conceiving it to be inherently existent. Thus, 'mine' in this context refers not to the objects that are being held as mine, which is the normal use of the word, but to the subject who is being held as the possessor. If 'mine' referred to the objects, such as one's clothes or one's body, then the observed object would be a phenomenon other than persons, and the mind grasping them to be inherently existent would be a self-grasping of phenomena, not a self-grasping of persons. Even so, it is not incorrect to say that objects such as one's clothes or one's body are examples of mine.

There is another twofold division of view of the transitory collection:

1 Innate view of the transitory collection
2 Intellectually-formed view of the transitory collection

Both the view of the transitory collection conceiving I and the view of the transitory collection conceiving mine have innate and intellectually-formed types. We have had the innate view of the transitory collection since beginningless time. It arises naturally in our mind through the force of imprints, and it is manifest in the minds of ordinary beings all the time, even during sleep. It is this innate view that is the root of samsara.

Like the innate view, the intellectually-formed view of the transitory collection is also a mind that grasps at one's own I as being inherently existent, but whereas the innate view develops naturally through the force of the imprints of ignorance, the intellectually-formed view arises as a result of contemplating wrong reasons or receiving misleading teachings. We tend to fabricate such false views of the I because we are very accustomed to the innate view of the transitory collection. The innate view, therefore, is the source of all the intellectually-formed views.

In *Guide to the Middle Way* Chandrakirti lists twenty intellectually-formed views of the transitory collection, four in relation to each of the five aggregates:

(1) The view holding our aggregate of form to be an inherently existent I

(2) The view holding our aggregate of form to be possessed by an inherently existent I

(3) The view holding our aggregate of form to be the basis upon which an inherently existent I depends

(4) The view holding our aggregate of form to be dependent upon an inherently existent I

(5) The view holding our aggregate of feeling to be an inherently existent I

(6) The view holding our aggregate of feeling to be possessed by an inherently existent I

(7) The view holding our aggregate of feeling to be the basis upon which an inherently existent I depends

(8) The view holding our aggregate of feeling to be dependent upon an inherently existent I

(9) The view holding our aggregate of discrimination to be an inherently existent I

(10) The view holding our aggregate of discrimination to be possessed by an inherently existent I

(11) The view holding our aggregate of discrimination to be the basis upon which an inherently existent I depends

(12) The view holding our aggregate of discrimination to be dependent upon an inherently existent I

(13) The view holding our aggregate of compositional factors to be an inherently existent I

(14) The view holding our aggregate of compositional factors to be possessed by an inherently existent I

(15) The view holding our aggregate of compositional factors to be the basis upon which an inherently existent I depends

(16) The view holding our aggregate of compositional factors to be dependent upon an inherently existent I

(17) The view holding our aggregate of consciousness to be an inherently existent I

(18) The view holding our aggregate of consciousness to be possessed by an inherently existent I

(19) The view holding our aggregate of consciousness to be the basis upon which an inherently existent I depends

(20) The view holding our aggregate of consciousness to be dependent upon an inherently existent I

Our aggregate of form is not an inherently existent I, but the first view holds it to be so; an inherently existent I does not possess our aggregate of form, but the second view holds our aggregate of form to be possessed by an inherently existent I; an inherently existent I does not depend upon our aggregate of form, but the third view holds our aggregate of form to be the basis upon which an inherently existent I depends; our aggregate of form does not depend upon an inherently existent I, but the fourth view holds our aggregate of form to be dependent upon an inherently existent I. The remaining sixteen views can be understood in the same way.

HOW TO ABANDON THE VIEW OF THE TRANSITORY COLLECTION

First we need to identify correctly and precisely the view of the transitory collection in our own experience. Then we have to realize that its conceived object, the inherently existent I, does not exist, and familiarize ourself with this knowledge for a long time in meditation. Through progressing in this meditation, eventually we shall abandon this view completely.

If the inherently existent I existed we would be able to find it through investigation, but no matter how closely we investigate – whether we search within our aggregates of body and mind or elsewhere – we shall never find it. From this we can safely conclude that the inherently existent I does not exist. Where previously we perceived a vividly appearing I, we now perceive a vacuity, an emptiness. This emptiness is the non-existence of the inherently existent I. It is the ultimate nature of our I. By familiarizing ourself with this absence, or non-existence, of the inherently existent I, we shall gradually reduce and eventually abandon altogether the view of the transitory collection grasping at such an I.

In *Commentary to Valid Cognition* Dharmakirti says:

Without its object being negated,
Self-grasping cannot be abandoned.

This means that to abandon the view of the transitory collection we need to realize the non-existence of the inherently existent self. This is like removing the fear of a snake by realizing that there is no snake. However, we should not think that in negating the conceived object of the view of the transitory collection we are driving the inherently existent I out of existence, because such an I has never existed. In this case, negating the conceived object is simply realizing that something we previously held to exist does not in fact exist.

Suppose a child is named 'Buddha' by his parents. The child would grow up thinking 'I am Buddha', but when he discovered that Buddha was someone who was free from the two obstructions he would examine his body and mind and realize he was not an actual Buddha but just an ordinary person with the name 'Buddha'. Although he might continue to call himself 'Buddha', he would know that this was merely a name and that it did not imply that he was actually a Buddha. Our situation is similar in that we have always thought of ourself as I, and assumed that, corresponding to this name, there was a real I. Like the child we should now examine our body and mind to see if this assumption is correct. If we search for this I we shall not find it, either within our body and mind or outside our body and mind. Thus, we shall realize that 'I' is just a name. The truly existent I we expect to find 'behind' the name does not exist at all. Thus, although we may continue to refer to ourself as 'I', we can be certain that it is just a name and that it in no way implies an inherently existent I.

Buddha explained that there are two types of self-grasping: self-grasping of persons and self-grasping of phenomena. The former is any mind that conceives a self or person to be inherently existent, and the second is any mind that conceives phenomena other than persons to be inherently existent. As mentioned before, the view of the transitory collection is a type of self-grasping of persons. Self-grasping of persons has two types: grasping at our own self as inherently existent and grasping at other persons as inherently existent, and it is only the former that is the view of the transitory collection. Both types of self-grasping of persons are the same in that they grasp at an inherently existent self, but they differ in their observed object. The first observes the self within one's own continuum and conceives it to be inherently existent, and the second observes the self of others and conceives it to be inherently existent.

How does the view of the transitory collection arise? In *Precious Garland* Nagarjuna says:

For as long as there is grasping at the aggregates
There is grasping at I.

This means that the view of the transitory collection grasping at an inherently existent I arises from grasping at our aggregates as inherently existent. When we observe our aggregates they appear as inherently existent, and we thereby develop a mind grasping at inherently existent aggregates. This is an instance of self-grasping of phenomena. In dependence upon grasping at our aggregates as inherently existent, we develop a mind grasping at our I as inherently existent – the view of the transitory collection. This is an instance of self-grasping of persons. If we understand this we shall realize that to abandon the view of the transitory collection completely we must realize not only selflessness of persons but also selflessness of phenomena. For example, if a person walking through a field at dusk sees a piece of rope and mistakes it for a snake he will develop fear, but once he realizes that there is no snake his fear will subside. However, if he does not remove the piece of rope there will be a danger of making the same mistake again in the future. In the same way, in the darkness of our ignorance we observe our aggregates and mistakenly conceive an inherently existent I, and because we grasp at this I we experience all the fears and sufferings of samsara. To remove these fears and sufferings we need to remove grasping at an inherently existent I by realizing that the inherently existent I does not exist; but if we do not also remove grasping at the aggregates by realizing the emptiness of our aggregates there will be a danger of the view of the transitory collection arising again. Therefore, to attain liberation from samsara we need to realize both selflessness of persons and selflessness of phenomena.

In *Guide to the Middle Way* Chandrakirti says:

I bow down to that compassion for living beings
Who from first conceiving 'I' with respect to the self,
Then thinking 'This is mine' and generating
    attachment for things,
Are without self-control like the spinning of a well.

In this verse Chandrakirti shows how we can develop compassion for all living beings by contemplating how they are trapped in samsara by the two types of view of the transitory collection. Thus, from the view of the transitory collection conceiving I, sentient beings develop the view of the transitory collection conceiving mine. From this they develop a strong sense of 'my pleasure', 'my pain', and so forth; and in this way they develop attachment for the things that please them and hatred for the things that displease them. From these develop all other delusions that cause them to create the karma to be reborn repeatedly in samsara. Once living beings take a samsaric rebirth they have to experience suffering without any choice, just as a bucket in a well swings uncontrollably from side to side and is thereby dented, scratched, and damaged. If we think deeply about this we shall develop renunciation for our own samsara and compassion for others. We shall see that to free ourself and others from the sufferings of samsara we must cut samsara at its root by eradicating the view of the transitory collection.

EXTREME VIEW

DEFINITION OF EXTREME VIEW

The definition of extreme view is a deluded view that observes the I that is the conceived object of the view of the transitory collection and grasps it either as permanent or as completely ceasing at the time of death.

In general, there are two extremes: the extreme of existence (or the extreme of permanence) and the extreme of non-existence (or the extreme of nothingness); but neither exists because whatever exists is necessarily the middle way free from the two extremes. However, even though the two extremes do not exist, minds grasping at these extremes do. Extreme view is such a mind.

The extreme of existence is a falsely imagined mode of existence that is superimposed onto phenomena whereby phenomena are held to be more concrete than they actually are. For example, a mind grasping at an inherently existent I, or a mind grasping at a permanent I, is grasping at the extreme of existence, or the extreme of permanence. The extreme of non-existence is a falsely imagined non-existence of something that exists. For example, if we make an exhaustive analytical search for our I and fail to find it, we may wrongly conclude that the I does not exist at all. Such a mind conceiving the non-existence of the I is grasping at the extreme of non-existence, or the extreme of nothingness. Although the I cannot be found under analysis, and therefore lacks inherent existence, it nevertheless exists conventionally. The I, therefore, is free from the extreme of existence in that it is not inherently existent, and free from the extreme of non-existence in that it is not completely non-existent. Moreover, the I is not a permanent unchanging entity that survives death unchanged, nor is it completely annihilated at death. Therefore, the I is free from the two extremes of permanence and nothingness, and so extreme view is mistaken.

To understand the view of the middle way we need sharp wisdom and clear and precise instructions. For example, we may understand that the body is not its parts, not the collection of its parts, and not separate from its parts; and from this conclude that the body is unfindable. However, to realize the emptiness of the body fully we must understand more than its unfindability. Through realizing the unfindability of the body we understand that the body is not inherently existent, and is therefore free from the extreme of existence; but to realize the emptiness of the body completely we must also understand how it is free from the extreme of non-existence by realizing that it is a mere imputation. Thus, even though the body lacks inherent existence and so cannot be found upon investigation, nevertheless it does exist conventionally. When we realize that there is no contradiction between the body being empty of inherent existence and the body existing conventionally, and when we understand how these two support each other, we shall have found the correct view of the middle way and then we shall have understood emptiness completely.

HOLDING FALSE VIEWS AS SUPREME

DEFINITION OF HOLDING FALSE VIEWS AS SUPREME

The definition of holding false views as supreme is a deluded view that holds a false view to be correct and superior to other views.

Because we cherish ourself so strongly we naturally feel that whatever we think is correct and superior to other points of view, and we find it difficult to accept that some of our views might be mistaken. Most arguments and wars occur because each party regards their view to be superior to their opponents' view. Whenever we grasp tightly to a mistaken view, thinking that it is a correct view and the best view, we are holding false views as supreme. An example is insisting that the view of the transitory collection is the correct view.

Holding a mistaken view to be supreme strengthens that view and makes it difficult for us to dislodge it. There are some people who disbelieve in past and future lives, but only because they have not given the subject serious consideration. When later they hear correct Dharma teachings proving the existence of past and future lives they quickly abandon their former wrong view and come to believe in past and future lives. However, a person who not only denies the existence of past and future lives but also holds his view to be supreme will not change his mind so easily. Therefore, if we discover that some of our views are at variance with those taught in Dharma we should at least try to make sure that we do not grasp at them too tightly. We must have the openness and flexibility of mind to let go of our wrong views when we hear correct explanations that disprove them.

HOLDING WRONG MORAL DISCIPLINES
AND CONDUCT AS SUPREME

DEFINITION OF HOLDING WRONG MORAL DISCIPLINES
AND CONDUCT AS SUPREME

The definition of holding wrong moral disciplines and conduct as supreme is a deluded view that holds any wrong moral discipline or conduct to be correct and considers it to be superior to other forms of moral discipline or conduct.

This deluded view has two types: holding wrong moral disciplines as supreme and holding wrong conduct as supreme.

Some religions advocate animal sacrifice as a means of pleasing the gods and attaining liberation. Others teach that treating the body harshly helps to overcome delusions, and so the followers of these traditions jump into fires, fast for long periods of time, lacerate themselves, or stand for a long time in cold water during winter. These views flourished widely in the past and still exist today. I myself saw ascetics in India who stood on one leg for three years in the belief that this would make them great Yogis. Why did they punish themselves so? It was because they believed that delusions are part of the body, and so if they could reduce the strength of the body they would be able to reduce the strength of their delusions. These are examples of views grasping at wrong moral disciplines or conduct as supreme. According to Buddhism such views are wrong paths because they do not lead to true liberation but cause us to waste our human life.

Deluded views such as these are usually the result of listening to misleading religious or philosophical teachings. We should be careful not to follow such mistaken teachings. Holding incorrect views about moral conduct and spiritual practice causes us to waste our time on inferior or perverse practices, and prevents us from making the best use of our precious human life. Some people may think that an authentic spiritual life entails living in poverty, constantly fasting, wearing poor clothing, and so forth, but Buddha taught that we should treat our body with care because it is the vehicle in which we progress to enlightenment and as such is very precious. A weak or mistreated body will not be able to support our spiritual development. Therefore, without being attached to our body we should feed it, clothe it, provide adequate shelter, and so on; and then concentrate our energy on training our mind. As Nagarjuna said:

Physical asceticism is of no benefit, but mental asceticism is very necessary.

By this he means that there is little purpose in enduring unnecessary physical pain, but that it is very important to endure the hardships involved in taming our mind.

WRONG VIEW

DEFINITION OF WRONG VIEW

The definition of wrong view is an intellectually-formed wrong awareness that denies the existence of an object that it is necessary to understand to attain liberation or enlightenment.

Not all wrong awarenesses are wrong views. For example, innate delusions, such as the innate view of the transitory collection, as well as all mistaken sense awarenesses, are wrong awarenesses but not wrong views. There are also many false views that are not wrong views. Denying the existence of yetis, for example, does not obstruct our progress towards liberation or enlightenment and is therefore not a wrong view. Examples of wrong views are denying the existence of past and future lives; denying the existence of the two truths; denying the existence of Buddha, Dharma, and Sangha; denying the existence of the four noble truths; and denying the existence of the five paths. Such wrong views block our progress to liberation and enlightenment. The effects of developing such wrong views are that we shall become very dull and ignorant, and that we shall be reborn in countries where there is no Buddhadharma or during a dark age when no Buddha has taught the doctrine. As wrong views are so harmful we should strive to overcome them by developing correct views.

It is important to realize that not all deluded views are wrong views. A wrong view is necessarily a negative mind, and is one of the ten non-virtuous actions. It consists of actively denying something that we need to believe in to attain liberation or enlightenment. Other deluded views, however, such as the innate view of the transitory collection, are neither negative states of mind nor non-virtuous actions. The innate view of the transitory collection is a neutral mind, neither negative nor positive, although it is the source of all our negative minds and of all our non-virtuous actions.

The Twenty Secondary Delusions

From the six root delusions, twenty secondary delusions develop:

1 Aggression
2 Resentment
3 Spite
4 Jealousy
5 Miserliness
6 Concealment
7 Pretension
8 Denial
9 Self-satisfaction
10 Harmfulness
11 Shamelessness
12 Inconsideration
13 Dullness
14 Distraction
15 Mental excitement
16 Non-faith
17 Laziness
18 Non-conscientiousness
19 Deluded forgetfulness
20 Non-alertness

AGGRESSION

The definition of aggression is an increase of the root delusion anger that wishes to hurt or harm others physically or verbally.

As long as anger is hidden within our heart and cannot be detected by others it is not aggression but the root delusion anger. If this anger becomes stronger, such that we start to think of ways of harming others physically or verbally and show external signs of anger such as menacing facial expressions, and if our behaviour comes under the influence of this anger, then the anger has become aggression.

RESENTMENT

The definition of resentment is a deluded mental factor that maintains the continuum of anger without forgetting it, and wishes to retaliate.

If someone harmed us a year ago and we still bear a grudge, this is resentment. Resentment is derived from the root delusion anger. First we develop anger, and then we hold onto that anger, not allowing ourself to forget the harm we experienced. Resentment is much more harmful than the root delusion anger or the secondary delusion aggression. Due to resentment people retaliate and become involved in disputes and wars which may continue for many years. Even if we develop aggression, if we soon forget our anger this is much less harmful than bearing a grudge for many years.

SPITE

The definition of spite is a mental factor that, motivated by resentment or aggression, wishes to speak harshly.

Harsh speech disturbs others' inner peace, destroys our good relationships with others, and causes others to get angry; but without the mental factor spite there would be no basis for harsh speech. Speaking harshly with a special, virtuous motivation, however, is not actual harsh speech.

JEALOUSY

The definition of jealousy is a deluded mental factor that feels displeasure when observing others' enjoyments, good qualities, or good fortune.

If our neighbour buys a new car, or our friend becomes close to someone else, and we become jealous, this will make our mind very uncomfortable whenever we think about their good fortune. There are three types of jealousy: jealousy observing others' possessions; jealousy observing others' good qualities, skills, knowledge, and so forth; and jealousy observing others' good reputation, fame, popularity, and so forth. Jealousy is the source of much anger, discontent, and disharmony. It feels like a thorn in our heart. When we are jealous our mind becomes narrow and obsessive, making it difficult for us to think of anything else or to see the situation from the other person's point of view. Jealousy is entirely futile because neither does it cause the other person's fortune or good qualities to decline, nor does it increase our own; all it does is to rob us of our own peace and happiness.

Jealousy is completely contradictory with the Bodhisattva's way of looking at things. Bodhisattvas constantly pray 'May all sentient beings possess happiness', so how can they feel displeasure when someone manages to obtain a little joy? In *Guide to the Bodhisattva's Way of Life* Shantideva says that people who are jealous of others' possessions and good qualities will never develop bodhichitta. Those with great wisdom never become jealous because they have a deep understanding of the faults of jealousy.

MISERLINESS

The definition of miserliness is a deluded mental factor that, motivated by desirous attachment, holds onto things tightly and does not want to part with them.

Due to miserliness we sometimes wish to hold onto our possessions forever, but since this is impossible we experience much suffering. If our possessions dwindle, or we are forced to give them away, we experience great pain. The more miserly we are, the more concerned we are about our possessions and the more worry and anxiety we suffer.

Miserliness is the opposite of the mind of giving. Sometimes miserliness prevents us from giving at all, and at other times it causes us to develop a sense of loss or regret when we do give. Although miserliness might appear to be a prudent attitude that ensures our material security in this life, from a long-term point of view it is very foolish. By preventing the wish to practise giving from arising, miserliness causes poverty in future lives. In the *Condensed Perfection of Wisdom Sutra* Buddha says:

Misers are reborn in the land of hungry ghosts;
And when reborn as human beings they experience
    poverty.

And in *Friendly Letter* Nagarjuna says:

There is no better friend for the future
Than giving – bestowing gifts properly
On ordained people, brahmins, the poor, and friends –
Knowing enjoyments to be transitory and essenceless.

If we want to enjoy good health, friends, relatives, and material resources in future lives we must practise giving now. As a result of being generous in this life we shall enjoy good conditions in future lives, so giving is our best friend for the future. To secure our well-being in this life we work very hard to accumulate material possessions, but we should not forget that to be happy in future lives we shall also need material resources then. The only way to secure these resources is to practise giving now.

If we find it difficult to give, we should meditate on the impermanence and essencelessness of our possessions and enjoyments. Milarepa said:

Since you have to depart alone, leaving everything
  behind,
It is more meaningful to leave everything now.

We cannot take our possessions with us when we die. No matter how tightly we hold onto them now, eventually they will all be passed on to others. If we wait until we die this will happen involuntarily and will have no meaning for us. Therefore, it is much better to give away our possessions now, while we are alive, and in this way accumulate some meaning from having owned them. In themselves samsaric objects have no essence, but by using them to practise giving they acquire meaning. If we understand the benefits of giving we shall develop delight and pleasure in giving.

CONCEALMENT

The definition of concealment is a deluded mental factor that, motivated by attachment to wealth or reputation, wishes to conceal our faults from others.

Although it would be unskilful to reveal publicly all our shortcomings, nevertheless we should not develop the wish to conceal our faults from others out of attachment or with a bad motivation.

PRETENSION

The definition of pretension is a deluded mental factor that, motivated by attachment to wealth or reputation, wishes to pretend that we possess qualities that we do not possess.

Pretension causes us to engage in the non-virtuous actions of lying and deceiving others, and so causes us to experience many problems.

DENIAL

The definition of denial is a deluded mental factor that does not wish to purify non-virtuous actions that we have committed or downfalls that we have incurred.

If we commit non-virtuous actions or incur downfalls of the Pratimoksha, Bodhisattva, or Tantric vows, we should immediately develop a wish to purify them by developing regret. If we do not do this, our non-virtuous actions and downfalls will increase every day and cause great obstacles to our spiritual development.

SELF-SATISFACTION

The definition of self-satisfaction is a deluded mental factor that observes our own physical beauty, wealth, or other good qualities, and, being concerned only with these, has no interest in spiritual development.

In *Friendly Letter* Nagarjuna explains five different types of self-satisfaction:

(1) Self-satisfaction with respect to status
(2) Self-satisfaction with respect to physical beauty
(3) Self-satisfaction with respect to knowledge, skills, and so forth
(4) Self-satisfaction with respect to youth and vitality
(5) Self-satisfaction with respect to power

These five types of self-satisfaction all deceive us eventually. Since status, beauty, and so forth are impermanent, if we allow ourself to become complacent on their account we shall only experience suffering when we eventually lose them.

Self-satisfaction makes our precious human life meaningless, and is the root of all non-conscientiousness. It prevents us from seeing our own faults and so makes it difficult for us to develop a wish to overcome them. For example, some people might feel that they have superior status or racial origins and therefore do not need to observe moral discipline and can do whatever they like, but the result of this way of thinking will only be that they will experience many difficulties. Self-satisfaction seriously impedes the attainment of spiritual realizations such as higher moral discipline, higher concentration, and higher wisdom.

HARMFULNESS

The definition of harmfulness is a deluded mental factor that wishes other sentient beings to suffer.

Harmfulness is the opposite of compassion. A harmful intent can arise through anger, jealousy, desirous attachment, or ignorance. For example, out of anger we may wish for someone to suffer, to experience problems, or even to die; out of jealousy we may find it impossible to bear the success or good fortune of others and wish for them to lose it; out of desirous attachment we may become attached to others' wealth and possessions, and even wish for them to die so that we can inherit them; and out of ignorance we may rejoice in the misfortune, or even the demise, of others. Also, out of ignorance some people hold wrong views, believing that animal sacrifice is a virtuous action, and as a result they develop the wish to kill animals. All these are examples of harmful intent.

Harmfulness is the principal object to be abandoned by Buddhists. One of the commitments of going for refuge is not to harm others. In the Sutras, Buddha says:

Those who harm others are not trainees in virtue.

This means that people who deliberately harm others are not practitioners of Buddha's teachings.

SHAMELESSNESS

The definition of shamelessness is a deluded mental factor that is the opposite of sense of shame.

Out of shamelessness we may break the commitments that we have taken in front of visualized Buddhas or our Spiritual Guide. Shamelessness leads us into non-virtuous paths, and as a result we experience suffering in this and many future lives.

INCONSIDERATION

The definition of inconsideration is a deluded mental factor that is the opposite of consideration for others.

Inconsideration and shamelessness are the basis of incurring all downfalls and of accumulating all non-virtuous karma. They lead us into lower rebirth and cause all our good qualities to degenerate. They cause many difficulties both for ourself and for others.

DULLNESS

The definition of dullness is a deluded mental factor that functions to make both the body and mind heavy and inflexible.

When dullness develops it is as if our mind has become enveloped by darkness and its object has become unclear, just as external objects become unclear when it is foggy or dark. Sometimes due to dullness Dharma teachings seem unclear to us; but in reality it is our mind that is unclear. Dullness is a cause of mental sinking and sleep, and is therefore a major obstacle to meditation. The reason we sometimes fall asleep when we are meditating is that, without being aware of it, we have developed dullness. We must be careful to distinguish dullness from mental sinking. Dullness is the cause of mental sinking and is necessarily a delusion, whereas mental sinking is not necessarily a delusion.

It is vitally important for those who are intent on making progress in meditation to overcome dullness. Without a method for counteracting dullness we shall find that this mental factor will naturally develop and cause the sharpness of our intelligence to decline, and our mind to become heavy, sluggish, and sleepy. As a result our body will also become heavy, our concentration will deteriorate, and we shall soon forget our object of meditation. Even if we do not forget the object, our meditation will be tainted by mental sinking and our concentration will no longer be flawless.

DISTRACTION

The definition of distraction is a deluded mental factor that wanders to any object of delusion.

Distraction makes us lose our concentration on our spiritual practice by causing our mind to wander to a contaminated object, such as a samsaric place, body, or enjoyment. The object of distraction can be an object of anger, an object of attachment, or an object of ignorance. Distraction is the worst obstacle to our spiritual development.

MENTAL EXCITEMENT

The definition of mental excitement is a deluded mental factor that wanders to any object of attachment.

Mental excitement is closely related to attachment. It seriously interrupts both analytical and placement meditation. Because we are so familiar with objects of attachment, when we are trying to make progress in our meditation mental excitement naturally develops within our mind and destroys our concentration.

NON-FAITH

The definition of non-faith is a deluded mental factor that is the opposite of faith.

Non-faith makes our mind like a dry seed from which no sprouts of spiritual realizations can grow. However much we study Dharma, if we lack faith we shall never gain any realizations. Therefore, to gain results from our Dharma study we must improve our faith in Dharma and in our Teachers.

LAZINESS

The definition of laziness is a deluded mental factor that, motivated by attachment to worldly pleasures or worldly activities, dislikes virtuous activity.

The laziness taught in Dharma and the laziness we talk of in everyday life are different. The mental factor laziness is necessarily a deluded mind. A dislike of engaging in non-virtuous actions is not a delusion but usually a virtuous mind. Similarly, a mind that lacks enthusiasm for neutral actions such as cleaning or cooking is also not necessarily deluded.

Just outside the entrance of the cave of Geshe Karakpa, one of the Kadampa Geshes, there was a thorn bush and, as the path was narrow, every time he went in and out he scratched himself. Each day he would decide to cut down the bush, but as his retreat schedule was so tight he never found time to do it. Month by month the bush grew larger until eventually it blocked the whole path. The local people thought that Geshe Karakpa was very lazy because he could not be bothered even to trim a bush, but in reality his inactivity was a sign not of laziness but of his effort in his spiritual practices.

Like non-faith, laziness is very harmful for Dharma practitioners. In this great aeon a thousand Buddhas will appear. The only difference between these Buddhas and us is that through their effort the Buddhas have attained great enlightenment, whereas we, through our laziness, remain in samsara.

NON-CONSCIENTIOUSNESS

The definition of non-conscientiousness is a deluded mental factor that wishes to engage in non-virtuous actions without restraint.

Non-conscientiousness is the opposite of conscientiousness, which functions to guard our mind against delusion and protects us from engaging in non-virtuous actions. Non-conscientiousness is the gateway to committing non-virtuous actions. It is one of the four doors of receiving downfalls. If we guard our mind by applying conscientiousness we shall avoid committing non-virtuous actions, and all our actions of body, speech, and mind will become pure; but if we allow non-conscientiousness to develop we shall act in an unrestrained manner and happily engage in negative actions.

In *Friendly Letter* Nagarjuna says:

The Teacher, Buddha Shakyamuni said
Conscientiousness is like nectar,
Non-conscientiousness is like death.

Conscientiousness is like nectar because it causes us to experience bliss and happiness now and in the future. Non-conscientiousness is like death because it destroys the meaning of having a human life. We consider death to be the worst that could befall us, but in reality living without conscientiousness is far worse. If we waste the precious opportunities afforded by this human life by not engaging in virtuous actions we are as if already dead. As Shantideva says in *Guide to the Bodhisattva's Way of Life*, what is the meaning in taking a human rebirth if we use it only to commit evil? Death is nowhere near as unpleasant as the long-term effects of our non-virtue.

DELUDED FORGETFULNESS

The definition of deluded forgetfulness is a deluded mental factor that makes us forget a virtuous object.

Not all forgetfulness is deluded. If we forget to eat breakfast, for example, this is not a delusion. Some forgetfulness, such as forgetting objects of attachment or anger, can even be virtuous. An example of deluded forgetfulness is when we forget the object of meditation because we are distracted towards an object of attachment.

Forgetfulness is one of the major obstacles to meditation. If we forget the object of meditation we have nothing to concentrate on. One of the five obstacles to be eliminated when training in tranquil abiding is forgetting the object of meditation, and its principal opponent is mindfulness. Mindfulness is the life force of meditation, and forgetting the object is the enemy that destroys the life of meditation.

NON-ALERTNESS

The definition of non-alertness is a deluded mental factor that, being unable to distinguish faults from non-faults, causes us to develop faults.

Non-alertness is the opposite of alertness. Some people may have a strong wish to follow a spiritual path but, because they lack alertness, continue to commit non-virtuous actions. If we lack the wisdom to distinguish what is virtuous from what is non-virtuous our actions will often be faulty even though we mean well.

Alertness is a type of wisdom that knows what is a fault and what is not a fault. When we meditate, alertness acts like a spy that checks to see whether our concentration is pure. It examines the mind to see if dullness, distraction, mental excitement, or mental sinking are developing. If we do not use alertness to keep a watch on our mind during meditation we shall not notice dullness and mental sinking when they arise, and so there is a great danger that we shall fall asleep during our meditation. Without alertness we shall not be able to overcome the obstacles that occur in meditation, and so our concentration will be flawed and we shall not attain tranquil abiding. Even during our daily activities, if we do not use alertness to keep a watch on our mind we may receive many downfalls.

In *Guide to the Bodhisattva's Way of Life* Shantideva says:

Moreover, for those whose minds lack alertness,
The wisdoms from listening, contemplating, and
   meditating
Will not be retained by their memory,
Any more than water will remain in a leaky pot.

Even those who have much learning and faith
And who have sincerely applied great effort
Will become defiled by moral downfalls
Through the fault of lacking alertness.

There are four main causes of breaking our moral discipline, known as the 'four doors of receiving downfalls'. The first is not knowing what the downfalls are, which is non-alertness. The other three are lack of respect for Dharma, strong delusions, and non-conscientiousness.

These twenty delusions are branches of the six root delusions. They are called 'secondary delusions' because they can arise from any one of the root delusions. The source of all delusions is the three poisons – desirous attachment, hatred, and ignorance. These are the main objects to be abandoned by those seeking liberation.

The Four Changeable
Mental Factors

The four changeable mental factors are:

1 Sleep
2 Regret
3 Investigation
4 Analysis

Depending upon their motivation these mental factors can be virtuous, non-virtuous, or neutral, which is why they are called 'changeable'.

SLEEP

The definition of sleep is a mental factor that is developed through dullness or its imprints and that functions to gather the sense awarenesses inwards.

Sleep is a subtle mind. When a subtle mind becomes manifest, gross minds such as sense awarenesses necessarily become non-manifest, which is why sleep has the function of gathering the sense awarenesses inwards. For ordinary beings sleep helps to restore the energy of the body and to bring the elements of the body into harmony, thereby making the body comfortable and prolonging life. For practitioners of Tantra the yoga of sleep helps the development of the clear light of bliss. However, if we are attached to sleep it causes us to increase our laziness.

Skilful Dharma practitioners use their understanding of sleep, dreams, and waking to understand the development of death, intermediate state, and rebirth, because sleep is similar to death, dreams are similar to the intermediate state, and waking is similar to rebirth. Sleep is also the basis of the development of all the things we experience in dreams.

REGRET

The definition of regret is a mental factor that feels remorse for actions done in the past.

There are three types of regret: virtuous, non-virtuous, and neutral. Regret for previously committed non-virtuous actions is virtuous regret because it encourages us to purify our past negative actions and acts as the first of the four opponent powers. This type of regret is developed by recognizing the faults and disadvantages of non-virtuous actions. Those who have not heard teachings on karma, however, will find it difficult to develop sincere regret, and therefore will not be able to purify their negative actions. One of the greatest gifts of Dharma is that it teaches us how to purify our past non-virtues.

We need to develop regret for past negative actions before their effects have ripened. There is no point in feeling regret for non-virtuous actions whose effects have already ripened because it is too late to do anything about them. For example, someone might have been born blind as a result of a non-virtuous action such as maliciously injuring someone's eyes in a previous life, but there is no point in their feeling regret for that action now because its effects have already ripened. Developing regret for negative actions that have already ripened only causes us to feel dejected. It is better patiently to accept our misfortune. We should think:

I have no choice but to experience these present effects of my past non-virtuous actions; but I will protect myself from such misfortune in the future by not accumulating any more negative karma.

Feeling regret for previously created virtuous actions is non-virtuous regret. Some Dharma practitioners may develop this kind of regret by, for example, regretting having taken vows, or by becoming unhappy about having commitments, or by regretting having made an offering. For example, if we take the eight Mahayana precepts in the morning, and in the evening feel hungry and develop regret for having taken those precepts, this is non-virtuous regret. We should never develop such regret. Those who have taken ordination have to keep strict moral discipline and this occasionally causes them some inconvenience, but at such times they should not think that it would have been better not to have taken the vows.

Neutral regret is very common. For example, if we eat unhealthy food and then feel ill we regret having eaten it. This is neutral regret. Even though neutral regret is not non-virtuous it is generally better to avoid it because it can lead to unhappiness and serves no useful function. For example, if we start a business that subsequently fails, there is no point in our regretting having started it. Before doing anything we should carefully consider whether it is worthwhile, and whether we are able to carry the action through to completion. This is much better than acting rashly and regretting it later. There is a saying in Tibetan:

The wise person checks carefully beforehand;
The fool feels regret afterwards.

If despite careful planning our actions do not succeed, there is no need to become unhappy or to blame others. We should recognize that this is the result of our past negative actions and willingly accept it.

INVESTIGATION

The definition of investigation is a mental factor that examines an object to gain an understanding of its gross nature.

There are many ways in which we can examine, or search for, an object. For example, we can examine it superficially or in great detail. Usually if we are looking for something we stop searching as soon as we find it. For example, if we are looking for our car we know when we have found it and we do not investigate further, asking questions like 'What exactly is the car?' Only those engaged in philosophical analysis investigate an object in this way. We can all recognize our body quite easily because we have a superficial understanding of it, but only proponents of philosophical tenets who have investigated the body in depth come to conclusions about its ultimate nature. By asking questions like 'Is the body one of its parts or is it the collection of its parts?' we arrive at a conclusion about the real nature of the body. Some conclude that the body is findable, while others, notably the Madhyamika-Prasangikas, conclude that it is unfindable. Realizing the analytical unfindability of the body brings us close to realizing emptiness. This type of investigation is quite different from the investigations we conduct in everyday life.

There are two types of object to be investigated: conventional objects and ultimate objects. First we should investigate conventional objects. These are of many different types: gross, subtle, and very subtle natures. For example, a car, its parts, colour, and shape are all the gross nature of a car; the car depending upon its parts is the subtle nature of the car; and the car existing as mere name is the very subtle nature of the car. In *Guide to the Middle Way* Chandrakirti says:

> Nominal truths are the method for realizing ultimate
> truth.

Here, 'ultimate truth' refers to emptiness and 'nominal truths' to all other phenomena.

In general, we should first try to gain a rough understanding of Dharma subjects before analyzing them in great detail. If we try to make a detailed analysis of a subject before having gained a rough generic image of it through the force of investigation, we shall definitely encounter difficulties. Therefore, the correct way to proceed with Dharma study is first to try to understand gross objects by relying upon investigation, and then to try to understand subtle objects by relying upon analysis.

ANALYSIS

The definition of analysis is a mental factor that examines an object to gain an understanding of its subtle nature.

After we have understood an object superficially by investigating it, we need to sharpen our wisdom by analyzing the object in greater detail. For example, having attained a rough conceptual understanding of emptiness through investigation we then need to analyze emptiness in great detail to gain a clear and precise generic image of it. With this we can then go on to attain a yogic direct perceiver realizing emptiness.

When we begin to meditate on any object we perceive only a very rough mental image of it, but by continuing to meditate on it with analytical and placement meditation we gradually perceive the object more clearly until eventually we attain complete clear appearance of the object. This occurs when the generic image ceases and our mind transforms into a yogic direct perceiver. By continuing to meditate on the object, this yogic direct perceiver will eventually transform into the uncontaminated mind of a Buddha. The only way to progress from our initial superficial conceptual understanding of an object to the perfect wisdom of a Buddha is to depend upon investigation and analysis.

If we do not engage in analysis our understanding will remain at the level of a correct belief, which is not completely reliable and can be reversed. Therefore, we must engage in analysis to transform our correct beliefs into valid cognizers, and eventually into yogic direct perceivers.

Conclusion

This completes the explanation of *Understanding the Mind*. It is not enough simply to understand the mind – we need also to put this understanding into practice. The success of our practice depends upon three things: accumulating merit, because merit is the main condition for attaining Dharma realizations; purifying negative karma, because negative karma is the main obstacle to attaining Dharma realizations; and receiving the blessings of the Buddhas and Bodhisattvas, because blessings are the principal method for transforming our mind into the stages of the path. We can practise these three by reciting the prayers for the six preparatory practices that are included in the *Essence of Good Fortune* sadhana. This sadhana can be found in Appendix II.

Dedication

I have applied great effort and spent a long time composing this book, and the editors have also applied great effort. Through this action we have accumulated a vast collection of virtuous karma, or merit. Through the force of these virtues may pure Buddhadharma flourish extensively throughout the world; and thereby may all living beings become free from every kind of misery and find true and lasting happiness.

Appendix I
The Condensed Meaning
of the Text

The Condensed Meaning
of the Text

The explanation of *Understanding the Mind* begins with a presentation of object-possessors.

The definition of object-possessor is a functioning thing that expresses or cognizes an object.

There are three types of object-possessor:

1 Expressive sounds
2 Persons
3 Minds

The definition of expressive sound is an object of hearing that makes its expressed object understood.

There are three types of expressive sound:

1 Letters
2 Names
3 Phrases

The definition of letter is a vocalization that is a basis for the composition of names and phrases.

The definition of name is an object of hearing that principally expresses the name of any phenomenon.

The definition of phrase is an object of hearing that indicates a meaning by connecting a name with a predicate.

The definition of person is an I imputed in dependence upon any of the five aggregates.

Person, being, self, and I are synonyms.

There are three main divisions of person:

1 A twofold division into Buddhas and non-Buddhas
2 A twofold division into ordinary beings and Superior beings
3 A fivefold division into Buddhas, Bodhisattvas, Solitary Conquerors, Hearers, and migrating beings

The definition of mind is that which is clarity and cognizes.

There are five main divisions of mind:

1 A twofold division into conceptual minds and non-conceptual minds
2 A twofold division into sense awarenesses and mental awarenesses
3 A sevenfold division into direct perceivers, inferential cognizers, re-cognizers, correct beliefs, non-ascertaining perceivers, doubts, and wrong awarenesses
4 A twofold division into valid cognizers and non-valid cognizers
5 A twofold division into primary minds and mental factors

The definition of conceptual mind is a thought that apprehends its object through a generic image.

The definition of generic image is the appearing object of a conceptual mind.

There are three types of conceptual mind:

1 Conceptual minds that perceive the generic image of an object mainly through the force of listening or reading
2 Conceptual minds that perceive the generic image of an object mainly through the force of contemplating the meaning of that object

3 Conceptual minds that perceive the generic image
   of an object mainly through the force of previous
   imprints

There is also a twofold division of conceptual mind:

1 Correct conceptual minds
2 Wrong conceptual minds

The definition of non-conceptual mind is a cognizer to which
its object appears clearly without being mixed with a generic
image.

There are two types of non-conceptual mind:

1 Sense awarenesses
2 Non-conceptual mental awarenesses

There are three types of non-conceptual mental awareness:

1 Non-conceptual mental direct perceivers
2 Yogic direct perceivers
3 Non-conceptual mental awarenesses that are
   neither of these two

There is another twofold division of non-conceptual mind:

1 Correct non-conceptual minds
2 Wrong non-conceptual minds

The definition of sense awareness is an awareness that is
developed in dependence upon its uncommon dominant
condition, a sense power possessing form.

There are five types of sense awareness:

1 Eye awareness
2 Ear awareness
3 Nose awareness
4 Tongue awareness
5 Body awareness

The definition of eye awareness is an awareness that is
developed in dependence upon its uncommon dominant

condition, an eye sense power. This definition can be applied to the other four sense awarenesses by changing the uncommon dominant condition to the ear sense power, the nose sense power, the tongue sense power, or the body sense power.

The definition of dominant condition is that which principally assists the development of a sense or mental awareness.

There are two types of dominant condition:

1 Common dominant condition
2 Uncommon dominant condition

The definition of mental awareness is an awareness that is developed in dependence upon its uncommon dominant condition, a mental power.

The definition of mental power is a mentality that principally functions directly to produce the uncommon aspect of a mental awareness.

There are two types of mental awareness:

1 Conceptual mental awarenesses
2 Non-conceptual mental awarenesses

There is also a threefold division of mental awareness:

1 Non-virtuous mental awarenesses
2 Virtuous mental awarenesses
3 Neutral mental awarenesses

The definition of direct perceiver is a cognizer that apprehends its manifest object.

There are three types of direct perceiver:

1 Sense direct perceivers
2 Mental direct perceivers
3 Yogic direct perceivers

The definition of sense direct perceiver is a direct perceiver that is generated in dependence upon its uncommon dominant condition, a sense power possessing form.

There are five types of sense direct perceiver:

1 Eye sense direct perceivers
2 Ear sense direct perceivers
3 Nose sense direct perceivers
4 Tongue sense direct perceivers
5 Body sense direct perceivers

There is also a threefold division of sense direct perceiver:

1 Sense direct perceivers that are valid cognizers but not re-cognizers
2 Sense direct perceivers that are both valid cognizers and re-cognizers
3 Sense direct perceivers that are non-ascertaining perceivers

The definition of mental direct perceiver is a direct perceiver that is generated in dependence upon its uncommon dominant condition, a mental power.

There are three types of mental direct perceiver:

1 Mental direct perceivers induced by sense direct perceivers
2 Mental direct perceivers induced by meditation
3 Mental direct perceivers that are induced neither by sense direct perceivers nor by meditation

There are five types of mental direct perceiver induced by sense direct perceivers: mental direct perceivers apprehending forms, sounds, smells, tastes, and tactile objects.

The definition of yogic direct perceiver is a direct perceiver that realizes a subtle object directly, in dependence upon its uncommon dominant condition, a concentration that is a union of tranquil abiding and superior seeing.

There are two types of yogic direct perceiver:

1 Yogic direct perceivers in the continuum of Hinayanists
2 Yogic direct perceivers in the continuum of Mahayanists

There is also a fourfold division of yogic direct perceiver:

1 Yogic direct perceivers that are paths of preparation
2 Yogic direct perceivers that are paths of seeing
3 Yogic direct perceivers that are paths of meditation
4 Yogic direct perceivers that are Paths of No More Learning

There is another twofold division of yogic direct perceiver:

1 Yogic direct perceivers that realize the conventional nature of phenomena
2 Yogic direct perceivers that realize the ultimate nature of phenomena

The definition of inferential cognizer is a completely reliable cognizer whose object is realized in direct dependence upon a conclusive reason.

The definition of conclusive reason is a reason that is qualified by the three modes.

There are three types of inferential cognizer from the point of view of the type of reason upon which they depend:

1 Inferential cognizers through the power of fact
2 Inferential cognizers through belief
3 Inferential cognizers through renown

There is also a twofold division of inferential cognizer from the point of view of how they are generated:

1 Inferential cognizers arisen from listening
2 Inferential cognizers arisen from contemplation

The definition of re-cognizer is a cognizer that realizes what has already been realized through the force of a previous valid cognizer.

There are two types of re-cognizer:

1 Non-conceptual re-cognizers
2 Conceptual re-cognizers

There are three types of non-conceptual re-cognizer:

1 Re-cognizers that are sense direct perceivers
2 Re-cognizers that are non-conceptual mental direct perceivers
3 Re-cognizers that are yogic direct perceivers

There are two types of conceptual re-cognizer:

1 Conceptual re-cognizers induced by direct perceivers
2 Conceptual re-cognizers induced by inferential cognizers

There are three types of conceptual re-cognizer induced by direct perceivers: those induced by sense direct perceivers; those induced by mental direct perceivers; and those induced by yogic direct perceivers.

The definition of correct belief is a non-valid cognizer that realizes its conceived object.

There are two types of correct belief:

1 Correct beliefs that do not depend upon a reason
2 Correct beliefs that depend upon a reason

The definition of non-ascertaining perceiver is a cognizer to which a phenomenon that is its engaged object appears clearly without being ascertained.

There are two types of non-ascertaining perceiver:

1 Non-ascertaining sense direct perceivers
2 Non-ascertaining mental direct perceivers

The definition of doubt is a mental factor that wavers with respect to its object.

There are two types of doubt:

1 Deluded doubts
2 Non-deluded doubts

There is also a threefold division of doubt:

1 Doubts tending towards the truth
2 Doubts tending away from the truth
3 Balanced doubts

There is another threefold division of doubt:

1 Virtuous doubts
2 Non-virtuous doubts
3 Neutral doubts

The definition of wrong awareness is a cognizer that is mistaken with respect to its engaged object.

There are two types of wrong awareness:

1 Non-conceptual wrong awarenesses
2 Conceptual wrong awarenesses

There are two types of non-conceptual wrong awareness:

1 Wrong sense awarenesses
2 Wrong non-conceptual mental awarenesses

A wrong sense awareness can be mistaken with respect to its object in any of seven different ways: being mistaken with respect to its object's shape, colour, activity, number, time, measurement, or entity.

There are two types of conceptual wrong awareness:

1 Intellectually-formed wrong awarenesses
2 Innate wrong awarenesses

There are four causes of wrong sense awareness:

1 A deceptive quality of the object
2 A deceptive situation
3 A defective sense power
4 A fault in the preceding awareness

There are three types of valid:

1 Valid Teachers
2 Valid teachings
3 Valid cognizers

The definition of valid Teacher is a Teacher who knows fully and without error what objects are to be abandoned and what objects are to be practised, and who, out of compassion, reveals this knowledge to others.

The definition of valid teaching is an instruction that principally explains without error the objects to be abandoned and how to abandon them, and the objects to be practised and how to practise them.

The definition of valid cognizer is a cognizer that is non-deceptive with respect to its engaged object.

There are two types of valid cognizer:

1 Direct valid cognizers
2 Inferential valid cognizers

The definition of direct valid cognizer is a non-deceptive cognizer that apprehends its manifest object.

The definition of manifest object is an object whose initial realization by a valid cognizer does not depend upon logical reasons.

There are three types of direct valid cognizer:

1 Valid sense direct cognizers
2 Valid mental direct cognizers
3 Valid yogic direct cognizers

The definition of inferential valid cognizer is a non-deceptive cognizer that realizes its hidden object by depending upon a conclusive reason.

The definition of hidden object is an object whose initial realization by a valid cognizer depends upon correct logical reasons.

There are three types of inferential valid cognizer:

1 Inferential valid cognizers through the power of fact
2 Inferential valid cognizers through belief
3 Inferential valid cognizers through renown

The definition of non-valid cognizer is a cognizer that is deceptive with respect to its engaged object.

There are two types of non-valid cognizer:

1 Non-conceptual non-valid cognizers
2 Conceptual non-valid cognizers

The definition of primary mind is a cognizer that principally apprehends the mere entity of an object.

Primary mind, mentality, and consciousness are synonyms.

There are six types of primary mind:

1 Eye consciousness
2 Ear consciousness
3 Nose consciousness
4 Tongue consciousness
5 Body consciousness
6 Mental consciousness

The definition of mental factor is a cognizer that principally apprehends a particular attribute of an object.

A primary mind and its mental factors possess five similarities:

1 Basis
2 Object
3 Aspect
4 Time
5 Substance

There are fifty-one mental factors, which are divided into six groups:

1 The five all-accompanying mental factors
2 The five object-ascertaining mental factors
3 The eleven virtuous mental factors
4 The six root delusions
5 The twenty secondary delusions
6 The four changeable mental factors

The five all-accompanying mental factors are:

1 Feeling
2 Discrimination
3 Intention
4 Contact
5 Attention

The definition of feeling is a mental factor that functions to experience pleasant, unpleasant, or neutral objects.

There are three types of feeling:

1 Pleasant feelings
2 Unpleasant feelings
3 Neutral feelings

There is also a twofold division of feeling from the point of view of their uncommon dominant condition:

1 Bodily feelings
2 Mental feelings

There is another twofold division of feeling from the point of view of their nature:

1 Contaminated feelings
2 Uncontaminated feelings

The definition of discrimination is a mental factor that functions to apprehend the uncommon sign of an object.

There are six types of discrimination:

1 Discriminations associated with eye consciousness
2 Discriminations associated with ear consciousness
3 Discriminations associated with nose consciousness
4 Discriminations associated with tongue consciousness
5 Discriminations associated with body consciousness
6 Discriminations associated with mental consciousness

There is also a twofold division of discrimination:

1 Mistaken discriminations
2 Non-mistaken discriminations

There is another twofold division of discrimination:

1 Clear discriminations
2 Unclear discriminations

The definition of intention is a mental factor that functions to move its primary mind to the object.

There are three types of intention:

1 Non-virtuous intentions
2 Virtuous intentions
3 Neutral intentions

There are three types of non-virtuous action:

1 Non-virtuous bodily actions
2 Non-virtuous verbal actions
3 Non-virtuous mental actions

There is another threefold division of intention:

1 Meritorious actions
2 Non-meritorious actions
3 Unfluctuating actions

There is a threefold division of both meritorious and non-meritorious actions: those that are throwing karma; those that are completing karma; and those that are karma whose results are experienced in the same life.

The definition of contact is a mental factor that functions to perceive its object as pleasant, unpleasant, or neutral.

There are six types of contact:

1 Contact associated with eye consciousness
2 Contact associated with ear consciousness
3 Contact associated with nose consciousness
4 Contact associated with tongue consciousness
5 Contact associated with body consciousness
6 Contact associated with mental consciousness

The definition of attention is a mental factor that functions to focus the mind on a particular attribute of an object.

There are two types of attention:

1 Correct attention
2 Incorrect attention

There is another twofold division of attention:

1 Appropriate attention
2 Inappropriate attention

The five object-ascertaining mental factors are:

1 Aspiration
2 Firm apprehension
3 Mindfulness
4 Concentration
5 Wisdom

The definition of aspiration is a mental factor that focuses on a desired object and takes an interest in it.

There are four types of aspiration:

1 Wishing to meet an object
2 Wishing not to be separated from an object
3 Wishing to obtain an object
4 Wishing to be released from an object

Each of these can be virtuous, non-virtuous, or neutral, depending upon its motivation.

There is also a twofold division of aspiration:

1 Mistaken aspirations
2 Non-mistaken aspirations

The definition of firm apprehension is a mental factor that makes its primary mind apprehend its object firmly.

There are two types of firm apprehension:

1 Correct firm apprehensions
2 Mistaken firm apprehensions

The definition of mindfulness is a mental factor that functions not to forget the object realized by the primary mind.

There are two types of mindfulness:

1 New mindfulness
2 Old mindfulness

There is another twofold division of mindfulness:

1 Mindfulness with movements of mental sinking
  and mental excitement
2 Mindfulness without movements of mental sinking
  and mental excitement

The definition of concentration is a mental factor that makes
its primary mind remain on its object single-pointedly.

There are nine levels of concentration from the point of view
of realm:

1 Concentration of the desire realm
2 Concentration of the first form realm
3 Concentration of the second form realm
4 Concentration of the third form realm
5 Concentration of the fourth form realm
6 Concentration of infinite space
7 Concentration of infinite consciousness
8 Concentration of nothingness
9 Concentration of peak of samsara

There are nine levels of desire realm concentration:

1 Placing the mind
2 Continual placement
3 Replacement
4 Close placement
5 Controlling
6 Pacifying
7 Completely pacifying
8 Single-pointedness
9 Placement in equipoise

There are two types of concentration from the point of view
of their effect:

1 Mundane concentrations
2 Supramundane concentrations

There is another twofold division of concentration from the point of view of their object:

1 Concentrations observing conventional objects
2 Concentrations observing ultimate objects

The definition of wisdom is a virtuous, intelligent mind that makes its primary mind realize its object thoroughly.

There are three types of wisdom:

1 Wisdom arisen from listening
2 Wisdom arisen from contemplation
3 Wisdom arisen from meditation

There is also a sevenfold division of wisdom:

1 Great wisdom
2 Clear wisdom
3 Quick wisdom
4 Profound wisdom
5 The wisdom of expounding Dharma
6 The wisdom of spiritual debate
7 The wisdom of composing Dharma books

The eleven virtuous mental factors are:

1 Faith
2 Sense of shame
3 Consideration for others
4 Non-attachment
5 Non-hatred
6 Non-ignorance
7 Effort
8 Mental suppleness
9 Conscientiousness
10 Equanimity
11 Non-harmfulness

The definition of faith is a mental factor that functions principally to eliminate non-faith.

259

There are three types of faith:

1 Believing faith
2 Admiring faith
3 Wishing faith

The definition of sense of shame is a mental factor that functions to avoid inappropriate actions for reasons that concern oneself.

There are three types of sense of shame:

1 Sense of shame that restrains us from inappropriate bodily actions
2 Sense of shame that restrains us from inappropriate verbal actions
3 Sense of shame that restrains us from inappropriate mental actions

There is also a twofold division of sense of shame:

1 Sense of shame that restrains us from inappropriate actions out of concern simply for ourself
2 Sense of shame that restrains us from inappropriate actions out of concern for the specific undesirable results for ourself

The definition of consideration for others is a mental factor that functions to avoid inappropriate actions for reasons that concern others.

There are three types of consideration for others:

1 Consideration for others that restrains us from inappropriate bodily actions
2 Consideration for others that restrains us from inappropriate verbal actions
3 Consideration for others that restrains us from inappropriate mental actions

There is also a twofold division of consideration for others:

1 Consideration for others that restrains us from inappropriate actions out of concern simply for others
2 Consideration for others that restrains us from inappropriate actions out of concern for the specific undesirable results for others

The definition of non-attachment is a mental factor that functions as the direct opponent of attachment.

There are three types of non-attachment:

1 Non-attachment to samsaric places
2 Non-attachment to samsaric enjoyments
3 Non-attachment to samsaric bodies

There is another threefold division of non-attachment:

1 Non-attachment to this life
2 Non-attachment to samsara
3 Non-attachment to solitary peace

The definition of non-hatred is a mental factor that functions as the direct opponent of hatred.

There are three types of non-hatred:

1 Non-hatred towards those who harm us
2 Non-hatred towards inanimate objects that cause us suffering
3 Non-hatred towards resultant suffering

The definition of non-ignorance is a mental factor that functions as the direct opponent of ignorance.

There are four types of non-ignorance:

1 Non-ignorance arisen from listening
2 Non-ignorance arisen from contemplation
3 Non-ignorance arisen from meditation
4 Non-ignorance arisen from imprints

The definition of effort is a mental factor that makes its primary mind delight in virtue.

There are four types of effort:

1 Armour-like effort
2 Effort of non-discouragement
3 Effort of application
4 Effort of non-satisfaction

There is also a fivefold division of effort:

1 Armour-like effort
2 Effort of non-discouragement
3 Effort of application
4 Effort of non-satisfaction
5 Effort of irreversibility

There is also a threefold division of effort:

1 Armour-like effort
2 Effort of gathering virtuous Dharmas
3 Effort of benefiting others

There are four powers:

1 The power of aspiration
2 The power of steadfastness
3 The power of joy
4 The power of rejection

The definition of mental suppleness is a flexibility of mind induced by virtuous concentration.

There are two types of mental suppleness:

1 Subtle mental suppleness
2 Gross mental suppleness

The definition of conscientiousness is a mental factor that, in dependence upon effort, cherishes what is virtuous and guards the mind from delusion and non-virtue.

There are two types of conscientiousness:

1 Conscientiousness that is a virtuous root of mundane paths
2 Conscientiousness that is a virtuous root of supramundane paths

The definition of equanimity is a mental factor that functions to keep the primary mind free from mental sinking and mental excitement.

There are three types of equanimity:

1 Equanimity that requires gross effort
2 Equanimity that requires subtle effort
3 Equanimity that requires no effort

The definition of non-harmfulness is a mental factor that wishes sentient beings not to suffer.

There are two types of non-harmfulness, or compassion:

1 Compassion wishing sentient beings to be free from suffering
2 Compassion wishing sentient beings to be free from the causes of suffering

There is another twofold division of compassion:

1 Mere compassion
2 Superior compassion

The definition of virtue is a phenomenon that functions as a main cause of happiness.

There are five types of virtue:

1 Natural virtue
2 Virtue by association
3 Virtue by motivation
4 Virtue by subsequent relation
5 Ultimate virtue

The definition of non-virtue is a phenomenon that functions as a main cause of suffering.

There are five types of non-virtue:

1 Natural non-virtue
2 Non-virtue by association
3 Non-virtue by motivation
4 Non-virtue by subsequent relation
5 Ultimate non-virtue

The definition of delusion is a mental factor that arises from inappropriate attention and that functions to make the mind unpeaceful and uncontrolled.

There are six causes of delusion:

1 The seed
2 The object
3 Inappropriate attention
4 Familiarity
5 Distraction and being influenced by others
6 Bad habits

There are three types of delusion from the point of view of realm:

1 Delusions of the desire realm
2 Delusions of the form realm
3 Delusions of the formless realm

There are nine levels, from big-big to small-small, of each of the delusions of the desire realm, and of each of the delusions of each level of the form and formless realms, making eighty-one levels of delusion in all.

There is also a twofold division of delusion from the point of view of their cause:

1 Innate delusions
2 Intellectually-formed delusions

There is another twofold division of delusion from the point of view of entity:

1 Root delusions
2 Secondary delusions

The six root delusions are:

1 Desirous attachment
2 Anger
3 Deluded pride
4 Ignorance
5 Deluded doubt
6 Deluded view

The definition of desirous attachment is a deluded mental factor that observes its contaminated object, regards it as a cause of happiness, and wishes for it.

There are three types of desirous attachment from the point of view of time:

1 Desirous attachment to past objects
2 Desirous attachment to present objects
3 Desirous attachment to future objects

From the point of view of entity, desirous attachment can be divided into three – big, middling, and small – or into eighty-one – the nine levels of desirous attachment of each of the nine realms. These are all included within three:

1 Desire realm desirous attachment
2 Form realm desirous attachment
3 Formless realm desirous attachment

There is another threefold division of desirous attachment from the point of view of its object:

1 Desirous attachment to samsaric places
2 Desirous attachment to samsaric enjoyments
3 Desirous attachment to samsaric bodies

The definition of anger is a deluded mental factor that observes its contaminated object, exaggerates its bad qualities, considers it to be undesirable, and wishes to harm it.

There are nine types of anger from the point of view of entity, from big-big to small-small.

There is another ninefold division of anger from the point of view of how it is generated:

1 Anger towards someone or something that harmed us in the past
2 Anger towards someone or something that is harming us now
3 Anger towards someone or something that might harm us in the future
4 Anger towards someone or something that harmed our friends or relatives in the past
5 Anger towards someone or something that is harming our friends or relatives now
6 Anger towards someone or something that might harm our friends or relatives in the future
7 Anger towards someone or something that helped our enemy in the past
8 Anger towards someone or something that is helping our enemy now
9 Anger towards someone or something that might help our enemy in the future

The definition of deluded pride is a deluded mental factor that, through considering and exaggerating one's own good qualities or possessions, feels arrogant.

There are seven types of deluded pride:

1 Pride over inferiors
2 Pride over equals
3 Pride over superiors
4 Pride in identity
5 Pretentious pride

6 Emulating pride
7 Wrong pride

The definition of ignorance according to Asanga and Vasu-bandhu is a mental factor that is confused about the nature of an object and that functions to induce wrong awareness, doubt, and other delusions.

The definition of ignorance according to Chandrakirti and Dharmakirti is a mental factor that is the opposite of the wisdom apprehending selflessness.

There are two types of ignorance:

1 Ignorance of conventional truths
2 Ignorance of ultimate truths

There is another twofold division of ignorance:

1 Ignorance of actions and their effects
2 Ignorance of emptiness

The definition of deluded doubt is a two-pointedness of mind that interferes with the attainment of liberation or enlightenment.

There are three types of doubt in general:

1 Doubts tending towards the truth
2 Doubts tending away from the truth
3 Balanced doubts

The definition of deluded view is a view that functions to obstruct the attainment of liberation.

There are five types of deluded view:

1 View of the transitory collection
2 Extreme view
3 Holding false views as supreme
4 Holding wrong moral disciplines and conduct as supreme
5 Wrong view

The definition of view of the transitory collection is a type of self-grasping of persons that grasps one's own I as being an inherently existent I.

There are two types of view of the transitory collection:

1 View of the transitory collection conceiving I
2 View of the transitory collection conceiving mine

There is another twofold division of view of the transitory collection:

1 Innate view of the transitory collection
2 Intellectually-formed view of the transitory collection

There are twenty intellectually-formed views of the transitory collection, four in relation to each of the five aggregates.

The definition of extreme view is a deluded view that observes the I that is the conceived object of the view of the transitory collection and grasps it either as permanent or as completely ceasing at the time of death.

The definition of holding false views as supreme is a deluded view that holds a false view to be correct and superior to other views.

The definition of holding wrong moral disciplines and conduct as supreme is a deluded view that holds any wrong moral discipline or conduct to be correct and considers it to be superior to other forms of moral discipline or conduct.

The definition of wrong view is an intellectually-formed wrong awareness that denies the existence of an object that it is necessary to understand to attain liberation or enlightenment.

The twenty secondary delusions are:

1 Aggression
2 Resentment
3 Spite
4 Jealousy
5 Miserliness
6 Concealment
7 Pretension
8 Denial
9 Self-satisfaction
10 Harmfulness
11 Shamelessness
12 Inconsideration
13 Dullness
14 Distraction
15 Mental excitement
16 Non-faith
17 Laziness
18 Non-conscientiousness
19 Deluded forgetfulness
20 Non-alertness

The definition of aggression is an increase of the root delusion anger that wishes to hurt or harm others physically or verbally.

The definition of resentment is a deluded mental factor that maintains the continuum of anger without forgetting it, and wishes to retaliate.

The definition of spite is a mental factor that, motivated by resentment or aggression, wishes to speak harshly.

The definition of jealousy is a deluded mental factor that feels displeasure when observing others' enjoyments, good qualities, or good fortune.

The definition of miserliness is a deluded mental factor that, motivated by desirous attachment, holds onto things tightly and does not want to part with them.

The definition of concealment is a deluded mental factor that, motivated by attachment to wealth or reputation, wishes to conceal our faults from others.

The definition of pretension is a deluded mental factor that, motivated by attachment to wealth or reputation, wishes to pretend that we possess qualities that we do not possess.

The definition of denial is a deluded mental factor that does not wish to purify non-virtuous actions that we have committed or downfalls that we have incurred.

The definition of self-satisfaction is a deluded mental factor that observes our own physical beauty, wealth, or other good qualities, and, being concerned only with these, has no interest in spiritual development.

The definition of harmfulness is a deluded mental factor that wishes other sentient beings to suffer.

The definition of shamelessness is a deluded mental factor that is the opposite of sense of shame.

The definition of inconsideration is a deluded mental factor that is the opposite of consideration for others.

The definition of dullness is a deluded mental factor that functions to make both the body and mind heavy and inflexible.

The definition of distraction is a deluded mental factor that wanders to any object of delusion.

The definition of mental excitement is a deluded mental factor that wanders to any object of attachment.

The definition of non-faith is a deluded mental factor that is the opposite of faith.

The definition of laziness is a deluded mental factor that, motivated by attachment to worldly pleasures or worldly activities, dislikes virtuous activity.

The definition of non-conscientiousness is a deluded mental factor that wishes to engage in non-virtuous actions without restraint.

The definition of deluded forgetfulness is a deluded mental factor that makes us forget a virtuous object.

The definition of non-alertness is a deluded mental factor that, being unable to distinguish faults from non-faults, causes us to develop faults.

The four changeable mental factors are:

1 Sleep
2 Regret
3 Investigation
4 Analysis

The definition of sleep is a mental factor that is developed through dullness or its imprints and that functions to gather the sense awarenesses inwards.

The definition of regret is a mental factor that feels remorse for actions done in the past.

The definition of investigation is a mental factor that examines an object to gain an understanding of its gross nature.

The definition of analysis is a mental factor that examines an object to gain an understanding of its subtle nature.

Appendix II
Essence of Good Fortune

PRAYERS FOR THE SIX PREPARATORY PRACTICES
FOR MEDITATION ON THE STAGES OF
THE PATH TO ENLIGHTENMENT

Introduction

Developing the realizations of the stages of the path to enlightenment depends upon four things: accumulating merit, purifying negativities, receiving the blessings of the Buddhas, Bodhisattvas, and Spiritual Guides, and training the mind in the actual meditation on the stages of the path. The supreme method for accomplishing the first three is the six preparatory practices. These are:

1 Cleaning the meditation room and setting up a shrine with representations of Buddha's body, speech, and mind.
2 Arranging suitable offerings.
3 Sitting in the correct meditation posture, going for refuge, generating and enhancing bodhichitta.
4 Visualizing the Field for Accumulating Merit.
5 Accumulating merit and purifying negativity by offering the practice of the seven limbs and the mandala.
6 Requesting the Field for Accumulating Merit in general and the Lamrim lineage Gurus in particular to bestow their blessings.

The essence of these six preparatory practices is contained in the following prayers, which should be recited with each session of meditation.

Essence of Good Fortune

Mentally purifying the environment

May the whole ground
Become completely pure,
As level as the palm of a hand,
And as smooth as lapis lazuli.

Mentally arranging pure offerings

May all of space be filled
With offerings from gods and men,
Both set out and imagined,
Like offerings of the All Good One.

Visualizing the objects of refuge

In the space in front, on a lion throne, on a cushion
of lotus, sun, and moon, sits Buddha Shakyamuni,
the essence of all my kind Teachers, surrounded by
the assembly of direct and indirect Gurus, Yidams,
Buddhas, Bodhisattvas, Hearers, Solitary Conquerors,
Heroes, Dakinis, and Dharma Protectors.

Generating the causes of going for refuge

I and all my kind mothers, fearing samsara's torments,
turn to Buddha, Dharma, and Sangha, the only sources
of refuge. From now until enlightenment, to the Three
Jewels we go for refuge.

Short prayer of going for refuge

I and all sentient beings, until we achieve enlightenment,
‚Go for refuge to Buddha, Dharma, and Sangha.

(7x, 100x, etc.)

Generating bodhichitta

Through the virtues I collect by giving and other perfections,
May I become a Buddha for the benefit of all.   (3x)

Purifying and receiving blessings

From the hearts of all refuge objects, lights and nectars
stream down and dissolve into myself and all living
beings, purifying negative karma and obstructions,
increasing our lives, our virtues, and Dharma realizations.

Generating the four immeasurables

May everyone be happy,
May everyone be free from misery,
May no one ever be separated from their happiness,
May everyone have equanimity, free from hatred and
    attachment.

Inviting the Field for Accumulating Merit

You, Protector of all beings,
Great Destroyer of hosts of demons,
Please, O Blessed One, Knower of All,
Come to this place with your retinue.

Prayer of seven limbs

With my body, speech, and mind, humbly I prostrate,
And make offerings both set out and imagined.
I confess my wrong deeds from all time,
And rejoice in the virtues of all.
Please stay until samsara ceases,
And turn the Wheel of Dharma for us.
I dedicate all virtues to great enlightenment.

Offering the mandala

The ground sprinkled with perfume and spread with
flowers,
The Great Mountain, four lands, sun and moon,
Seen as a Buddha Land and offered thus,
May all beings enjoy such Pure Lands.

I offer without any sense of loss
The objects that give rise to my attachment, hatred, and
confusion,
My friends, enemies, and strangers, our bodies and
enjoyments;
Please accept these and bless me to be released directly
from the three poisons.

IDAM GURU RATNA MANDALAKAM NIRYATAYAMI

Requests to the Field for Accumulating Merit and the Lamrim lineage Gurus

So now my most kind root Guru,
Please sit on the lotus and moon on my crown
And grant me out of your great kindness,
Your body, speech, and mind's attainments.

*Visualize that your root Guru comes to the crown of your
head and makes the following requests with you:*

I make requests to you, Buddha Shakyamuni,
Whose body comes from countless virtues,
Whose speech fulfils the hopes of mortals,
Whose mind sees clearly all existence.

I make requests to you, Gurus of the lineage of extensive
deeds,
Venerable Maitreya, Noble Asanga, Vasubandhu,
And all the other precious Teachers
Who have revealed the path of vastness.

I make requests to you, Gurus of the lineage of profound
   view,
Venerable Manjushri, Nagarjuna, Chandrakirti,
And all the other precious Teachers
Who have revealed the most profound path.

I make requests to you, Gurus of the lineage of Secret
   Mantra,
Conqueror Vajradhara, Tilopa, and Naropa,
And all the other precious Teachers
Who have revealed the path of Tantra.

I make requests to you, Gurus of the Old Kadam
   lineage,
The second Buddha Atisha, Dromtönpa, Geshe Potowa,
And all the other precious Teachers
Who have revealed the union of vast and profound paths.

I make requests to you, Gurus of the New Kadam
   lineage,
Venerable Tsongkhapa, Jampäl Gyatso, Khädrubje,
And all the other precious Teachers
Who have revealed the union of Sutra and Tantra.

I make requests to you, Venerable Kelsang Gyatso,
Protector of a vast ocean of living beings,
Unequalled Teacher of the paths to liberation and
   enlightenment,
Who accomplish and explain everything that was
   revealed
By the Fourth Deliverer of this Fortunate Aeon.

I make requests to you, my kind precious Teacher,
Who care for those with uncontrolled minds
Untamed by all the previous Buddhas,
As if they were fortunate disciples.

Requesting the three great purposes

Please pour down your inspiring blessings upon myself
and all my mothers so that we may quickly stop all
perverse minds, from disrespect for our kind Teacher
to the most subtle dual appearance.

Please pour down your inspiring blessings so that we may
quickly generate pure minds, from respect for our kind
Teacher to the supreme mind of Union.

Please pour down your inspiring blessings to pacify all
outer and inner obstructions.   (3x)

Receiving blessings and purifying

From the hearts of all the holy beings, streams of light and
nectar flow down, granting blessings and purifying.

Prayer of the Stages of the Path

The path begins with strong reliance
On my kind Teacher, source of all good;
O Bless me with this understanding
To follow him with great devotion.

This human life with all its freedoms,
Extremely rare, with so much meaning;
O Bless me with this understanding
All day and night to seize its essence.

My body, like a water bubble,
Decays and dies so very quickly;
After death come results of karma,
Just like the shadow of a body.

With this firm knowledge and remembrance
Bless me to be extremely cautious,
Always avoiding harmful actions
And gathering abundant virtue.

Samsara's pleasures are deceptive,
Give no contentment, only torment;
So please bless me to strive sincerely
To gain the bliss of perfect freedom.

O Bless me so that from this pure thought
Come mindfulness and greatest caution,
To keep as my essential practice
The doctrine's root, the Pratimoksha.

Just like myself all my kind mothers
Are drowning in samsara's ocean;
O So that I may soon release them,
Bless me to train in bodhichitta.

But I cannot become a Buddha
By this alone without three ethics;
So bless me with the strength to practise
The Bodhisattva's ordination.

By pacifying my distractions
And analyzing perfect meanings,
Bless me to quickly gain the union
Of special insight and quiescence.

When I become a pure container
Through common paths, bless me to enter
The essence practice of good fortune,
The supreme vehicle, Vajrayana.

The two attainments both depend on
My sacred vows and my commitments;
Bless me to understand this clearly
And keep them at the cost of my life.

By constant practice in four sessions,
The way explained by holy Teachers,
O Bless me to gain both the stages,
Which are the essence of the Tantras.

May those who guide me on the good path,
And my companions all have long lives;
Bless me to pacify completely
All obstacles, outer and inner.

May I always find perfect Teachers,
And take delight in holy Dharma,
Accomplish all grounds and paths swiftly,
And gain the state of Vajradhara.

You may do your meditation here or at any appropriate point within the Prayer of the Stages of the Path.

Mantra recitation

After our meditation we contemplate that from the heart of Buddha Shakyamuni, the principal Field of Merit in front of us, infinite light rays emanate, reaching all environments and all beings. These dissolve into light and gradually gather into the Field of Merit. This dissolves into the central figure, Buddha Shakyamuni, who then dissolves into our root Guru at the crown of our head, instantly transforming him into the aspect of Guru Buddha Shakyamuni. He then diminishes in size, enters through our crown, and descends to our heart. His mind and our mind become one nature. We recite the mantra:

OM MUNI MUNI MAHA MUNIYE SÖHA   (7x, 100x, etc.)

Dedication prayers

Through the virtues I have collected
By practising the stages of the path,
May all living beings find the opportunity
To practise in the same way.

However many living beings there are
Experiencing mental and physical suffering,
May their suffering cease through the power of my merit,
And may they find everlasting happiness and joy.

May everyone experience
The happiness of humans and gods,
And quickly attain enlightenment,
So that samsara is finally extinguished.

For the benefit of all living beings as extensive as space,
May I attain great wisdom like that of Manjushri,
Great compassion like that of Avalokiteshvara,
Great power like that of Vajrapani.

The Buddhadharma is the supreme medicine
That relieves all mental pain,
So may this precious Dharma Jewel
Pervade all worlds throughout space.

May there arise in the minds of all living beings
Great faith in Buddha, Dharma, and Sangha,
And thus may they always receive
The blessings of the Three Precious Gems.

May there never arise in this world
The miseries of incurable disease, famine, or war,
Or the dangers of earthquakes, fires,
Floods, storms, and so forth.

May all mother beings meet precious Teachers
Who reveal the stages of the path to enlightenment,
And through engaging in this path
May they quickly attain the ultimate peace of full
  enlightenment.

Through the blessings of the Buddhas and Bodhisattvas,
The truth of actions and their effects,
And the power of my pure superior intention,
May all my prayers be fulfilled.

If we are unable to recite all these prayers for the six prepa-
ratory practices in every meditation session, we should at least
always remember Guru Buddha Shakyamuni at the crown of
our head, recalling that his mind is the synthesis of all
Buddha Jewels, his speech the synthesis of all Dharma Jewels,

and his body the synthesis of all Sangha Jewels. Then with strong faith we should go for refuge by reciting the short prayer of going for refuge, generate bodhichitta with the words, 'Through the virtues … for the benefit of all', offer the mandala, request the three great purposes, and receive blessings and purify.

If we perform these three practices every time we sit down to meditate – namely, accumulating merit, purifying negative karma, and making requests to receive blessings and inspiration – we will have accomplished the three purposes of engaging in preparatory practices. At the conclusion of every meditation session, we should dedicate our merit.

Colophon: These prayers were compiled from traditional sources by Geshe Kelsang Gyatso Rinpoche. The verse of request to Geshe Kelsang Gyatso was composed by the Dharma Protector Duldzin Dorje Shugdän and included in the prayers at the request of Geshe Kelsang's faithful disciples.

Glossary

Aggregate In general, all functioning things are aggregates because they are an aggregation of their parts. In particular, a person of the desire realm or form realm has five aggregates: the aggregates of form, feeling, discrimination, compositional factors, and consciousness. A being of the formless realm lacks the aggregate of form but has the other four. A person's form aggregate is his or her body. The remaining four aggregates are aspects of his mind. See also *Contaminated aggregate*. See *Heart of Wisdom*.

Asanga A great Indian Buddhist Yogi and scholar of the fifth century, author of *Compendium of Abhidharma*.

Aspiring bodhichitta A bodhichitta that is a mere wish to attain enlightenment for the benefit of all living beings. See also *Bodhichitta*.

Basis of imputation All phenomena are imputed upon their parts; therefore, any of the individual parts, or the entire collection of the parts, of any phenomenon is its basis of imputation. A phenomenon is imputed by mind in dependence upon its basis of imputation appearing to that mind. See *Heart of Wisdom*.

Beginningless time According to the Buddhist world view, there is no beginning to mind, and so no beginning to time. Therefore, all sentient beings have taken countless previous rebirths.

Blessing 'Jin gyi lab pa' in Tibetan. The transformation of our mind from a negative state to a positive state, from an unhappy state to a happy state, or from a state of weakness to a state of strength, through the inspiration of holy beings such as our Spiritual Guide, Buddhas, and Bodhisattvas.

Bodhichitta Sanskrit word for 'mind of enlightenment'. 'Bodhi' means 'enlightenment', and 'chitta' means 'mind'. There are two types of bodhichitta – conventional bodhichitta and ultimate bodhichitta. Generally speaking, the term 'bodhichitta' refers to conventional bodhichitta, which is a primary mind motivated by great compassion that spontaneously seeks enlightenment to benefit all living beings. There are two types of conventional bodhichitta – aspiring bodhichitta and engaging bodhichitta. Ultimate bodhichitta is a wisdom motivated by conventional bodhichitta that directly realizes emptiness, the ultimate nature of phenomena. See also *Aspiring bodhichitta* and *Engaging bodhichitta*. See *Joyful Path of Good Fortune* and *Meaningful to Behold*.

Bodhisattva A person who has generated spontaneous bodhichitta but who has not yet become a Buddha. See *Joyful Path of Good Fortune* and *Meaningful to Behold*.

Buddha A being who has completely abandoned all delusions and their imprints. There are many people who have become Buddhas in the past, and many people will become Buddhas in the future. See also *Buddha Shakyamuni*. See *Joyful Path of Good Fortune*.

Buddha nature The root mind of a sentient being, and its ultimate nature. Buddha nature, Buddha seed, and Buddha lineage are synonyms. All sentient beings have Buddha nature and therefore the potential to attain Buddhahood.

Buddha Shakyamuni The fourth of one thousand founding Buddhas who are to appear in this world during this Fortunate Aeon. The first three were Krakuchchanda, Kanakamuni, and Kashyapa. The fifth Buddha will be Maitreya. See *Introduction to Buddhism*.

Buddhadharma See *Dharma*.

Buddhist Anyone who from the depths of his or her heart goes for refuge to the Three Jewels – Buddha Jewel, Dharma Jewel, and Sangha Jewel. See *Introduction to Buddhism*.

Central channel The principal channel at the very centre of the body, along which the channel wheels are located. See *Clear Light of Bliss*.

Chakra Sanskrit word for 'channel wheel'. A focal centre where secondary channels branch out from the central channel. Meditating on these points can cause the inner winds to enter the central channel. See *Clear Light of Bliss*.

Chandrakirti A great Indian Buddhist scholar and meditation master who composed, among many other books, the well-known *Guide to the Middle Way*, in which he clearly elucidates the view of the Madhyamika-Prasangika school according to Buddha's teachings given in the *Perfection of Wisdom Sutras*. See *Ocean of Nectar*.

Charavaka A non-Buddhist nihilist school current in Buddha's day, which denied inferential cognizers, rebirth, the laws of karma, and so forth, and which encouraged a hedonistic attitude to life. See *Ocean of Nectar*.

Chittamatra The lower of the two schools of Mahayana tenets. 'Chittamatra' means 'mind only'. They are so-called because they assert that all phenomena are merely the nature of mind. A Chittamatrin is a proponent of Chittamatra tenets. See *Meaningful to Behold* and *Ocean of Nectar*.

Clear light A manifest very subtle mind that perceives an appearance like clear, empty space. See *Clear Light of Bliss*.

Compassion A mind that cannot bear the suffering of others and wishes them to be free from it. See also *Great compassion*. See *Joyful Path of Good Fortune*.

Contaminated aggregate Any of the aggregates of form, feeling, discrimination, compositional factors, and consciousness of a samsaric being. See also *Aggregate*. See *Heart of Wisdom*.

Conventional nature See *Ultimate nature*.

Conventional truth Any phenomenon other than emptiness. Conventional truths are true with respect to the minds of ordinary beings, but in reality they are false. See *Heart of Wisdom*.

Dakini Land The Pure Land of Heruka and Vajrayogini. In Sanskrit it is called 'Keajra' and in Tibetan 'Dagpa Khachö'. See *Guide to Dakini Land*.

Deity 'Yidam' in Sanskrit. A Tantric enlightened being.

Dharma Buddha's teachings and the inner realizations that are attained in dependence upon practising them. 'Dharma' means 'protection'. By practising Buddha's teachings, we protect ourself from suffering and problems.

Dharmakirti A great Indian Buddhist Yogi and scholar who composed *Commentary to Valid Cognition*, a commentary to *Compendium of Valid Cognition*, which was written by his Spiritual Guide, Dignaga.

Dignaga A great Indian Buddhist Yogi and scholar who composed a number of works on logic and cognition, the most famous being *Compendium of Valid Cognition*.

Empowerment A special potential power to attain any of the four Buddha bodies that is received by a Tantric practitioner from his or her Guru, or from other holy beings, by means of Tantric ritual. It is the gateway to the Vajrayana. See *Tantric Grounds and Paths*.

Engaging bodhichitta A bodhichitta held by the Bodhisattva vows. See also *Bodhichitta*.

286

Enlightenment Usually the full enlightenment of Buddhahood. There are three levels of enlightenment: small enlightenment, or the enlightenment of a Hearer; middling enlightenment, or the enlightenment of a Solitary Realizer; and great enlightenment, or the enlightenment of a Buddha. An enlightenment is a liberation and a true cessation. See *Joyful Path of Good Fortune.*

Essence of Good Fortune A sadhana consisting of prayers for the six preparatory practices. See also *Preparatory practices.* For a full commentary, see *Joyful Path of Good Fortune.*

Foe Destroyer 'Arhat' in Sanskrit. A practitioner who has abandoned all delusions and their seeds by training on the spiritual paths, and who will never again be reborn in samsara. In this context, the term 'Foe' refers to the delusions.

Four noble truths True sufferings, true origins, true cessations, and true paths. They are called 'noble' truths because they are supreme objects of meditation. Through meditation on these four objects, we can realize ultimate truth directly and thus become a noble, or Superior, being. Sometimes referred to as the 'four truths of Superiors'. See also *Sixteen characteristics of the four noble truths.* See *Joyful Path of Good Fortune.*

Generation stage A realization of a creative yoga prior to attaining the actual completion stage, which is attained through the practice of bringing the three bodies into the path, in which one mentally generates oneself as a Tantric Deity and one's surroundings as the Deity's mandala. Meditation on generation stage is called a 'creative yoga' because its object is created, or generated, by correct imagination. See *Tantric Grounds and Paths.*

Geshe A title given by Kadampa monasteries to accomplished Buddhist scholars. Contracted form of the Tibetan 'ge wai she nyen', literally meaning 'virtuous friend'.

Great compassion A mind wishing to protect all sentient beings from suffering. Generally there are three types: compassion observing sentient beings, compassion observing phenomena, and compassion observing the unobservable. The second is a great compassion induced by and accompanied by a realization of impermanence, and the third is a great compassion induced by and accompanied by a realization of emptiness. The first is a great compassion that is not qualified in either of these ways. See *Universal Compassion* and *Ocean of Nectar.*

Ground/Spiritual ground A clear realization that acts as the foundation of many good qualities. A clear realization is a realization held by spontaneous renunciation or bodhichitta. The ten grounds are the realizations of Superior Bodhisattvas: Very Joyful, Stainless, Luminous, Radiant, Difficult to Overcome, Approaching, Gone Afar, Immovable, Good Intelligence, and Cloud of Dharma. See also *Path/Spiritual path*. See *Ocean of Nectar* and *Tantric Grounds and Paths*.

Guide to the Bodhisattva's Way of Life A classic Mahayana Buddhist text composed by the great Indian Buddhist Yogi and scholar Shantideva, which presents all the practices of a Bodhisattva from the initial generation of bodhichitta through to the completion of the practice of the six perfections. For a full commentary, see *Meaningful to Behold*.

Guide to the Middle Way A classic Mahayana Buddhist text composed by the great Indian Buddhist Yogi and scholar Chandrakirti, which provides a comprehensive explanation of the Madhyamika-Prasangika view of emptiness as taught in the *Perfection of Wisdom Sutras*. For a full commentary, see *Ocean of Nectar*.

Hashang A Chinese monk of the twelfth century who propagated many wrong views in Tibet, including the view that the meaning of Buddha's teachings on emptiness was that we should empty our mind of all conceptions and meditate on nothingness. He was publicly defeated in debate by Kamalashila and banished from Tibet.

Hearer One of two types of Hinayana practitioner. Both Hearers and Solitary Conquerors are Hinayanists, but they differ in their motivation, behaviour, merit, and wisdom. In all these respects, Solitary Conquerors are superior to Hearers. See *Ocean of Nectar*.

Hell realm The lowest of the six realms of samsara. See *Joyful Path of Good Fortune*.

Heruka A principal Deity of Mother Tantra, who is the embodiment of indivisible bliss and emptiness. He has a blue-coloured body, four faces, and twelve arms, and embraces his consort Vajravarahi. See *Essence of Vajrayana*.

Hinayana Sanskrit word for 'Lesser Vehicle'. The Hinayana goal is to attain merely one's own liberation from suffering by completely abandoning delusions. See *Joyful Path of Good Fortune*.

Impermanent phenomenon Phenomena are either permanent or impermanent. 'Impermanent' means 'momentary', thus an impermanent phenomenon is a phenomenon that is produced and disintegrates within a moment. Synonyms of impermanent phenomenon are 'functioning thing' and 'product'. There are two types of impermanence: gross and subtle. Gross impermanence is any impermanence that can be seen by a ordinary sense awareness – for example the ageing and death of a sentient being. Subtle impermanence is the momentary disintegration of a functioning thing.

Imprint There are two types of imprint: imprints of actions and imprints of delusions. Every action we perform leaves an imprint on the mental consciousness, and these imprints are karmic potentialities to experience certain effects in the future. The imprints left by delusions remain even after the delusions themselves have been abandoned, rather as the smell of garlic lingers in a container after the garlic has been removed. Imprints of delusions are obstructions to omniscience, and are completely abandoned only by Buddhas.

Imputation, mere According to the Madhyamika-Prasangika school, all phenomena are merely imputed by conception in dependence upon their basis of imputation. Therefore, they are mere imputation and do not exist from their own side in the least. See *Heart of Wisdom*.

Inherent existence An imagined mode of existence whereby phenomena are held to exist from their own side, independent of other phenomena. In reality, all phenomena are empty of inherent existence because they depend upon their parts. See *Heart of Wisdom*.

Inner winds Special subtle winds related to the mind that flow through the channels of our body. Our body and mind cannot function without these winds. See *Clear Light of Bliss*.

Je Tsongkhapa (AD 1357-1419) An emanation of the Wisdom Buddha Manjushri, whose appearance in fourteenth-century Tibet as a monk, and the holder of the lineage of pure view and pure deeds, was prophesied by Buddha. He spread a very pure Buddhadharma throughout Tibet, showing how to combine the practices of Sutra and Tantra, and how to practise pure Dharma during degenerate times. His tradition later became known as the 'Gelug', or 'Ganden Tradition'. See *Heart Jewel* and *Great Treasury of Merit*.

Kadampa A Tibetan word in which 'Ka' means 'word' and refers to all Buddha's teachings, 'dam' refers to Atisha's special Lamrim instructions known as the 'stages of the path to enlightenment', and 'pa' refers to a follower of Kadampa Buddhism who integrates all the teachings of Buddha that they know into their Lamrim practice. See also *Kadampa Buddhism* and *Kadampa Tradition*.

Kadampa Buddhism A Mahayana Buddhist school founded by the great Indian Buddhist Master Atisha (AD 982-1054). See also *Kadampa* and *Kadampa Tradition*.

Kadampa Tradition The pure tradition of Buddhism established by Atisha. Followers of this tradition up to the time of Je Tsongkhapa are known as 'Old Kadampas', and those after the time of Je Tsongkhapa are known as 'New Kadampas'. See also *Kadampa* and *Kadampa Buddhism*.

Khädrubje One of the principal disciples of Je Tsongkhapa, who did much to promote the tradition of Je Tsongkhapa after he passed away. See *Great Treasury of Merit*.

Liberation 'Nirvana' in Sanskrit. Complete freedom from samsara and its cause, the delusions. See *Joyful Path of Good Fortune*.

Lorig Tibetan word for 'types of mind'.

Madhyamika A Sanskrit word, literally meaning 'Middle Way'. The higher of the two schools of Mahayana tenets. The Madhyamika view was taught by Buddha in the *Perfection of Wisdom Sutras* during the second turning of the Wheel of Dharma and was subsequently elucidated by Nagarjuna and his followers. There are two divisions of this school, Madhyamika-Svatantrika and Madhyamika-Prasangika, of which the latter is Buddha's final view. See *Meaningful to Behold* and *Ocean of Nectar*.

Mahamudra A Sanskrit word, literally meaning 'great seal'. According to Sutra, this refers to the profound view of emptiness. Since emptiness is the nature of all phenomena, it is called a 'seal', and since a direct realization of emptiness enables us to accomplish the great purpose – complete liberation from the sufferings of samsara – it is also called 'great'. According to Secret Mantra, or Vajrayana, great seal is the union of spontaneous great bliss and emptiness. See *Great Treasury of Merit* and *Clear Light of Bliss*.

Mahayana Sanskrit word for 'Great Vehicle', the spiritual path to great enlightenment. The Mahayana goal is to attain Buddhahood for the benefit of all sentient beings by completely abandoning delusions and their imprints. See *Joyful Path of Good Fortune*.

Mahayana path A clear realization in the mental continuum of a Bodhisattva or a Buddha. There are five Mahayana paths: the Mahayana path of accumulation, the Mahayana path of preparation, the Mahayana path of seeing, the Mahayana path of meditation, and the Mahayana Path of No More Learning. The first four are necessarily in the continuum of a Bodhisattva and the last is necessarily in the continuum of a Buddha. See *Ocean of Nectar*.

Maitreya The embodiment of the loving kindness of all the Buddhas. At the time of Buddha Shakyamuni, he manifested as a Bodhisattva disciple. In the future, he will manifest as the fifth founding Buddha.

Manjushri The embodiment of the wisdom of all the Buddhas. At the time of Buddha Shakyamuni, he manifested as a Bodhisattva disciple.

Mantra A Sanskrit word, literally meaning 'mind protection'. Mantra protects the mind from ordinary appearances and conceptions. There are four types of mantra: mantras that are mind, mantras that are inner wind, mantras that are sound, and mantras that are form. In general, there are three types of mantra recitation: verbal recitation, mental recitation, and vajra recitation. See *Tantric Grounds and Paths*.

Merit The good fortune created by virtuous actions. It is the potential power to increase our good qualities and produce happiness.

Mundane paths Contaminated actions that lead to samsaric rebirth. There are two types: the ten non-virtuous actions that lead to the lower realms, and the ten virtuous actions and contaminated concentrations that lead to the higher realms.

Nagarjuna A great Indian Buddhist scholar and meditation master who revived the Mahayana in the first century AD by bringing to light the teachings on the *Perfection of Wisdom Sutras*. See *Ocean of Nectar*.

Nirvana See *Liberation*.

Obstructions to liberation Obstructions that prevent the attainment of liberation. All delusions, such as ignorance, attachment, and anger, together with their seeds, are obstructions to liberation. Also called 'delusion-obstructions'.

Obstructions to omniscience The imprints of delusions that prevent simultaneous and direct realization of all phenomena. Only Buddhas have overcome these obstructions.

Path/Spiritual path An exalted awareness conjoined with non-fabricated, or spontaneous, renunciation. Spiritual path, spiritual ground, spiritual vehicle, and exalted awareness are synonyms. See also *Ground/Spiritual ground*.

Perfection of Wisdom Sutras Sutras of the second turning of the Wheel of Dharma, in which Buddha revealed his final view of the ultimate nature of all phenomena – emptiness of inherent existence. See *Heart of Wisdom* and *Ocean of Nectar*.

Phenomena source A phenomenon that appears only to mental awareness.

Pratimoksha Sanskrit word for 'individual liberation'. See *The Bodhisattva Vow*.

Preparatory practices Practices that prepare the mind for successful meditation, such as purifying the mind, accumulating merit, and receiving blessings. See also *Essence of Good Fortune*.

Prostration An action of showing respect with body, speech, or mind. See *The Bodhisattva Vow*.

Pure Land A pure environment in which there are no true sufferings. There are many Pure Lands. For example, Tushita is the Pure Land of Buddha Maitreya; Sukhavati is the Pure Land of Buddha Amitabha; and Dakini Land, or Keajra, is the Pure Land of Buddha Vajrayogini and Buddha Heruka. See *Living Meaningfully, Dying Joyfully*.

Purification Generally, any practice that leads to the attainment of a pure body, speech, or mind. More specifically, a practice for purifying negative karma. See *The Bodhisattva Vow*.

Refuge Actual protection. To go for refuge to Buddha, Dharma, and Sangha means to have faith in these Three Jewels and to rely upon them for protection from all fears and suffering. See *Joyful Path of Good Fortune*.

Sadhana A ritual that is a method for attaining spiritual realizations. It can be associated with Sutra or Tantra.

Schools of Buddhist tenets Four philosophical views taught by Buddha according to the inclinations and dispositions of disciples. They are the Vaibashika, Sautrantika, Chittamatra, and Madhyamika schools. The first two are Hinayana schools and the second two are Mahayana schools. They are studied in sequence, the lower tenets being the means by which the higher ones are understood. See *Meaningful to Behold* and *Ocean of Nectar*.

Secret Mantra Synonymous with Tantra. Secret Mantra teachings are distinguished from Sutra teachings in that they reveal methods for training the mind by bringing the future result, or Buddhahood, into the present path. Secret Mantra is the supreme path to full enlightenment. The term 'Mantra' indicates that it is Buddha's special instruction for protecting our mind from ordinary appearances and conceptions. Practitioners of Secret Mantra overcome ordinary appearances and conceptions by visualizing their body, environment, enjoyments, and deeds as those of a Buddha. The term 'Secret' indicates that the practices are to be done in private, and that they can be practised only by those who have received a Tantric empowerment. See *Tantric Grounds and Paths*.

Seed-letter The sacred letter from which a Deity is generated. Each Deity has a particular seed-letter. For example, the seed-letter of Manjushri is DHI, of Tara is TAM, of Vajrayogini is BAM, and of Heruka is HUM. To accomplish Tantric realizations, we need to recognize that Deities and their seed-letters are the same nature.

Self-cherishing A mental attitude that considers oneself to be supremely important and precious. It is regarded as a principal object to be abandoned by Bodhisattvas. See *Eight Steps to Happiness*.

Sentient being Any being who possesses a mind that is contaminated by delusions or their imprints. Both 'sentient being' and 'living being' are terms used to distinguish beings whose minds are contaminated by either of these two obstructions from Buddhas, whose minds are completely free from these obstructions.

Shantideva (AD 687-763) A great Indian Buddhist scholar and meditation master. He composed *Guide to the Bodhisattva's Way of Life*. See *Meaningful to Behold*.

Sixteen characteristics of the four noble truths Buddha taught that each of the four noble truths has four special characteristics. The four characteristics of true sufferings are: impermanent, suffering, empty, and selfless; the four characteristics of true origins are: cause, origin, strong producer, and condition; the four characteristics of true cessations are: cessation, peace, supreme attainment, and definite abandoner; and the four characteristics of true paths are: path, antidote, accomplisher, and definite abandoning. See *Ocean of Nectar*.

Solitary Conqueror A type of Hinayana practitioner. Also known as 'Solitary Realizer'. See also *Hearer*.

Solitary peace A Hinayana nirvana.

Superior being 'Arya' in Sanskrit. A being who has a direct realization of emptiness. There are Hinayana Superiors and Mahayana Superiors.

Supramundane path Any path leading to liberation or enlightenment – for example, the realizations of renunciation, bodhichitta, and the correct view of emptiness. Strictly speaking, only Superior beings possess supramundane paths. See *Tantric Grounds and Paths*.

Sutra The teachings of Buddha that are open to everyone to practise without the need for empowerment. These include Buddha's teachings of the three turnings of the Wheel of Dharma.

Tangkha A traditional painting of a holy being.

Tantra See *Secret Mantra*.

Training the mind 'Lojong' in Tibetan. A special lineage of instructions that came from Buddha Shakyamuni through Manjushri and Shantideva to Atisha and the Kadampa Geshes, which emphasizes the generation of bodhichitta through the practices of equalizing and exchanging self with others combined with taking and giving. See *Universal Compassion* and *Meaningful to Behold*.

Tummo Sanskrit word for 'inner fire'. An inner heat located at the centre of the navel channel wheel. See *Clear Light of Bliss*.

Ultimate nature All phenomena have two natures – a conventional nature and an ultimate nature. In the case of a table, for example, the table itself, and its shape, colour, and so forth are all the conventional nature of the table. The ultimate nature of the table is the table's lack of inherent existence. The conventional nature of a phenomenon is a conventional truth, and its ultimate nature is an ultimate truth. See *Heart of Wisdom*.

Ultimate truth The ultimate nature of all phenomena, emptiness.

Uncompounded space Lack of obstructive contact. So called because it is not produced by causes and conditions and so is permanent. See *Heart of Wisdom*.

Vajra recitation A mantra recitation produced from inner winds that is practised in conjunction with Vajrayana practices. See *Tantric Grounds and Paths*.

Vajrayana Mahamudra See *Mahamudra*.

Vajrayogini A female Highest Yoga Tantra Deity who is the embodiment of indivisible bliss and emptiness. She is the same nature as Heruka. See *Guide to Dakini Land*.

Vasubhandu A great Indian Buddhist scholar of the fifth century who was converted to the Mahayana by his older brother, Asanga. He wrote *Treasury of Abhidharma* (Skt. *Abhidharmakosha*).

Vinaya Sutras Sutras in which Buddha principally explains the practice of moral discipline, and in particular the Pratimoksha moral discipline.

Wheel of Life A diagram depicting the twelve dependent-related links and the four noble truths. See *Joyful Path of Good Fortune*.

Winds See *Inner winds*.

Yogi/Yogini The Sanskrit word 'Yogi' usually refers to a man, and 'Yogini' to a woman, who has attained the union of tranquil abiding and superior seeing.

Bibliography

Geshe Kelsang Gyatso is a highly respected meditation master and scholar of the Mahayana Buddhist tradition founded by Je Tsong-khapa. Since arriving in the West in 1977, Geshe Kelsang has worked tirelessly to establish pure Buddhadharma throughout the world. Over this period he has given extensive teachings on the major scriptures of the Mahayana. These teachings are currently being published and provide a comprehensive presentation of the essential Sutra and Tantra practices of Mahayana Buddhism.

Books

The following books by Geshe Kelsang are all published by Tharpa Publications.

The Bodhisattva Vow. The essential practices of Mahayana Buddhism. (2nd. edn., 1995)

Clear Light of Bliss. The practice of Mahamudra in Vajrayana Buddhism. (2nd. edn., 1992)

Eight Steps to Happiness. The Buddhist way of loving kindness. (2000)

Essence of Vajrayana. The Highest Yoga Tantra practice of Heruka body mandala. (1997)

Great Treasury of Merit. The practice of relying upon a Spiritual Guide. (1992)

Guide to Dakini Land. The Highest Yoga Tantra practice of Buddha Vajrayogini. (2nd. edn., 1996)

Heart Jewel. The essential practices of Kadampa Buddhism. (2nd. edn., 1997)

Heart of Wisdom. An explanation of the *Heart Sutra*. (4th. edn., 2001)

Introduction to Buddhism. An explanation of the Buddhist way of life. (2nd. edn., 2001)

Joyful Path of Good Fortune. The complete Buddhist path to enlightenment. (2nd. edn., 1995)

Living Meaningfully, Dying Joyfully. The profound practice of transference of consciousness. (1999)

Meaningful to Behold. The Bodhisattva's way of life. (4th. edn., 1994)

The Meditation Handbook. A practical guide to Buddhist meditation. (3rd. edn., 1995)

Ocean of Nectar. Wisdom and compassion in Mahayana Buddhism. (1995)

Tantric Grounds and Paths. How to enter, progress on, and complete the Vajrayana path. (1994)

Transform Your Life. A blissful journey. (2001)

Understanding the Mind. An explanation of the nature and functions of the mind. (2nd. edn., 1997)

Universal Compassion. Transforming your life through love and compassion. (3rd. edn., 1997)

Sadhanas

Geshe Kelsang has also supervised the translation of a collection of essential sadhanas, or prayer booklets.

Assembly of Good Fortune. The tsog offering for Heruka body mandala.

Avalokiteshvara Sadhana. Prayers and requests to the Buddha of Compassion.

The Bodhisattva's Confession of Moral Downfalls. The purification practice of the *Mahayana Sutra of the Three Superior Heaps.*

Condensed Essence of Vajrayana. Condensed Heruka body mandala self-generation sadhana.

Dakini Yoga. Six-session Guru yoga combined with self-generation as Vajrayogini.

Drop of Essential Nectar. A special fasting and purification practice in conjunction with Eleven-faced Avalokiteshvara.

Essence of Good Fortune. Prayers for the six preparatory practices for meditation on the stages of the path to enlightenment.

Essence of Vajrayana. Heruka body mandala self-generation sadhana according to the system of Mahasiddha Ghantapa.

Feast of Great Bliss. Vajrayogini self-initiation sadhana.

Great Compassionate Mother. The sadhana of Arya Tara.

Great Liberation of the Mother. Preliminary prayers for Mahamudra meditation in conjunction with Vajrayogini practice.

The Great Mother. A method to overcome hindrances and obstacles by reciting the *Essence of Wisdom Sutra* (the *Heart Sutra*).

Heartfelt Prayers. Funeral service for cremations and burials.

Heart Jewel. The Guru yoga of Je Tsongkhapa combined with the condensed sadhana of his Dharma Protector.

The Hundreds of Deities of the Joyful Land. The Guru yoga of Je Tsongkhapa.

The Kadampa Way of Life. The essential practice of Kadam Lamrim.

Liberation from Sorrow. Praises and requests to the Twenty-one Taras.
Mahayana Refuge Ceremony and Bodhisattva Vow Ceremony.
Medicine Buddha Sadhana. The method for making requests to the Assembly of Seven Medicine Buddhas.
Meditation and Recitation of Solitary Vajrasattva.
Melodious Drum Victorious in all Directions. The extensive fulfilling and restoring ritual of the Dharma Protector, the great king Dorje Shugdän, in conjunction with Mahakala, Kalarupa, Kalindewi, and other Dharma Protectors.
Offering to the Spiritual Guide (*Lama Chöpa*). A special Guru yoga practice of Je Tsongkhapa's tradition.
Pathway to the Pure Land. Training in powa – the transference of consciousness.
Prayers for Meditation. Brief preparatory prayers for meditation.
A Pure Life. The practice of taking and keeping the eight Mahayana precepts.
The Quick Path. A condensed practice of Heruka Five Deities according to Master Ghantapa's tradition.
Quick Path to Great Bliss. Vajrayogini self-generation sadhana.
Treasury of Blessings. The condensed meaning of Vajrayana Mahamudra and prayers of request to the lineage Gurus.
Treasury of Wisdom. The sadhana of Venerable Manjushri.
Vajra Hero Yoga. A brief essential practice of Heruka body mandala self-generation, and condensed six-session yoga.
The Vows and Commitments of Kadampa Buddhism.
Wishfulfilling Jewel. The Guru yoga of Je Tsongkhapa combined with the sadhana of his Dharma Protector.
The Yoga of Buddha Amitayus. A special method for increasing lifespan, wisdom, and merit.
The Yoga of White Tara, Buddha of Long Life.

To order any of our publications, or to
receive a catalogue, please contact:

Tharpa Publications
Conishead Priory
Ulverston
Cumbria LA12 9QQ
England

Tel: 01229-588599
Fax: 01229-483919

E-mail: tharpa@tharpa.com
Website: www.tharpa.com

Tharpa Publications
47 Sweeney Road
P.O. Box 430
Glen Spey, NY 12737, USA

Tel: 845-856-5102 or
888-741-3475 (toll free)
Fax: 845-856-2110

Email: tharpa-us@tharpa.com
Website: www.tharpa.com

Study Programmes of Kadampa Buddhism

Kadampa Buddhism is a Mahayana Buddhist school founded by the great Indian Buddhist Master Atisha (AD 982-1054). His followers are known as 'Kadampas'. 'Ka' means 'word' and refers to Buddha's teachings, and 'dam' refers to Atisha's special Lamrim instructions known as 'the stages of the path to enlightenment'. By integrating their knowledge of all Buddha's teachings into their practice of Lamrim, and by integrating this into their everyday lives, Kadampa Buddhists are encouraged to use Buddha's teachings as practical methods for transforming daily activities into the path to enlightenment. The great Kadampa Teachers are famous not only for being great scholars, but also for being spiritual practitioners of immense purity and sincerity.

The lineage of these teachings, both their oral transmission and blessings, was then passed from Teacher to disciple, spreading throughout much of Asia, and now to many countries throughout the Western world. Buddha's teachings, which are known as 'Dharma', are likened to a wheel that moves from country to country in accordance with changing conditions and people's karmic inclinations. The external forms of presenting Buddhism may change as it meets with different cultures and societies, but its essential authenticity is ensured through the continuation of an unbroken lineage of realized practitioners.

Kadampa Buddhism was first introduced into the West in 1977 by the renowned Buddhist Master, Venerable Geshe Kelsang Gyatso. Since that time, he has worked tirelessly to spread Kadampa Buddhism throughout the world by giving extensive teachings, writing many profound texts on Kadampa Buddhism, and founding the New Kadampa Tradition (NKT), which now has nearly four hundred Kadampa Buddhist Centres worldwide. Each Centre offers study programmes on Buddhist psychology, philosophy, and meditation instruction, as well as retreats for all levels of practitioner. The emphasis is on integrating Buddha's teachings into daily life to solve our human problems and to spread lasting peace and happiness throughout the world.

The Kadampa Buddhism of the NKT is an entirely independent Buddhist tradition and has no political affiliations. It is an association of Buddhist Centres and practitioners that derive their inspiration and

298

guidance from the example of the ancient Kadampa Buddhist Masters and their teachings, as presented by Geshe Kelsang.

There are three reasons why we need to study and practise the teachings of Buddha: to develop our wisdom, to cultivate a good heart, and to maintain a peaceful state of mind. If we do not strive to develop our wisdom, we will always remain ignorant of ultimate truth – the true nature of reality. Although we wish for happiness, our ignorance leads us to engage in non-virtuous actions, which are the main cause of all our suffering. If we do not cultivate a good heart, our selfish motivation destroys harmony and good relationships with others. We have no peace, and no chance to gain pure happiness. Without inner peace, outer peace is impossible. If we do not maintain a peaceful state of mind, we are not happy even if we have ideal conditions. On the other hand, when our mind is peaceful, we are happy, even if our external conditions are unpleasant. Therefore, the development of these qualities is of utmost importance for our daily happiness.

Geshe Kelsang Gyatso, or 'Geshe-la' as he is affectionately called by his students, has designed three special spiritual programmes for the systematic study and practice of Kadampa Buddhism that are especially suited to the modern world – the General Programme (GP), the Foundation Programme (FP), and the Teacher Training Programme (TTP).

GENERAL PROGRAMME

The General Programme provides a basic introduction to Buddhist view, meditation, and practice that is suitable for beginners. It also includes advanced teachings and practice from both Sutra and Tantra.

FOUNDATION PROGRAMME

The Foundation Programme provides an opportunity to deepen our understanding and experience of Buddhism through a systematic study of five texts:

1 *Joyful Path of Good Fortune* – a commentary to Atisha's Lamrim instructions, the stages of the path to enlightenment.
2 *Universal Compassion* – a commentary to Bodhisattva Chekhawa's *Training the Mind in Seven Points*.
3 *Heart of Wisdom* – a commentary to the *Heart Sutra*.
4 *Meaningful to Behold* – a commentary to Venerable Shantideva's *Guide to the Bodhisattva's Way of Life*.
5 *Understanding the Mind* – a detailed explanation of the mind, based on the works of the Buddhist scholars Dharmakirti and Dignaga.

The benefits of studying and practising these texts are as follows:

(1) *Joyful Path of Good Fortune* – we gain the ability to put all Buddha's teachings of both Sutra and Tantra into practice. We can easily make progress on, and complete, the stages of the path to the supreme happiness of enlightenment. From a practical point of view, Lamrim is the main body of Buddha's teachings, and the other teachings are like its limbs.

(2) *Universal Compassion* – we gain the ability to integrate Buddha's teachings into our daily life and solve all our human problems.

(3) *Heart of Wisdom* – we gain a realization of the ultimate nature of reality. By gaining this realization, we can eliminate the ignorance of self-grasping, which is the root of all our suffering.

(4) *Meaningful to Behold* – we transform our daily activities into the Bodhisattva's way of life, thereby making every moment of our human life meaningful.

(5) *Understanding the Mind* – we understand the relationship between our mind and its external objects. If we understand that objects depend upon the subjective mind, we can change the way objects appear to us by changing our own mind. Gradually, we will gain the ability to control our mind and in this way solve all our problems.

TEACHER TRAINING PROGRAMME

The Teacher Training Programme is designed for people who wish to train as authentic Dharma Teachers. In addition to completing the study of twelve texts of Sutra and Tantra, which include the five texts mentioned above, the student is required to observe certain commitments with regard to behaviour and way of life, and to complete a number of meditation retreats.

All Kadampa Buddhist Centres are open to the public. Every year we celebrate Festivals in the USA and Europe, including two in England, where people gather from around the world to receive special teachings and empowerments and to enjoy a spiritual vacation. Please feel free to visit us at any time! For further information, please contact:

UK NKT Office
Conishead Priory
Ulverston
Cumbria LA12 9QQ
England

Tel/Fax: 01229-588533

Email: kadampa@dircon.co.uk
Website: www.kadampa.org

US NKT Office
Kadampa Meditation Center
47 Sweeney Road, P.O. Box 447
Glen Spey, NY 12737, USA

Tel: 845-856-9000
Fax: 845-856-2110

Email: info@kadampacenter.org
Website: www.kadampacenter.org

Index

The letter 'g' indicates an entry in the glossary.

definition 36
dominant condition 40
gross, subtle, very subtle 18,
    70, 114, 127
immediate condition 40
non-virtuous, virtuous, neutral
    37
mental consciousness 44
mental direct perceiver 37, 46-8
    definition 46
    induced by sense direct
        perceiver 37, 46
    induced by meditation 46, 47,
        50
    that are neither 46, 47
    non-ascertaining 68, 69
    non-conceptual 29
    re-cognizer 47, 62
    valid 99
mental excitement 128, 168, 230
mental factors (see also
        individual ones) 103-6
    definition 103
    function 103
    relationship with primary
        mind 103
mental power 22, 36-7, 46
mental sinking 128, 168-9, 229
mentality (see also deluded
        mentality; primary mind) 36,
        37, 103
merit 240, g
middle way 218
Milarepa 225
mind (see also individual types)
    cause of happiness and
        suffering 3-4
    causes 21-2
    continuum 1
    creator 4-5
    definition 16
    gross, subtle, very subtle (see
        also mental awareness) 18-9,
        235
    levels of understanding 1

locations 18
main divisions 19
nature and functions 1, 3, 16,
    17
parts 211
relationship with body 17,
    19-20
root 18-9
sevenfold division 41-88
mindfulness 63, 126-8, 183, 201,
    233
    basis for 120, 125, 166
    new and old 127-8
    root of meditation 25
    twofold division 128
mirage 84
miserliness 224-6
mistaken awareness 72, 79
moment 61
moral discipline 135, 167, 201,
    234
    of restraint 143, 144
motivation 12, 125, 173, 175
mundane attainments 131, 155
mundane paths 167, g

name 11-2, 57
    mere 11, 208, 214-5
Nagarjuna 38, 220, g
negative actions (see non-
    virtuous actions)
nirvana (see liberation) g
nominal truth (see also
    conventional truth) 238
non-alertness 233-4
non-ascertaining perceiver 75,
    90, 120, 125
    deceptive 95
    definition 68
    ear awareness 68-9, 71
    eye awareness 69
    five types 69-71
    mental direct perceiver 68, 69
    sense direct perceiver 43, 44,
        68-9, 100, 125